# Praise for
# *Reclaiming UGLY!*

"The wisdom of this book is borne of a deeply personal story told with such clarity and love that we are thankfully implicated and freed by it all at the same time. Vanessa's writing is a mirror where each page rescues a bit more of our reflections from the lies and dangers of lookism. The framework here is ultimately one that teaches us how to recover what in us has been made out as ugly by this society, to interrupt the harm to each other we perpetuate in its name, and how, ultimately, we reclaim an ethic of care, deep honor, and protection. Vanessa has given us a generous, liberating provocation and invitation with *Reclaiming UGLY!* that we would do ourselves a service to receive."

—PRENTIS HEMPHILL, author, therapist, founder of The Embodiment Institute, and host of the *Finding Our Way* podcast

"With *Reclaiming UGLY!*, Vanessa Rochelle Lewis is offering us her hand as we look in the mirror and learn to see the beauty there, and the beauty in everyone, shirking off societal norms that deny our multitudinous, miraculous nature. Looking at the creation, maintenance, and impact of uglification through a lens that includes the personal, cultural, and factual, Vanessa shows us a way forward toward compassion and revolutionary love."

—ADRIENNE MAREE BROWN, *New York Times* best-selling author of *Pleasure Activism*

"Healing comes only when we face the deep harms of which we have been subject and perpetrator. *Reclaiming UGLY!* is an invitation to heal both the internal and external wounds of uglification. With a grace born of profound empathy, Vanessa never blames us for drinking from the chalice of shame and cruelty as she knows we all have thirsted for belonging, care, and love amidst oppressive structures that have left us few options. *Reclaiming UGLY!* is a necessary drink of liberatory possibility; a world formed of immense beauty and transformative love; a world we each get to co-create. Lucky us."

—SONYA RENEE TAYLOR, *New York Times* best-selling author of *The Body Is Not an Apology*

# Reclaiming UGLY!

# Reclaiming

# UG
# G
# LY!

## A Radically Joyful Guide to Unlearn Oppression and Uplift, Glorify, and Love Yourself

*Vanessa Rochelle Lewis*

North Atlantic Books
Huichin, unceded Ohlone land
Berkeley, California

Published by
North Atlantic Books
Huichin, unceded Ohlone land
Berkeley, California

Cover design by Jasmine Hromjak
Book design by Happenstance Type-O-Rama
Printed in the United States of America

*Reclaiming UGLY!: A Radically Joyful Guide to Unlearn Oppression and Uplift, Glorify, and Love Yourself* is sponsored and published by North Atlantic Books, an educational nonprofit based in the unceded Ohlone land Huichin (Berkeley, CA) that collaborates with partners to develop cross-cultural perspectives; nurture holistic views of art, science, the humanities, and healing; and seed personal and global transformation by publishing work on the relationship of body, spirit, and nature.

North Atlantic Books's publications are distributed to the US trade and internationally by Penguin Random House Publisher Services. For further information, visit our website at www.northatlanticbooks.com.

Library of Congress Cataloging-in-Publication Data
Names: Lewis, Vanessa Rochelle, author.
Title: Reclaiming ugly! : a radically joyful guide to unlearn oppression
  and uplift, glorify, and love yourself / Vanessa Rochelle Lewis.
Description: Huichin, unceded Ohlone land Berkeley, California : North
  Atlantic Books, [2024] | Includes bibliographical references and index.
  | Summary: "A blend of self-help, social analysis, and personal
  narrative that deconstructs what we've been told is ugly and taboo and
  empowers readers to heal, connect, and revolt against uglification"--
  Provided by publisher.
Identifiers: LCCN 2023019326 (print) | LCCN 2023019327 (ebook) | ISBN
  9781623175863 (trade paperback) | ISBN 9781623175870 (ebook)
Subjects: LCSH: Ugliness.
Classification: LCC BH301.U5 .L495 2024 (print) | LCC BH301.U5 (ebook) |
  DDC 111/.85--dc23/eng/20230919
LC record available at https://lccn.loc.gov/2023019326
LC ebook record available at https://lccn.loc.gov/2023019327

1 2 3 4 5 6 7 8 9 KPC 29 28 27 26 25 24

This book includes recycled material and material from well-managed forests. North Atlantic Books is committed to the protection of our environment. We print on recycled paper whenever possible and partner with printers who strive to use environmentally responsible practices.

*Reclaiming UGLY!* **envisions a world in which everybody is included, centered, protected, and cared for, and everybody's person- hood is supported to grow, heal, rest, love, imagine, become, and actualize their most authentic and pleasure-centered dreams.**

**This book is a Love Revolution.**

In honor of Stacey Park Milbern, Marissa Snoddy, and Jeron HP Alexander.

These three beautiful souls transitioned from this realm during the writing of this book, and the world is forever transformed because of them. Their lives, activism, leadership, and he(art) helped so many people Uplift, Glorify, and Love Themselves—including myself.

# Contents

# 1

# Grounding in Intention

Welcome to *Reclaiming UGLY! A Radically Joyful Guide to Unlearn Oppression and Uplift, Glorify, and Love Yourself.*

Thank you for picking this book up, opening it, and investing the energy, courage, vulnerability, and care it takes to engage with a theme like this. Talking about ugliness is hard, especially when your looks, body, and identity may have been weaponized against you by bullies and loved ones alike. It's also critical to healing from the impacts of being uglified, and to creating a world where other people don't have to experience the same harm. I'm so happy that you are ready to join me on the journey of reclaiming every single precious part of yourself from the devastating process, experience, and culture of uglification.

As a person who is very much alive and breathing in this wild and busy emotional tanglewood of a world in which we cohabitate, I respect you deeply for being here. I know that you have bills to pay, chores to get done, meals to prepare, friendships and intimacies to nurture, children to raise, bodies to care for, pleasure to indulge in, and a slew of other time-consuming responsibilities. You can be doing anything in the world right now, but you're here with me, dreaming and scheming for better.

It's hard to set aside the time we need to focus on our healing, tend to the spiritual and psychological parts of resistance, or simply know what it is we want from life (as opposed to what we're told to want)—which are all things that this book will request of you. It's even more difficult to do this tender and emotional labor when the premise is not just healing from the hardships we have experienced, but also healing the parts of us that are actively inclined to justify the harms, violence, and unfair judgments we perpetuate against ourselves and others.

This book will explore our attitudes about ugliness, beauty, right, and wrong, as well as the impacts and consequences of those attitudes, but also why we have those values, how they serve us (even those of us who face marginalization and oppression), and how they hurt us, the people we care about, and so many other people. While there will be some systemic analysis in the following pages, this book is far more about you, the people you love, the life you've led, and the world we can all create when we choose to Uplift, Glorify, and Love Ourselves while creating a world where others can as well. I will share an abundance of personal stories, affirmations, and critical reflection questions for you to ask yourself along the way.

One of my former boyfriends used to love to tell me, "Vanessa, you deserve better than the best you've ever known." You, dear reader, also deserve so much more and so much better than the best life has given you thus far. You deserve pure, unadulterated, and unapologetic bliss and ease. I believe that this is all our birthright, but oppression and class-based hierarchies have, unfortunately, convinced us that it's something we need to earn and make others earn. Can you imagine a world where we all consented to making joy and inclusion accessible to all bodies? A world where people don't have to prove their worth or advocate to be treated fairly? A world that recognizes kindness and structural inclusivity as a critical part of our collective survival and economy? I can, and as you read this book, I hope that you can imagine it with me. Hip Hop Hooray for pragmatic optimism.

We all know what it's like to be uglified by others and to uglify others. We have all experienced, at some point in our lives, being treated as if we were disposable, problematic, ugly, trash, a bother, and less than worthy of goodness and safety. And most of us have treated other people that way, or at least witnessed someone treat others in such a horrific manner. However, as poorly as some of us have been treated, we have also had enough love, care, and safety in our lives that we have developed the tools and confidence to lift our heads up, scowl down at any cruel words we encounter, cry or cuss when we need to, strategize for justice, and keep going. Essentially, we're empowered enough to dust our shoulders off and demand better. Here's the thing, though: too many of us aren't. Too many of us did not grow up receiving the safety, nurture, and encouraging pep talks to know we get to have standards or expectations.

Some of us have never had the opportunity to experience what justice or resolution feels like when it doesn't come at the expense of our safety or voice. Some of us, especially those most frequently bullied in classrooms, on playgrounds, in boardrooms and courthouses, and while simply walking down the street, almost never experience the apologies or hugs we need to keep moving forward. Those of us who weren't protected as children, who weren't safe with the adults that raised us, and who were constantly attacked by our peers know what it's like to experience uglifying words that are attached to fists, open palms, feet stomping down on us, weapons as threats, and life-threatening legislations or prison sentences.

We know the dangerous and terrifying consequences of living in a body that someone meaner and more protected than us perceives as ugly; of possessing a gender, sexual orientation, disability, race, nationality, or religion that other folks believe should be destroyed or illegalized; and the violence, hardships, cruelty, struggles, and abuse that happens when too many privileged people agree with those assertions.

We don't all experience uglification the same way, and we don't all have the same skill and capacity to clap back or defend ourselves. The language and concepts of this book cannot be treated as universal or simplified into black-and-white ideas. We must account for our different lived experiences, privileges, and oppressions while doing the work of fighting uglification, and strive to be compassionate and uplifting of those who know exclusion and violence the most. That said, regardless of our lived experiences and backgrounds, we all have the right to Reclaim UGLY and the responsibility to not uglify others. Change belongs to all of us and cannot happen without all of us.

## We Deserve Better

I want to be real with you, fam. Your beauty, ugly, brilliance, and fuckups mean nothing to me. I don't care what you look like, where you come from, what you ate for breakfast this morning, or how high maintenance someone else told you you are: **you deserve better.** I don't care if you've lied, stolen, cheated, snuck into the movie theatres, sold all the drugs in the world, or slept with everyone else's partners: **you deserve better.** And I don't care if you know me and we've had conflicts that were never resolved, if you are a former abuser, or if you threw a bottle at me while I was walking down the street and called me Chewbacca (which actually happened): **you still deserve better.**

It's okay to reject any voice that tries to convince you that you don't deserve better. We already know that traumatized and marginalized people, aka the vast majority of us, will try their best to shoot you down with the same intensity that they've been shot down. Uglification has conditioned us to normalize abuse and critique as culture and to believe we have to prove to someone else that we have done the work to be worthy of better treatment.

Some folks, including our loved ones and the organizations designed to help those of us in need, will outright tell you that you don't deserve better, that you're asking for too much, that you're acting entitled. They will critique you for speaking up for yourself and asking for justice or equity. Sometimes these messages will even come from the people who love you and want the best for you. They will tell you that you have to work harder than your body can, that you have to sacrifice your well-being and rest, that you have to suppress your desires and authenticity, that you have to lose weight, put on heels, deny your gender, change your hair, and strive to be perceived as cisgender to get something nice in life.

When you receive these messages, remember that **you deserve better**. There is no shame in knowing that you are worthy of more: more than simple survival or even resilience, more than being tired and exhausted all the time, more than choosing between joy or wellness and having enough money to pay your bills. You deserve more than listening to people constantly misgender you, forget your pronouns, or debate whether your existence is real or not; more than people putting you down for how you look, how your body moves and takes up space, or how you desire to experience being alive on this magical planet. You deserve more than some industry telling you that any part of your precious and perfect body needs to change so that you can finally be treated with the respect and kindness you deserve; more than wondering if you or your loved ones are going to face deportation, get arrested, or be killed by the cops or some racist vigilantes who don't know that they deserve better as well, and more than risking your safety every time you go on a date or fall in love. You deserve more than dying early from stress, trauma, poverty, and violence.

Oppression is not just something that scholars and social justice advocates write about. It's not just a concept that queers, racial justice advocates, and feminists complain about online. It's not just a thing that happens to people in countries with recognized dictators. It is real, present in our everyday realities, motivating our choices, informing how we perceive ourselves and others, and is viciously and connivingly killing us.

Whether it be through gunshots, fists, loneliness, rejection, cruelty, suicide, or the slow drain of working more than you sleep, oppression is killing us. If you are BIPOC; a trans, nonbinary, or queer person; a fat, sick, or disabled person; a person living with an abusive partner or parent; or someone impacted by the classist, racist, and xenophobic structures of policing, immigration, and economic neglect—it is crucial to me that you know that succumbing to the structures and trauma of oppression is not your fate, doesn't have to be your fate, shouldn't even have to be something you contemplate. **You deserve better. You deserve to live.**

We can create better. We have the power to make choices, create protocols and systems, and develop cultural values that protect ourselves and each other from the violence around us and the hateful ideologies we've socialized to perceive as "just the way things are." We have the skill and insight to create spaces, cultures, values, and even systemic practices that will keep us alive. We have the capacity and collaborative brilliance to build, write, paint, perform, dance, design, facilitate, organize, meme, and legislate the more and better that are attainable, that we know we need if we want to survive the changes happening to the earth that feeds and shelters us, and that we deserve. Let me repeat myself, **WE DESERVE BETTER!**

Oppression is not just the callous flick of a legislative vote or the daunting histories of colonization that slaughtered our ancestors. It's a system of choices that billions of people continue to make. You and I are among those billions. Oppression as we know it is a choice. There are parts of oppression that are completely out of our unique control or are a result of choices that have been made long before us, but there are so many other parts, some huge and some tiny, that we can shift and change through the everyday choices we make, the things we say, and the actions we refute.

In this book, you'll learn more about the ways we choose to consent to and participate in oppression—and how we can make very different choices. You'll learn about the possibilities and imaginations we can tap into that will let us take a break from the fight of survival—especially those of us with enslaved and colonized ancestries who have been fighting every day of our lives. And we will practice celebrating ourselves for choosing to Reclaim UGLY and helping facilitate a world where others can as well.

We deserve to be proud of ourselves for leaning into the courage to try something different when almost everyone we know pressures us to sustain and adhere to the same old, familiar status quo. We deserve to explore the luscious world around us with less fear, less anxiety, less stress, less worry, and so much more loving support, nurturing creativity, and affirming freedom. And we deserve to be free and better—truly free from the invisible but very real, very cultural, and very legislative chains that compel us into practices of harm and violence toward ourselves.

We deserve better. We deserve a world where we can all Uplift, Glorify, and Love Ourselves: equitably, in the ways that we choose, and through avenues and practices that support the liberation of others.

## The Apology You Deserve

If someone has had the audacity and gall to call you ugly or bully you for your appearance, I am so sorry.

If someone in your life chose to look at your precious and perfect face—your first portal of self-expression, the place where you feed yourself and scream out your rage, the venue of your smile and your most flirtatiously wanton eyes, the canvas adorned and alive with the shifting colors of emotion as they sparkle across your skin—and they, cruelly, unfairly, and without permission, pointed out every imperfection they thought they saw, nitpicked your complexion, critiqued the shape of your eyes or nose, told you your lips were too wide or small, commented on your facial hair, and spilled out all their unnecessary judgments about whether your face was appropriately smiling, assertive, confident, friendly, sweet, or expressing enough remorse, guilt, or grief: I am so sorry.

If anyone, at any point, without your consent, deigned themselves worthy of telling you their thoughts about your body or your health, about whether you needed to lose or gain weight, increase your muscle mass, or surgically amplify your curves: I'm sorry. If a loved one purchased you a gym membership without asking if that's what you wanted or kept pressuring you to change your hairstyle, wear more or less makeup, and/ or whiten your teeth: I'm sorry. If a friend or partner pressured you to exercise with them when you didn't want, stared intently at the amount of food that was or wasn't on your plate, or even commented on what was in your grocery cart or lunch pail: I'm sorry. I'm sorry if a stranger on the internet may have implied that you deserve to die because of your body weight, disability, gender, or life choices. These are cruel behaviors, sometimes wrapped up in a veneer of love or concern, but harmful nonetheless. Regardless of how often they may have been directed at you, they are not your burden to carry, and you deserve all the apologies.

I'm so sorry if an individual, or group of individuals in some position of authority, leadership, or intimacy, ever told you your delicious personality was too much, not enough, overdramatic, aggressive, bitchy, contrary, too timid, or in need of some suppression or repair. I'm sorry for the times you were silenced because someone didn't experience you as articulate enough when you spoke up, or because they reduced your perspective or research to "an agenda" because of your race, gender, sexual orientation, disability, or parenthood.

I'm sorry if you had to hold your precious child after they came home crying, whimpering the horrible and unfair things their classmates or teachers said to them, and bearing bruises and broken hearts because we still believe that bullying is inevitable. It's not. You and your child deserve better.

This part is also important: I'm sorry for the times when you were the bully, when you felt so hopeless and powerless that you used another person's suffering or disenfranchisement to make you feel better, when you repeated something horrible to your loved one because you didn't know better or were too stressed or terrified to say what you really felt, and when you negatively impacted someone's financial and living stability because of the ways uglification and capitalist elitism have colonized your imagination and taught you to prioritize some and deprioritize others.

I'm sorry for all the experiences you missed out on due to having internalized the messages of uglification. I mourn with you for the joy and relationships you may have experienced if you were open to recognizing beauty in different ways. I'm sorry for the years of pleasure and bliss you could have experienced if you weren't uglifying your body, your desires, or the people you secretly crave to be around. Uglification steals so much magic, possibility, and fulfillment from us, and it's not okay. You are worthy of a life radiant with joyful happenings and connection.

It is important that we recognize, name, and unpack the ways we experience uglification. Contemporary social justice, healing justice, and identity-politic movements have given us the space, voice, and language to talk about the unfair harms and violence we experience. But there aren't that many safe and courageous spaces for us to talk about the harms we perpetuate, the times we are cruel or judgmental because of our upbringings, and the people who suffered at the expense of our learning and growth. We won't see the better we need and deserve until we create those spaces and we offer ourselves and each other the grace to tell our awkward, uncomfortable, fumbling, and ugly truths.

We must tell the stories of the cruelties and injustices we experience to denormalize the attitudes and behaviors that facilitate them, to stigmatize those cruelties and injustices in an impactful way, and to hold the world accountable to doing better. But it cannot just be a conversation about the harm we experience. If we truly want to see change, we also must tell the truths about the times we've looked at other people with disgust and distaste because of our judgments about their appearance and personhood. We have to be courageous enough to discuss the occasions when we've leaned over to whisper something nasty in our friend's ear about the looks of someone we didn't like or the times when we've chosen to limit someone else's opportunity because of our biases and prejudices.

We need to be vulnerable and compassionate with ourselves about the times we've pressured our children and partners to be someone other than who they authentically are or pursue what they desire, because we believed them to be a representative of our selves. There is no asking other people to be accountable, regardless of how much more privilege they have than you, if you cannot be accountable to the times when you lashed out at people simply because you were frustrated or mad about something else, and never took the time to apologize. We have to discuss our uglifying behaviors and values in a real way, a transformative way, and not a simple finger-pointing, name-the-villain way. Criminalization has yet to produce anything but more violence and harm.

People who have raped others need to be able to process the fact that they made that choice and to unpack the why, so we can figure out what cultural work we need to do to prevent other rapes. Abusers need the space to explore their humanity, and what part of their emotional and psychological ecosystem has led them to choose abuse. Bullies cannot stop bullying until they can empathize with the parts of themselves that choose those behaviors.

We humans do horrible things to other people, all of us, and as long as we continue to subscribe to an us vs. them binary mentality, those horrible things will persist and we won't be able to heal the hurt and anger that oppression has pushed into the crevices of so many of our hearts. That is why reclaiming ugly is not just about addressing beauty standards, it's an invitation into the compassionate self-exploration needed to understand why we perpetuate, tolerate, and condone uglification. It may sound naïve or delusional, but if we consistently uglify ourselves and others for our behavior without creating space for true curiosity, we'll never actually end the cycles of harm and uglification that have been plaguing human existence since, well, we've come into existence.

Sometimes even the most justice oriented and benevolent hearted of us can find ourselves assessing and critiquing other people through the same colonized, repressed, patriarchal, and brutal ideologies that have been viciously imposed on us. We can be lookist and fatphobic. We can be xenophobic and white-supremacist. We can practice rape and disposability culture. We can be more in touch with our trauma than our hope and dreams. And we can mobilize around militaristic and binaried standards of what is and isn't social justice, who is and isn't acceptable to be in community with, who we are willing to align ourselves with and who we turn up our noses at. We were taught these rituals of judgment and condemnation via the starch rules of right and wrong in childhood, the dangerous binaries of history books and religious studies, and even through the simplified mores of children's television programming and cultural mythology. We learned through discipline and punishment. We learned by watching how the adults who reared and educated us related to themselves and each other. Adulthood sometimes coerces us into justifying behaviors and attitudes that we may have, at one point in our lives, thought of as unreasonable and unfair; and we end up hurting the people we love and discriminating against strangers and friends alike as a result of that coercion. Too many times, we turn our claws—claws we didn't exactly ask for, claws we grew to survive a ruthless and callous social climate, claws that we think will keep us safe but that actually scratch already tender and bruised flesh—on ourselves, our babies, our siblings, our people, and we suffer in harsh, lonely, and devastatingly unnecessary ways.

Engaging with this book is an opportunity to tenderly sit with yourself and assess if you are helping create a world where you yourself and other people, both near and far, have the support and spaciousness to uplift, glorify, and love themselves out of suffering—or if you are making it a little bit harder for the people around you to enjoy being alive and present. In writing *Reclaiming UGLY*, I examined my own past, the times I've been uglified and the times I've uglified others. I will share some of those tender and vulnerable stories. These stories are not to inspire shame or secondary trauma. They are here because they need to be spoken and heard so that we can not only understand them but also name and bury the tools, beliefs, and practices that facilitate them.

To access that dream of systemizing and normalizing the better we deserve, we have to take care of ourselves in the now by determining and centering what our better means and looks like in the moment. In honor of that care, I would like to offer trigger warnings for intimate partner violence, suicide, the prison-industrial complex, rape, medical violence, white supremacy, misogyny—including misogynoir and transmisogyny—and murder. As a survivor of many traumatic incidents, I experience a lot of pain when I hear about other people's pain and hardship. Here is a list of strategies I practice to take care of my triggers and traumas when they show up. I hope they will support you to be present with yourself and what may come up as you read this book. I like to think about them as my defenses against the relentless havoc that systemic oppression and uglification imparts on my body. They help me reclaim my calm, my body, and my imagination when it feels like stress and anxiety are taking over. Practicing them helps me ensure I am centering and providing the more and better that I'm advocating.

# Reclaiming UGLY Self-Compassion Sustainability Practices

As you begin to engage with this book, keep these tips in mind and come back to these pages often to ground yourself and remember that you deserve more.

## 1. Stay present with your body and bless it with your attention.

Sometimes when we are triggered, caught up in the emotionality of painful history, or even overwhelmed with empathy, our bodies can shut down, disconnect from our agency and values, and go into autopilot. This is called *disassociation*, and it's usually a result of how our consciousness has learned from previous traumatic experiences to protect itself from that which may be overwhelming or terrifying. The hard thing about disassociating during tense situations is that we may misunderstand or miss out on the embodied, intuitive, and wise messages that will tell us what we need to stay safe in the moment.

When we can be present with ourselves, these internal messages are so potent. They can help keep us grounded in our power and protected from the ways uglification and other acts and practices of violence exasperate our mental health, our perceptions of other people and uncomfortable situations, and the workings of our bodily organs. While stress facilitates great harm and even kills, practicing grounded presence and self-awareness can save your life and prevent so many other people's death.

If you are someone who struggles to ground when triggered, I encourage you to turn reading this book into an experiment: use it as a lower-stakes opportunity to practice respecting your body as a messenger, healer, and defender against stress. If you decide to take me up on the idea to treat this book as an experiment, here are a few things to note as you read:

- What feelings, thoughts, and desires come up as you encounter certain stories, questions, analysis, poems, and memory triggers?

- When you are hyperaware of your breath, when is it faster or more labored than usual, and when do you find yourself experiencing headaches because you aren't taking in enough oxygen?

- Are you so caught up in a story that you're not paying attention to your thirst or hunger, holding in liquids that your body needs to release, or not fully present to what's going on around you?

- Are you empathizing with someone else's story so intensely that you feel anger, shame, or a lack of safety?

I've learned that regardless of where I am and what I'm doing, if I'm feeling anxiety, it helps me to sit up straight, push my shoulders back and my chest out, relax my belly and jaw, and allow myself to slowly process each inhale and exhale of breath. The slowing down of breath, especially the outward breath, lessens any tension aches I may be feeling and eases a racing heart.

If I have knots or tightness in my tummy or feel dizzy or faint, I like to lie down with my head on a pillow and my feet and legs elevated. From there I lovingly massage my thighs, hips, and belly, breathe in deep and slow, and softly offer myself words of grounding affirmation. I might tell myself that I'm alright over and over, until I believe it with my whole body and the panic is gone. I try to stay unclenched and loose as possible, bounce or walk around, and invite looseness to help me reject the ways that stress will try its best to take over my organs, thought patterns, and choices.

If you find yourself approaching a panic attack, remember that your flesh, including your brain and heart, belongs solely to your consciousness in this moment—not your memories, fears, anger, shame, self-doubt, empathy, or someone else's opinion. Claiming your breath and body is a way to make sure you remain in charge of you.

## 2. Keep water nearby and drink it frequently, especially if you are a sweet, tender crybaby like me.

However they come, our flowing tears are a powerful and necessary release. They bathe us. They carry protective salts. They baptize us into the transcendence of our own choices. They wash away previous hurts. They cleanse and moisturize our eyes as we prepare to continue living our magical lives. Tears can also dehydrate us, pulling very necessary resources from our skin, flesh, and energy.

As you read this book, consume the water, teas, and fruits that will support your body to hold you whole throughout this healing and reflection process. You are precious, important, and more than worthy of staying hydrated and refreshed. The water will also support the lucidity of your thoughts and expansiveness of your imagination; it will keep you in the present, nurture you as you explore the nuance of your emotions, and remind you of your fluidity.

If your feelings get too heavy, take a bath, shower, or foot bath. Put Epsom salt and your favorite flowers or herbs in the water with you. Breathe the steam in through your nose and mouth. The water inside you will establish harmony with the water outside you. Pretend like you are a water witch. When you are distressed, you can summon water to your soil and gently use it to grow fibrous plants for healing change, you can rinse away the muck that no longer serves you, or you can drown in a shame storm that takes everyone else around you out as well. I'm cheering you on to use the water of your emotions as tool and medicine!

## 3. Move and meow when your body wants to and the way it wants to.

Make sounds, like meows, sighs, roars, yawns, or even Mariah Carey high-pitched whistles, when your body feels compelled. Give yourself the opportunity to release noise and breath without worrying about how you sound or how other folks may respond to you. Be as growly, ugly, and bold as you need. Get the gunk out your throat and the junk out your heart.

Gentle stretching can also do so much to keep us emotionally limber while we manage the stress and anxiety of traumatic memories, including empathizing with other people's difficult stories. Don't get stuck in the book. When you are inclined to shift, give yourself the freedom to respond. Move in a way that feels safe, pleasurable, and easily accessible to you. If your body allows you to, lift your arms over your head and reach for the sky every hour or so. Twist your torso from side to side. If you are a person who walks, walk around your home or yard, bend over, smell a plant or stare at a meandering insect, and let your body hang and sway.

Feel the sensations of the ground underneath your feet. Remember that the earth holds your weight without limit, complaint, or critique. The earth birthed you, feeds you, and loves you. It does not care about how your body moves, how much you move, and the pace at which you move. It is there for your joy, pleasure, coexistence with other creatures. For many of us who are fat and/or disabled, reclaiming our right to indulge in healing movement, body intuition, and earth magic, rigorous or not, can be an extraordinary feat. In my thirties I learned that I enjoy brief stints of running up hills, that I thrive on the challenge and short burst of competitive energy, that my muscles craved the burn of a fast run, and learning those things about myself shocked the shame and trauma of fatphobia out of me.

As you read this book and deep into the future, please remember that you are a sensuous being. Enjoy the texture of wind and sun-warmth caressing your skin, the tickle of grass or carpet between your toes, the shift of energy flexing throughout your flesh, and the decadence of one part of your body touching and even jiggling against another part as you move. I personally love the ripple sensation of one chubby inner thigh lobe slapping against another when I do certain dances. I adore the breathlessness I feel after karaoke-screaming Mary J. Blige songs at the top of my lungs. I crave the ease and contentment I feel after a class of facilitated restorative or Anusvara yoga. And I will literally fight to retain the psychological and emotional spaciousness I feel after a long, slow, and meandering walk while listening to my favorite audiobook or the old-school funk, soul, and R&B I was raised on.

By making these suggestions, I am not requesting that you exercise, nor am I expressing concern about your health. But like the way we digest food, we also digest ideas. Movement on your own terms and grounded in your own pleasure and accessibility will definitely help aid your holistic engagement with the ups and downs of this text and the external stressors of life. We fat people and disabled people deserve to enjoy our bodies without the fatphobia and healthism that constantly assault and police us. Even more so, we deserve the grounded ease that comes from having an active and intentionally loving relationship with our bodies and the ways they move. Even if it's a two-minute sprint, running has been a way to reclaim my precious flesh from the uglification it has endured. Passionate lovemaking with myself, another person, or the earth (ask me about that rock I sat on the last time I was at the river) is another way. As you read this book, I hope you find a way to reclaim your relationship to your body and its needs as well.

## 4. Protect your energy and headspace.

This book is an invitation for you to uplift your needs, desires, joy, and humanity. It's an opportunity to practice glorifying your magnificent self with the same fierce commitment that some people glorify deities, riches, success, and even other people. It's a request that you create the time to explore loving yourself in new and precious ways, to be in intimate and passionate relationship with yourself, to practice embracing every ounce of you, including and especially those bits that are hard to love.

As you explore what it means to love all of you with care and consideration for who you are and what you need to feel safe and joyful, I highly recommend that you decide who and which ideas get to enter your realm of sacred healing and growth. You don't need to justify who and what you do and don't allow into your life. You deserve peace. Try your absolute best to avoid people and media whose words and behavior are counterproductive to your ability to have an uninterrupted loving relationship with yourself.

Don't let naysayers, haters, or someone else's internalized oppression get in the way of you having a more liberated and joyful relationship with yourself. If you know your mom is going to critique your lifestyle, appearance, or career/love choices when she calls, don't answer the phone. If you know your homeboy is going to make snarky comments about your intelligence or desirability, cancel that hang-out date. If you know that social media is going to be filled with stories of grief that you just don't have emotional room for, play a nonviolent video game instead. Why not listen to a soothing jazz or classical station instead of a radio station with insensitive commercials and deejays who don't know how to be funny without being cruel?

Keep handy the phone number of someone who loves you specifically the way you want to be loved. Not everyone who loves or cares about us knows how to translate that love into a healing or generative experience. Some people don't yet know how to respect our boundaries, honor our pronouns, or provide us with the compassionate generosity we need. These are not the people to reach out to during moments of trigger or intensity. Choose someone who knows how to hold you when you're in a fragile space, someone who can be honest with you without ripping you to shreds, someone who can respect your vision for what healing and support looks like in the moment.

Please don't use this as an excuse to critically judge what you need or where you believe you are. If you're concerned about your choices or level of self-awareness, take this moment in time as an opportunity to be present with yourself right now, including the parts of yourself you want to set free. Treat this as a getting-to-know-yourself process, an intimate and precious romance with yourself, an opportunity to remember the magic, creativity, and feral wildness of who you were before society and respectability may have tempered your freedom. When you are ready, invite the participation of people who can help you take care of yourself the way you want and need. Regardless of what's going on in your life, you are the senior-most expert at loving you. No one knows you better. Your happiness, ease, and pleasure are always a sign of the right direction. You don't have to work for it. You don't have to earn it.

## 5. Have long, sprawling conversations with yourself.

I have a journaling prompt that I frequently offer myself, especially during moments of panic or when I'm uncertain about my feelings or a decision I need to make. I carve out a comfortable amount of space and time, grab a notebook or use my cell phone to text myself, and I facilitate a written conversation with myself.

I ask myself questions about how I feel, how I feel about that feeling, why I feel that way, and what I want to do with it. Sometimes I give myself very helpful advice. I'm able to say the things that are difficult for me to remember when I'm triggered, hurt, enraged, or spiraling deep into victimization. When I've felt hurt by others, I've been able to talk myself out of sending long, unnecessary emails to people who wouldn't actually care or receive them well, and I have figured out what I needed to feel better in the minute and in the long term. During these conversations, I get to be sweet to myself, learn myself better, and hold myself accountable to what my values and beliefs are today, in the moment.

I want to encourage you all to do something similar for yourselves. Talk to yourself. Journal. Take notes. Ask yourself questions. I've sprinkled creative reflection prompts aplenty throughout the book. Play with the ones that call to you. If you are a romantic person like me, consider engaging with them as a romantic experience. When we find ourselves falling in deep love with new people, practices, ideas, and interest, we often want to learn everything we can about them. We want to know their history, how they became who or what they are, how to treat them or it well. This is an opportunity for you to do the same with yourself.

Reclaiming ugly is about unpacking and understanding uglification. But it's much, much more about reclaiming a deep, unapologetic, compassionate, and loving relationship with ourselves in our most human wholeness. It's about knowing ourselves, so we can be the people we truly want to be while creating a world that is safe and expansive enough for us all. I believe that the better we treat ourselves, the better we treat others, our planet, and all the seeds and beings this planet produces. But to treat ourselves well, we have to know ourselves outside the gaze of oppression and shame. So use this as an opportunity to court, romance, befriend, and fall passionately in love with you.

## 6. Fill yourself and your surroundings up with yummy, yummy goodness.

Yes, family, transform instances of discomfort into opportunities to indulge in the things, practices, and experiences that invite you to feel good, inside and out. When your heart feels overwhelmed with the grief of everything, or if you find yourself starting to shame-spiral, please take a break and pursue some sort of intentionally thought-out, instinctual, and ethically hedonistic comfort, and portion it out with a pleasurable abundance. This sort of care is both reclamation and a strategy to decrease the impacts of uglification and the inclination to uglify yourself and others. It's swamping agony with beauty. We deserve beauty.

Reclaiming ugly is not a rejection of beauty. It's an expansion of what we have been taught to perceive as beautiful and what we allow ourselves to enjoy. It's a reminder that beauty is a personal and autonomous instance of consent, and not a universal standard or objective assessment. What is beautiful, delicious, and magical to me may not and does not need to be perceived as such by anyone else, and no one should attempt to overlord or dominate another person's experience of beauty and joy. With that said, I encourage you, dear reader, to decide the experiences of beauty that will serve your comfort and joy, inspire feelings of creativity and safety, and lift you up when the murk is too overwhelming. What's most exciting is that you and only you get to choose what beauty and joy mean for yourself—and you can choose to pursue and explore them as often as you desire, you can change your mind about what does and doesn't work for you, and you can modify your joy and beauty recipe as you grow and experience more of life and healing. I recommend *Pleasure Activism* by adrienne maree brown and *Eat Mangoes Naked* by SARK as literary tools to help you define and lean into what feels good for you. In the meantime, if recognizing what pleasure feeds you is a struggle, as it often is for people who have experienced a lot of abusive and unwanted domination or who are in the middle of trigger and panic, I have a few suggestions to offer. Use them as a diving board to jump into your own fantasies of paradise in the moment!

One suggestion, especially for folks who struggle with anxiety and panic, is reading this book underneath a weighted blanket in a comfortable room that is filled with crystals, plants, paintings, snacks, and the sounds of serotonin-inducing musical frequencies. This will facilitate a sacred, meditative experience, and the plant, art, sound, and stone energy will energize and nurture you in the most delicious of ways. If you're always busy, overwhelmed, running around, or sitting in front of a computer, you may consider reading this book at a park, amid the sounds of children playing and life humming, with your back propped up against a tree, and smoking some herbs that calm you down and bliss you out. My favorite is a joint made of mullein, damiana, and cannabis. Music is a bit of heart and brain decadence that I also forget when I'm in the heavy midst of things. Everything that Gina Breedlove and Beautiful Chorus release lend themselves to be soothing balms of belonging and meditative self-love, and Jill Scott's "Hate on Me" picks me up out of every possible emotional gutter to remind me of the fact that those gutters are usually created by someone else and that I can say no, and Lil Nas X and Lizzo remind me that I can be my freest self.

If you like aromatics, perhaps you have herbal oils, steams, teas, incense, or sage nearby to burn. Cook or boil something that will transform your space. Beauty is about more senses than those experienced by the eyes, the ears, and the heart. Stimulate your senses with smells and textures that bring about all the warm fuzzies and stimulate spaciousness and slowness needed to truly breathe. Indulge in snacks. Perhaps they are the foods that give you energy or cleanse your blood, as our bodies need and deserve, but they may also be the comfort foods that help you relax, escape from the wild world we live in, and remember sweet moments from the past. Choose the beauty and bliss that will help you experience the life and moment you crave.

## 7. Be gentle and compassionate with yourself so that you can be genuine and honest with yourself.

The call to reclaim ugly is not only a request to reclaim the parts of yourself that have been uglified by the systems, values, and subscribers of oppression; it is also a call to recognize and intervene with the ways you practice uglification. Uglification is something we all do in a myriad of conscious and unconscious ways, including me. We've been trained to accept receiving it from others and to use it as a tool to make interpersonal, political, and self-directed assessments from the moment we start learning what it means to be a human.

Early on, we're taught how to be presentable and beautiful; how to best represent our families, religions, races, and genders; and how to not "act ugly" or embarrass our loved ones or other people with whom we share cultural/racial identity. We're taught that there are consequences for stepping out of line, and that we should be terrified of them and do everything possible to avoid them. Then we're taught how to recognize when others step out of those same arbitrary lines and to be angry or uncomfortable with those people. We're taught the different ways we can dispense consequences (like bullying, exclusion, chastisement, concern trolling, and shaming) to rein in people who step out of line and to hold them accountable for breaking the social contracts of good, beauty, normality, and culture. Consider a time when you were chastised for a behavior that felt right or good because someone in your family or at your church or school told you that your behavior was un-Christian, un-Muslim, unladylike, unmanly, not <insert racial identity> enough, or un-something-else that someone expected of you and others like you. Can you remember an occasion when you were discouraged to befriend someone because of how other people judged them, maybe even a time when you chose not to befriend or date someone you liked because you were afraid of the social repercussions?

Throughout childhood we are taught, through media, gossip, and messages from our families/religions, which type of people to pursue friendships with, which traits to avoid in others, and how to be someone that others will find acceptable to like, love, and desire in public. Rarely are we taught how to be ourselves, listen to our own hearts, and make our own autonomous determinations around who we want to befriend, admire, or find attractive. Those of us who are encouraged to pursue that sort of freedom are lucky and should share their stories far and wide. We need as many examples as possible of adults nurturing the empowered autonomy and self-determination of children.

Those of us who weren't supported to be decision-makers or taught how to be free and open-minded thinkers will often center our very natural thirst for acceptance and admiration, even if it's at the expense of our authentic joy. This is because the world teaches us to crave success and external affirmation, to say that we made it, we were accepted, and we have something better than other people from where we originated, rather than to make choices that facilitate happiness. In fact, media and religious parables alike often vilify or make jokes of people who have found happiness outside the beaten norm. Consider the constant jokes about cat ladies, wacky aunts who live in the country, and weed-smoking hippies—all caricature tropes of people who have chosen lifestyles outside the regular, all people who we're taught to perceive as other, different, crazy.

We often make choices based on those learnings. We're taught who to distrust and who to automatically assume is safe. We're taught that certain standards of appearance, accomplishment, and existence should be celebrated, and that others are grounds for dismissal or rebuke. Because of this, we've all unkindly laughed at people who deserved their peace. We've judged people who honor their freedom. We've said and done things that have hurt someone we loved for exploring their truth. We have bullied people into complacency with the norms we've accepted or watched while someone else did it, unsure of how to speak up or if it is our place to intervene. Some of us may have even abused people in an effort to control them and make them be who we believe they should be. All of us have done things that are more violent than we want to acknowledge, and it's because of unchecked uglification. We all need to heal the parts of us that have been uglified and the parts of us that are inclined to uglify others. We deserve better.

What's important to name, however, is that none of us, nor our actions, exist in a vacuum. A person cannot hold the sole accountability for anything or any situation. When we choose to make a person fully and wholly responsible, we dismiss the power of the systems and economies that not only foster violence and uglification but rely on them to exist. We deny the impact of experiencing repetitive trauma in a world that rarely facilitates opportunities and resources for people to heal. We ignore the roles we, even those of us who are oppressed, play in sustaining and benefiting from systems of oppression, and hence the roles we play in the violence and trauma they facilitate. When this happens, we end up protecting the actual source of harm and throwing an actual human being, a fellow survivor, under the bus. This does not effect change. Throwing people away does not interrupt harm. Nor does beating yourself up when you realize the harm you've caused, the injustices you've perpetuated, and the times you have been the steward of someone else's uglification. If you recognize yourself as a steward of uglification while reading this text, please know that you are not alone and that shame or self-flagellation will not alleviate anything you have done in the past. That is something that only healing, self-love, humility, and repair can do for you.

So, family, as you read this book and explore your own reclaiming ugly journey, please bless yourself with the space, gentleness, community support, and self-compassion to heal from the past. Give yourself room to relearn who you are, to catch up with the healing and growth you've already done, and to choose how to move forward in a way that is aligned with curiosity, awareness, and a pleasure that starts inside you and extends to everyone you meet. If you can't stop thinking about people you have harmed and your heart is telling you to act, get consent to negotiate restitution. Learn what repair is needed and welcomed. And apologize to yourself and them from a place of patience and abundance, from a desire to do better and an acknowledgment that they and you both deserve better. If guilt shows up, feel it, learn from it, but don't build a home there. Guilt is a temporary emotion, which makes its capacity for honesty just as temporary. Real change relies on real healing, and that takes a lot of time and intentionality. Please be good to you. You deserve the best and so do the people with whom you choose to love, collaborate, and be in community.

• • •

I would like to take a moment to be transparent and vulnerable with you. I am deeply impacted by other people's thoughts about me—especially my character. Being an intentionally kind, just, loving, and compassionate person is important to me, and being loved by my chosen community and family—especially as a chronically ill and neurodivergent person—is fundamental to my survival. I know how hard life is when the people

around you don't love or like you, and I am terrified of being in that position. More so, I am terrified of causing the people I choose to call beloved
or community unnecessary pain.

But as a human being, I also know that hurting people is inevitable;
and I have hurt so many people. I have hurt people due to my lack of healing and groundedness. I have hurt people by looking at them through the
gaze of my insecurity and fears of rejection or exclusion, instead of seeing
their humanity and good intentions. I have hurt people with unfair accusations when I felt triggered, instead of asking questions. I have hurt
people by not fully listening to their truths and only responding to what
I wanted to hear, or what my most traumatized brain heard. I have hurt
people by unknowingly regurgitating my own socialized uglifications
of others at them. I have hurt people by immediately believing the half-
truths that people have told me about them, and spreading those half-
truths through the fires of my own sense of justice. I have hurt people
by abandoning them during moments of crisis or turmoil. I have hurt
people by only acknowledging their privileges and using that information to judge them. I have hurt people intentionally, as an act of revenge,
retribution, or self-protection, when I felt harmed. I have hurt people by
refusing to apologize.

I have hurt people unintentionally; for example, I've stepped on people's feet, literally, and I once accidentally stapled my friend's arm while
being silly. I have hurt people by not understanding that no means no, as
opposed to no meaning try to convince them harder. I have hurt people
by telling truths that weren't mine to tell and using their stories as examples to push a point. I have hurt people by not understanding or realizing
how much they love me. I have hurt people by not showing up when I
said I would or in the way I said I would. I have hurt people by celebrating
them when they did not want or consent to be celebrated.

I have hurt people by honoring and not honoring my own truths:
by agreeing to participate in projects, activities, and relationships that I
didn't want to participate in or didn't really have capacity for. I have hurt
people by making choices rooted in not wanting to hurt their feelings. I
have hurt people by deciding to end jobs and relationships that no longer

served my joy or happiness. I have hurt people by saying no to the things they wanted from me, including time. I have hurt people by putting up boundaries when my boundaries weren't in alignment with their needs or desires. I have hurt people by speaking up to them, or speaking to people who could help intervene, when I was feeling harmed or unprotected. I have hurt people by being too afraid, or not confident enough, to be honest.

Some people, including people I love, will be hurt by some of the stories I share in this book. Some people will feel shame when they recognize in my stories some of the harm and mistakes they have made. Please be compassionate with yourself.

I sometimes conflate hurting people with being a bad person—but please hear me deep in your heart when I say that this is not true. There are times when people are hurt because of something we have said or done, but that does not mean our words or actions are wrong. Our hurt is a result of our lived experiences, how others have treated us, how we are and are not healing/healed, what we are and are not sensitive to, and what we project onto our experiences or someone else. Sometimes people are hurt because they feel entitled to us and our resources and are unable to accept our no or our standards. Sometimes people are hurt because they want to be hurt—that's where they are at in the moment and that's how they choose to live their lives. And sometimes people are hurt because we fucked up and made choices that unfairly, unjustly, unkindly caused pain.

I believe it is my responsibility to make choices that foster freedom and equity, to be a healing and compassionate person. But I know that I cannot take on everyone's hurt. Neither can you. That said, when you care, when you are empathetic, it's so hard not to take on responsibility for others' pain.

When I hurt people, shame takes ahold of me and drags me into the seven fabricated hells of low self-esteem, guilt, and shame so dense it occasionally transforms into ideation. These emotions, or the behaviors they produce, do not help give me the courage to apologize or make corrective actions, nor do they heal the impacts of my choices. Because

I know that my shame doesn't serve me or isn't in alignment with the person I want to be, I must work hard, regularly and intentionally, to be kind and compassionate to myself when I fuck up or cause harm.

I use the Reclaim UGLY framework to help myself navigate shame and guilt when it comes up for me, which is all the damn time. Perhaps it will also work for you. Here is my strategy:

1. **I Reclaim Myself:** I am a dynamic human being who cares about other people and I am trying my best. I will make mistakes but I am not the sum of my mistakes. Learning that I have caused harm or fucked up is not the worst news in the world, it's not an indication of my worth or social value. Instead, it's an opportunity to learn, show up with the care for others I believe in, listen to the people who have harmed me, and grow. I want to grow and I trust my beloveds to hold me, and sometimes even lead me, during that growing process.

2. **I Uplift Myself:** So I fucked up and caused harm. That doesn't make me a horrible person. It makes me human. But what makes me a wonderful person is my ability to listen to others, receive feedback, and make changes. Because I'm willing to do this, instead of lean into defensiveness and put the blame on others, I am actually a wonderful person to be around and build with. Go, Vanessa, go! I can be the person I want to be!

3. **I Glorify Myself:** I am talented, powerful, and capable of implementing the changes necessary to create a safer environment for myself, my loved ones, and the people I collaborate with. I am a portal for collective healing because I'm so invested in my own healing! If I were perfect, I could not heal, I could not grow, I could not aspire. Thank goodness I am not perfect. Thank goodness for my softness, my big heart, and my fleshy-electric brain that refuses to be stuck. <Insert a song of self-praise>

**4. I Love Myself:** I deserve sweetness and care in order to face, admit to, and navigate the difficult impacts of my behavior. Beating myself up and shame spiraling is not loving to myself. I must say sweet, encouraging things to myself. I must bless my body with things that feel good, like hot showers, nature walks, cuddling with my lovers, delicious foods, and rest. Even though it's so hard, coming from a crime-and-punishment culture, I have to love and nurture myself into the beauty of self- and collective compassion and accountability.

Another way that I reclaim ugly through self-kindness and self-compassion is remembering the fact that I have a purpose. I exist, in my body, in this moment in time, for a reason—and it has nothing to do with being productive or in service to others. My purpose, which is naturally and innately a part of my flesh and spirit, gets activated when I get spaciousness from the exhaustion of oppression and the depression of constant triggers and trauma. It gets hungry to exist. It gets fueled up by its power. And it becomes too irresistible to suppress, much less allow myself to linger in a cesspool of shame and lack of accountability.

Remembering that I have a purpose inspires me to heal, grow, dream of ways to do better, and to actually do the better, right then, when I need it. My purpose helps me identify what integrity, rightness, and morality mean to me, instead of getting dragged down into names that another person has called me, expectations that aren't in alignment with my purpose or values, or even concepts of heaven or hell / good or bad that society has been taught through different versions of church and government.

My purpose reminds me of how I want to move, how I want to treat a situation, and how I want to right my wrongs and interact with other people. It keeps me free. It keeps me away from the fiery jaws of uglification—including the ways I, or others, may direct uglification toward me amid conflict and confusion.

Friends, your purpose is a gift from the divine, a brilliant tool that can keep you safe, a reverent magic that can light your way when the voices around you are murky. We can recognize our purpose when we feel like we are walking in our power, our pleasure, and our pride. Our pleasure perks up when we sit patiently with our truths and honor them.

Our purpose does not have to be talent, productivity, or capitalism. Consider how people who are dependent on others, regardless of age, make their caretakers so happy just by continuing to be alive. Our pets hold us through the hardest of storms, and we don't put them to work. Babies remind us of the awe and wonder of the world, and we don't expect them to prove their value. We consent to it being innate. Sometimes we heal from stress and ailment simply by sleeping next to someone we trust and love.

I believe that our purposes are why we are here on this planet and why we existed when we transition out of this life. Our lives, all our lives, are sacred. When the world forgets that we are sacred, connecting with our purpose can help us remember just how critical and precious we are, regardless. Say it with me now: "I am sacred. I am precious. I belong here. I am worthy of love. I deserve better and I am capable of better. I must stay alive, present, and open to experience the better that is my birthright."

Below are a series of critical-thinking prompts that I often ask myself when I am stuck in a place I don't want to be. I hope they support you with your own freedom and remembering.

---

## CRITICAL-THINKING PROMPTS FOR REVOLUTIONARY SELF-REFLECTION AND LIBERATION JOURNALING

- What do you in the world? (These can be things you do for money or trade, for your own passion and pleasure, for art and movement work, or for family and loved ones.)

- What brings you the most pleasure, fulfillment, and pride?

- How much do you understand your purpose and/or reason for being on this earth? How do you honor your purpose through the things you do in this world? How do your life circumstances affect your ability to live your purpose?

- How are you impacted by oppression, injustice, and uglification in your life? How have they been used against you? How are you privileged by them?

- How have you been ambivalent or unaware?

- What do you need to learn about power, privilege, and oppression—and what steps will you take to learn that information?

- How will you prepare yourself to be present with AND answer any calls to action if your purpose changes, evolves, re-reveals itself to you, or becomes more accessible to you because of this new learning?

- What power or influence do you have to create cultural, systemic, or even ideological shifts—in your family and the communities, movements, and professions you navigate—to honor what you've learned about the world and your purpose?

- What support do you need from yourself and others to lean into your power and courage to implement those changes? What might get in the way, and who can you call on to strategically plan and circumvent any naysayers or disrupters?

- What can you do in spite of the gatekeepers and stewards of oppression, or anyone else who attempts to shame or persecute you out of your purpose and desire to do/live/experience better?

- What will you do to nurture your spirit and joy along the way?

# 2

# An Introduction to Uglification

Whether it was a stranger taking a photo of me and giggling during a bus ride, a fellow classmate at my middle school testifying that God made light because God hates darkness and consequently hates me for being so dark and burnt, one of my parents desperately asking me if I "wanted to be beautiful" in an attempt to convince me to lose weight, or some random teenaged boy screaming "eeeewwww gross" after hearing a rumor that I had a crush on him—I know the isolation, harassment, and exhaustion that comes with being perceived as ugly. I have known this experience since I was a five-year-old child starting elementary school, and that knowing left me devastated as a child and as a young adult. It wasn't until my mid to late twenties that I decided I no longer consented to live within that devastation.

By the time I reached the early part of my mid-thirties, when the unfortunate incident that inspired my curiosity about uglification and my action call to reclaim ugly happened, I was done caring about what other people had to say about my looks, health, or body—period. I was in a romantic relationship with myself and had decided that my opinion about my body was supreme to any voice that had the misgiving to suggest anything different. I had leaned into the difficulty and bliss of courting myself, fallen passionately and romantically in love with myself as I was, learned how to nurture that love through making my own choices, transformed so much of yesterday's wounds into gorgeous scar tissue, and spiritually tattooed several of those scars with self-compassion and reverence. I told myself over and over, with a fierce righteousness, that other people's perspectives of how I look is more about them and their gaze and has absolutely nothing to do with me or the way I rock my skin and curves. I was so damn happy during that era. I was living the life of my dreams. I had fully embraced the TRUTH that when it comes to my self-perception, there is no definitive beauty or human value outside my own determination, and I determine myself to be stunning, opulent with sex appeal, and so very seductive. I asserted that anyone who thinks differently was confused, and their confusion was not my problem.

I had everything I needed: best friends, homies, family, lovers, respected colleagues, and a partner who loved every juicy part of my plum-colored body and feral, artsy personality. I was rarely lonely or bored. I lived and loved in a home and community that, for the most part, felt good for my soul. I never questioned whether I was cute enough, entertaining enough, or wore the right outfit when I went to a party or event because I knew the people around me were not judging or assessing me for those things. I had worked in many incredible arenas, including the online editorial world, academia, the nonprofit industry, and even corporate America. When I felt insecurity about being sick and disabled, organizations like Sins Invalid, a disability justice performance art group that spoke to the erotic of my soul, and other social justice arts groups helped me feel like my dreams of creating meaningful and accessible art were more than accessible. Because, as a part of my romantic commitment to myself that I would only sustain joyful relationships and that anyone who popped the bubble of my fat, dark-skinned, disabled queer joy would get axed out of my life, there were no (at the time) haters or naysayers making my lived experience uncomfortable. I was living out loud, in public, and on every stage that I could book.

The thing about living publicly, however, is that all sorts of people eventually see you. Including people that don't mean you, or anyone else, any good. My photo was found and exploited by several male online personalities who not only didn't mean me any good, they couldn't even recognize my humanity. The men who found my photo looked at me and saw a tool, a joke, and a body to tread on.

Reclaiming ugly began for me in November 2018 after I read at a book launch for James Cagney, a dope-ass poet living in the Bay Area, and his phenomenal poetry collection, *Black Steel Magnolias in the Hour of Chaos Theory*. That night, I was looking fly. I wore a long thin red dress that draped like magic and honeysuckle across my curves, a black and red Harlem Renaissance style feather hair barrette, and some strappy high-heeled shoes that I was only able to wear because my partner held my hands the whole night. Because I had been severely sick and had brain fog for a while, it was my first time reading my poetry in front of an audience in many months, and I was so proud of my poetry. I got to hug, catch up with, and take photos with so many of my fellow and very beloved local poets. It was wonderful. So when I signed online early afternoon the next day and received a notice from Facebook that someone had uploaded a picture of me, I wasn't remotely surprised. I expected to see foxy pictures from James's launch and was fully prepared to swoon over them.

Instead, what I found was a sweet-faced photo of twenty-six- or twenty-seven-year-old me—a chubby, nerdy, perky community college English instructor smiling joyfully in front of a dry-erase board that I was in the middle of cleaning—that had been transformed into a very belittling meme. Since then, I've seen that photo used on many other occasions to make points about the desirability of Black women.

I remember the exact moment that photo was taken: "Smile, Ms. V!" chimed one of my more outspoken students, a Brazilian mother newer to the US who was taking my class with her adult daughter. We had just completed a fun class session full of vocabulary skits and silly grammar assignments. Photos, games, Theatre of the Oppressed, and other forms of play-based learning and intimacy building were joyful rituals in my classroom. As a former teachers' pet, I loved school, and as a Black person who grew up in the hood and attended a community college myself, I knew how harmful and humiliating the academic system could be for some students. My goal was to erase the coldness and gatekeeping nature that often left the students I served—students traumatized by their lack of success in middle and high school, new English language learners settling into the US as refugees of war and abuse, students with learning disabilities who were struggling to get their needs met in more traditional classes, and formerly incarcerated adults exploring the deep anxiety and pressure of reentry—feeling helpless and anxious about their ability to succeed, much less keep up. Facilitating a space that felt like Beloved Community and encouraging my students to feel comfortable, to believe they were worthy of shining and sparkling in the classroom, to love being in their bodies, and to enjoy learning was my passion. It still is. I want, and have always wanted, to create confident, happy students, and on the day that photo was taken, my heart was blissed out with success.

The day I took that photo, I felt sexy wearing my burgundy braids in a ponytail with a side drizzle of bangs and my lush cleavage out in a black vest and camisole. My skin was smooth and beaming with shea butter and jojoba oil. My cheekbones were reaching for the sky. My body language was relaxed and free. It was a very adorable picture of me, one that I still like. There was nothing spectacular or unique about it. I looked like any other happy young Black woman at work. But instead of being celebrated, appreciated, or even simply ignored, that photo of me was turned into something ugly. Nasty. Venomous.

That gorgeous photo full of memory, sweetness, and Black Girl Magic was co-opted and exploited by a series of strangers and transformed into a misogynoiristic weapon and a heeding: MaGes (*MaGE* stands for *marginalized genders*—referring to all genders except for cis men), specifically women who shared physical traits with me, were ugly. We were unquestionably unattractive, unwelcome in spaces frequented by supposedly more attractive people, and worthy of malicious laughter and public scorn. And sadly, my photo was used to hurt and poke at Black MaGes on multiple occasions.

On the first occasion brought to my attention, my photo was uploaded onto Facebook by a man who I have (perhaps pettily) renamed Pat Riarchy. Pat Riarchy was a party promoter and event organizer utilizing social media to recruit attractive-to-him female partygoers to hang out in a post-concert VIP lounge with the well-known southern rapper Gucci Mane. After, I suppose, receiving messages from women he did not deign beautiful or glamourous enough to maintain his industry credibility and kick it with rappers, he decided to make a statement using my face.

"Me looking for baddies," he wrote as a status with my picture attached. "The kind of women who respond."

He went on to explain that if you look like this (this being me) don't even think about sending him a request to attend one of his events.

Despite me emerging from a cocoon of illness and creative stagnancy, my career as a writer and performer was still in blossom. Most of my work centered around radical self-love and inviting other people, especially other fat people, LGBTQIA+ youth, survivors of intimate partner violence, and dark-skinned Black people, to love themselves with an equally determined and pleasurable ferociousness. I wanted to live in a world where people loved themselves too much to hurt themselves and other people, where we saw each other as sacred and vibrant in all our flavors of existence, where people choose to liberate themselves and their families from the values Pat Riarchy espoused.

Of course I have known many people who believed and behaved like Pat Riarchy throughout my life. They are a part of the reason why I do the work I do, so I was prepared for him. I did not feel insulted or hurt by his status. No yesteryear trauma, insecurity, or doubt about my self-worth showed up to hurt my heart or body. Instead, I saw red and felt the potent, self-loving rage of blood surge through my body and activate the part of my brain that signaled urgency and action. I wanted that status down, gone, and off the internet.

Fortunately, it never got to the point of being viral. No more than thirty or forty people had reacted to it by the time I saw it and less than fifteen people had commented on it. But fifteen people was still too many people. I did not want anyone else to see that post or engage with any feelings of shame or judgment it may have inspired for them—especially young people and other fat, Black, dark-skinned people. I would not and could not allow my photo to be used as a weapon to terrorize the people I had devoted my life to loving. My body would not be used to attack the ideals of self-worth, self-acceptance, and compassionate self-love that I so fiercely believed in. I was ready to fight the best way I knew how.

I private-messaged Pat Riarchy and asked him how he came across my picture, why he would use it to spread such a harmful message, and if he would immediately remove it. When he didn't respond, I wrote to all the people who commented on the photo, predominantly other Black women and a couple of Brown women, and asked them why they would condone his message. Why would they tolerate such misogynist cruelty? Why did they think my face and body was funny? Only one person responded. She apologized for her comments and told me to ignore Pat Riarchy because he was a fool who always made posts like that.

But I was long done with ignoring the Pat Riarchys of the world. I was completely over being silent. I was spitting teeth and nails that someone thought they could use me, my precious face, to hurt another person. My standards for self-love were beginning to transform from personal endeavors of self-nurture into the mama dragon screech of NO MORE. I would not hold the sole responsibility of loving myself while other people felt entitled to rendering my person as garbage and disposable. I sure as hell would not be made the poster girl for oppressive ugly standards. If it had been a few years earlier, maybe even a few months, I might have chosen silence and inactivity. But Pat Riarchy made the mistake of arbitrarily choosing my body on a day that I decided to climb high into my power, and that power would not be dampened by complacency, fear, threat, and apologies.

After a short period of repeatedly writing to Pat Riarchy and being ignored, though he read all my messages, I wrote a status about the experience for my extraordinary Facebook community of queers, activists, artists, and folks simply committed to loving other people and asked for support. That is when the metaphorical shit, I mean the most succulent and healthy shit of all the shits, hit the fan in the most heart-redeeming, uplifting, and lovely way.

My Facebook community of friends, people I had been sharing my heart, thoughts, and ideas with for many years, came through, and they came through with a determined and collaborative flourish. They stood up for me the way I wished people would stand up for me when I was a child, the way I have often wished I could stand up for myself. They moved with the swift and heavy hand of care and justice, and they flooded Pat Riarchy's inbox and status with critiques, insults, analysis, and compassionate requests. They were a breathing fortress of love and hellfire, and I felt like the most protected sweet baby angel alive. I was grateful. While Pat Riarchy's cruelty didn't facilitate tears, my Facebook friends had me drowning in rivulets of healing salt water.

Then Pat Riarchy finally wrote back.

Initially, he told me that he didn't realize I was a "real" person, that he was sorry for causing so much harm, that he would have never posted that photo if he knew I was such a positive and loved member of our community. He told me that he googled me, saw some of the things I had accomplished, and that he was proud of me.

That was not an acceptable answer to me, and I was not concerned with his pride. No one, regardless of what they do or do not contribute to community, deserves to be publicly ridiculed or automatically excluded, period. That is no different than saying someone deserves to be excluded or welcomed based on how they look, what their health status is, whether they have a college degree or not. These are all arbitrary and fallaciously created standards to justify who we privilege, who we protect, who we value, and who we don't.

Uglification teaches us that we get to choose who we treat well, who we include, and who we discriminate against and reject based on appearance, lived experiences, and other biases. Though Pat Riarchy may have thought he was affirming me with his list of my accolades after eventually googling me, he was only testifying to the resources, privileges, and support systems that have allowed me to become who I am and do the things I have done. I did not get to this place without a great amount of support; further praise and welcome that comes at the expense of someone else is just discrimination. If all my people ain't welcome to visit a venue, relax, and lay down roots, it isn't a place I want to be and it's not a true safe space for any of us. I want liberatory social change, not privilege. I want inclusion, not tokenization. A Black person being successful does not represent social change. A thousand Black success stories doesn't represent social change. Social change is when none of us are starving, unsheltered, body broken from overwork and not enough rest, or dealing with societal neglect and exclusion. His response was representative of the capitalistic, elitist, and patriarchal world we live in, and that world is not tolerable at all.

I gently explained to him that what *would* be a tolerable response was to collaborate with me to create some change. What if he were to speak up about how we bully people on the internet and call for a cultural overhaul, I asked. Or how about using his privilege and platform to spotlight all the people doing beautiful things in community. He seemed to be enthusiastically amenable, and my heart soared with pride and gratitude.

I thought, "How gorgeous is it to go from cruelty to the possibility of kindness with a simple conversation. Dialogue is such a beautiful tool of transformation."

However, I quickly found out that I was moving from a place of hopeful naïveté (it's the Aries and neurodivergence in me). While he was dreaming and scheming social justice birds and bees with me, Pat Riarchy was threatening, arguing with, and verbally assaulting my Facebook friends who spoke up on his status and mine. He not only said that he would turn some of them into memes, he also overtly told some people, specifically men and masculine-of-center people, that he would cause them physical harm and mentioned guns. He wrote that if someone had the right to be ugly, he had the right to call them ugly.

I sadly accepted that Pat Riarchy was not someone with whom I could negotiate much less collaborate at that point in his life. I also realized that I didn't need Pat Riarchy to speak up against the way we treat others. Instead, I decided to write about my experience and share it as far and wide as I possibly could. My friends with platforms kindly agreed to share my writing, and thousands of people learned about what happened and the nascent idea of uglification. But it would happen again, not too long afterward.

My photo was, and still is, the feature for a blog post entitled "The Typical Black Woman Is Unattractive," which was written by a Black man who identified himself as an Afro American Conservative Techy Geek and Afro Futurist.[1] The blog entry was a meditation on the many reasons why the author believes Black women to be unattractive and poor candidates for romantic partners. He spoke directly to Black men and encouraged them to go to college so that they could meet women of other ethnicities, who he lauded as more beautiful. He then juxtaposed the images of scantily clad non-Black female models with images of Black women, both women in crisis and people who were in professional dress, to illustrate his point of who is and isn't desirable.

I never imagined that anyone would go as far as to write an article imploring people to not date or love Black women, especially a Black man, regardless of preference. Nor did I imagine that someone would be google image searching "ugly black women" or "ugly black" anything until that experience. I wasn't just surprised, I was heartbroken.

I felt utterly bereft for my people: for the uglifying atrocities done to us that would leave any Black person thinking another Black person was ugly, for the circumstances that would lead one Black person to exploit another Black person's oppression for gain, and for the people who would be intimately exposed to folks who think and behaved the way Pat Riarchy and the blog author did.

Their actions were the result of a history that has conditioned so many Black men to loathe Black MaGes and blame us for their inability to access the promise of cis het white male privilege: uncompromised power over everyone else, including other men, and entitlement to people's respect, time, bodies, and lives. This is also the reason why my image, alongside all the other images of Black MaGes, showed up during that google search in late 2018.

They did not upload my picture to crack jokes about my appearance or describe who they were or were not attracted to; instead, they were making a clear statement about power, privilege, and who is and isn't valuable. Who is and isn't offered the false premise of safety or protection. Who is and isn't automatically worthy of the loving kindness and inclusion we all need and deserve to survive. Who is and isn't worthy of survival.

Because men like Pat Riarchy have platforms and the ability to control who accesses space, his behavior was not just mean. He wasn't just bullying people or making fun of people who looked a certain way. He wasn't simply being exclusive or holding a standard about who is and isn't beautiful enough to dally with rappers and other posh people. He was participating in the systems and infrastructures of oppression, and using uglification as a tool to validate his behavior and positions.

My neurodivergence makes clubs, parties, and other social spaces inaccessible for me; however there are many people who look like me, or who have features and bodies that are unquestioningly uglified, who would absolutely love to hang out in VIP lounges and meet the rich and the famous. I completely understand why. It's an arena to make many different types of connections: business deals and professional relationships are negotiated, friendships are fostered, sexual encounters and potential romances are initiated. The VIP area is a location of commerce, resource, and possibility. By innately limiting access to that arena based on who Pat Riarchy deemed sexually desirable, Pat Riarchy also gave himself the authority to decide who is and isn't worthy of the resources, relationships, and opportunities that could transpire.

Friends, this is the status quo, and the status quo is rooted in legacies of violent and supremacist exclusion. It is no different than the dean of a graduate program deciding that students cannot wear their hair in locs, braids, or other protective styles. It is the same thing as a real estate agent determining who to show which homes to based on class, race, or family history, and who to exclude. It is equivalent to a banker deciding to not give loans or provide them with irrationally jacked interest rates based on race, gender, or line of employment. It's just like a country club choosing people based on wealth, race, and ability to adhere to respectability politics. It's discrimination, but it's so much more.[2]

It's suppression determined by one individual, or a set of individuals, based on the way society and history has uglified different groups of people to glorify others.

Pat Riarchy created a small post that didn't have a significant impact on the world. But it had an extraordinary impact on me and my understanding of the world. It helped me realize that **who we determine to call ugly is not a frivolous or temporary thing**. It isn't simply words that we should reject or brush off our shoulders. It is the foundation of oppression, the justification of who we oppress and allow to be oppressed, and the reason why we protect and sustain systems that facilitate oppression.

Uglification surrounds us like a midnight smog full of toxic gas and cancerous radiation. It infiltrates nearly every part of our cultural experience, including our most sacred spaces, our families, our liberation and activist communities, our spiritual venues, our romantic and platonic partnerships, our work environments, our colleges and grade schools, our doctor appointments, social services, government, and our imaginations. It empowers the systemic and social neglect, the violence and poverty, and the trauma and stress that interfere with our ability to live.

Uglification is a hate strategy so sophisticated, so clever, it turns the most marginalized and systemically oppressed people against each other. It convinces us to blame ourselves and each other for what was done to us, for our struggles, for the violence we experience. It conditions us to hate and loathe our loved ones for who they are, what they look like, who they love, and the ways they have figured out how to survive. It derails human compassion and strips us of our ability to be accountable to ourselves, to each other, to our dreams, and to our ability to create a world that really and truly can serve our collective freedom and our joy.

I am in no way grateful to Pat Riarchy for weaponizing my face and body against other people or to the blog author for calling me ugly. But I am so grateful for the opportunity to say, "No More! We Deserve Better."

I am grateful for the opportunity to tell you the following things:

**1. You are not ugly (unless you want to be).** Someone may have called you ugly or implied that you are not beautiful enough, but that reflects who they are, what they have been through, and the ideals that they have internalized. People choose to see ugly. People choose to make, paint, render, and perceive different features, body parts, and locations as ugly. These are all subjective opinions that come from legacies of pain and oppression. It is a gaze people opt into and are coerced into. What we consider to be ugly is temporary and changes based on who is around us, what they currently believe, and how we feel about it. Someone calling you ugly is an irrational act of psychological violence and abuse and serves no purpose other than to discriminate and harm.

Ask yourself: What has happened to a person that makes them want to uglify other people and/or make folks feel bad about how they look? Why do they believe they are entitled to an opinion about your face, body, and appearance? How does their opinion impact your life or your joy? Why does their opinion matter to you? Do people who believe they should be able to tell you how to look deserve space in your life?

**2. You do not have the right to comment on other people's appearance.** (Unless they are rocking clothing or tattoos that signify hatred.) Uglification teaches us to seek out imperfection in other people and to assess them based on our perceived ideals of what is and isn't attractive. We expect people to want to be pleasing to our sensibilities and bias. When we do that, we project our values onto them instead of allowing them to be who they are in the moment. People get to decide how they want to look. They get to be okay with possessing the features that you don't like, including the features you have strived to change or remove.

People don't have to have a gender or subscribe to how you think people of their gender should present. People can grow hair anywhere their bodies grow hair, and keep that hair. People can age and look old. People can have a gut or double chin. People can have chipped teeth. People deserve to live their lives the way they want and change their appearance as frequently as they desire.

When you bully, pressure, or shame people into looking a certain way, turn their bodies into jokes, or make passing commentary, you are perpetuating violence against them and attacking their freedom. You are interfering with their ability to like and love themselves. Like people who catcall and who rape, you are forcing yourself onto someone without their consent.

Ask yourself: Why do you feel entitled to judge or assess someone else's appearance, including your partner/s, children, colleagues, potential employees, students, celebrities, or strangers? What ideals and values are you promoting, agreeing with, and consenting to with your expectations and standards of how people should and shouldn't look? Where do they come from? How did you learn them? How does perceiving someone else as ugly serve your happiness? Does someone else's looks impact their ability to do a job, or are you catering to your clients' biases and oppression?

**3. There is nothing wrong with who or what you find desirable and attractive.** Uglification teaches us that beauty is objective and determined by the validation and approval of other people. Human beauty, as well as attraction, is expansive, shifting, and influenced by so much more than how our bodies look, what our genders are, or how our brains function. It is rooted in how we exist within our bodies, how we treat the world around us, the way we show up in any unique moment. It comes from the ways we relate to each other, hold space for each other, and allow each other to be ourselves. Different people respond to so many different things, and that changes as time goes by.

You get to want and desire whoever you want. You do not have to limit your attractions to what the world tells you to find beautiful, to who your friends and family will approve or want from you to bodies that feel familiar or celebrated. You get to be attracted to people who make you feel gooey inside, who make you hungry for physical or emotional connection, who help ground you in your own truths. If you are a sexual or romantic person, it's beautiful to allow your heart to open to folks that make you swoon. There is nothing wrong with being attracted to a disabled person, a trans or nonbinary person, a fat person, a person of a different race, a person other people don't call cute or sexy. There is nothing wrong with watching your desires shift. It's possible to notice yourself attracted to people of genders you didn't think you would want before.

Ask yourself: Whose happiness are you invested in—yours, your potential lovers', or the peanut gallery with inconsiderate opinions? What is the point of romance and sex if not for pleasure? Why should anyone else determine your attraction? Have you ever pursued or dated someone because of how they looked, even though you weren't attracted to them? Has your heart ever gone *thadump* for someone your friends didn't notice? Are you limiting your happiness and bliss based on irrational concerns that don't serve your joy? Are you missing out on the human of your dreams because of fear? Don't you deserve better? Are you secretly dating someone you really like or limiting your connection to a sexual one because of your judgmental friends or a fear of being queer? Don't you and that other person deserve better?

**4. Someone's lack of attraction to you is not about you and doesn't indicate a failure to be attractive.**   The idea that someone may or may not be out of our league is a figment of uglification's most dastardly ingenuity. Desire and attraction have absolutely nothing to do with imaginary caste systems or fabricated beauty categories. People are attracted to who they are attracted to, and people are absolutely attracted to you. They may not be who you are attracted to or what you want from a lover, but that does not negate that they are a valuable and magical human being, with friends, loved ones, and dreams, and in possession of a big, flaming crush on you. Whether you care about their feelings or not, their feelings still matter. You not wanting them does not say anything about who they are, whether they are cute enough to be desired or loved, and what kinds of beauty standards they meet. Your feelings are not an assessment of their worth. Your feelings are completely about you and what you want.

Similarly, someone's lack of interest in you has nothing to do with you. If someone is not open to get to know you, it does not mean you aren't good enough. You are good enough, gorgeous enough, smart enough, special enough. It's about where the other person is at and what feels good to them. Honoring other people's disinterest, regardless of the reason, is a way to practice consent culture. We cannot project our feelings and emotional needs to feel enough or valuable onto another person, regardless of how the world uglifies us or what we've experienced.

We can choose to be open to and curious about the people who see us, think we are gorgeous as we are, and won't expect us to maintain external beauty standards that might be hard to achieve or not what we personally aspire toward. We can choose to stop centering people who are only open to certain types of people, and explore what it's like to prioritize the people who see the beauty in who we are, exactly as we are, in the moment. Having someone love us the way we want to be loved, in a way that makes us feel free and inspires our comfort, pleasure, and joy, and who we can't help but love back, is more compelling than someone everyone else wants.

Ask yourself: Do you need other people to be attracted to you or return your desire? When people don't return your interest, do you decide it's because there is something wrong with you or that you aren't good enough? When people say no, do you attempt to make yourself more like what you think they want or attempt to prove that other people want you? When people aren't into you, do you internalize it as a failure on your end? When you're not attracted to another person, do you believe it's because there is something wrong with them? Have you ever not been attracted to someone and still thought they were gorgeous and kind? Can you respect someone's no? Is it possible that someone's inclination to uglify others just because they aren't attracted to them or to prioritize toxic beauty standards can make them unattractive? Are you secretly, or openly, not attracted to people with bodies or facial features like yours? Do you think about what other people think when you choose who to date? Do you think that what your partner looks like reflects some status you've achieved? Do you choose to date people to make a point?

**5. Your body is your body.**    Your body belongs to you. It is yours to be explorative, experimental, and creative with. You can dye your hair any color you want and wear the wildest style you desire, unless you equate the hairstyles of people of color with wild—that's just white supremacy, fetishization, and appropriation. You can reclaim your ancestral robes. You can rock facial and body hair like jewels born of your own flesh. You can be as huge, lush bodied, and generous of rolls, edges, and craters as the Grand Canyon. You can choose to be fatter. You can choose to lose weight. You can choose to pierce every bit of skin you can find. You can get surgical elf-ear implants. You can split your tongue.

You can have as much sex as you desire or not have sex at all. You can masturbate as frequently as you want. You can spend all your free time naked. You can date all the people who consent in any way they consent to. You can be submissive or dominant or kinky in all the ways. You can choose to belong to another person. You can choose to support another person in untraditional ways. You can be a parent. You can have twelve children. You can be single. You can never have children.

You can be disabled and be a parent. You can be fat and disabled and be a parent. You can be a sex worker and be a parent. You can be a proud slut and be a parent. You can be trans and be a parent. You can be trans. You can be trans regardless of what your parents say. You can be trans and keep it a secret until you feel comfortable and safe to tell others. You can be trans with no pressure to tell others.

You can be nonbinary or bigender. You can refuse gender. You can love gender. You can change your gender as much as you want. You can be intersex and love it. You can be intersex and identify with a specific gender. You can be intersex and trans and agender.

Your body is your body. It does not belong to your parents, your partners, your children's expectations of how you should look, your neighbors, or a political movement. They do not belong to your career, your self-esteem, your religion, or patriarchy. You don't have to be smart or in competition with other people. You get to be you.

**6. You can choose to embrace ugliness.**   Ugliness doesn't have to be an insult or monstrous, nor does it need to be another person's oppressive and entitled opinion about our bodies. Reject other people's opinions about what is and isn't ugly. Ignore and disengage from them. Let them have their opinion, and know that it has nothing to do with you. There are so many strands of color in the universe, and we, as individuals, get to decide how we want to play with them.

We can decide today that embracing ugliness solely means rejecting patriarchy and all the violent, judgmental, and exclusive things he does with his power. We can decide that we no longer consent to other people's ugly standards and explore other ways to be in relationship with ourselves, other people, and the world that holds us all alive and sacred. Embracing ugliness is the political, personal, and deeply spiritual practice of choosing, every day, every moment, to reject the pressure of who you are expected to be, and exploring what feels good, pleasurable, and right for you.

Embracing ugliness is not social reform, nor is it social justice. It's taking the agency, with the strategies and materials we have right now, to create the world we want to experience. It's recognizing the cultural behaviors and values of that world, exploring how we want to be treated in that world or how we want to experience our lives, and centering that experience in the moment. If we want to be treated with respect, we don't make the people around us change themselves—we remove from our world anyone who disrespects us. That might take time. You might have to become an adult first, find another job, explore a strategy to escape safely, change the people you pursue, or examine how you understand respect or how you treat others; but the first step is embracing that you deserve better than what you're experiencing, that you don't have to improve yourself to earn the better you deserve, and that no one else's opinion about your worth or how you should be yourself matters (unless, again, your way of being is hateful and violent).

Embracing ugliness is refusing to participate in traditional power dynamics—harmful and nonconsensual power dynamics, period— or steward the status quo. You can choose to not comply with the classist, elitist, and inconsiderate expectation that committed, talented, and knowledgeable workers went to college. There are so many ways to learn, gain, process, and practice education. There are so many phenomenal teachers and teachings that have never existed on a college campus or have been excluded from campuses. Centering a college education is uglifying all the other types of teachers, including the teachers structurally excluded from the university, as inferior to a state- and capitalism-sanctioned institution. We deserve better. Hire people without a degree. Hire people who don't "fit in" with the aesthetic of other people who work at your organization. Hire people who don't currently fit into the seats at your office, and create space that fits them.

What if we only invested in MaGe leadership? What if we moved past concepts of equity that clearly don't work, and centered the hiring of nontraditional employees and an attempt to reject the violence of uglification? What if that leadership would make the rest of the world safer, more protected, and more comfortable? What if we suddenly started enjoying our jobs, our lives, our families? What if we noticed that war stopped and gun violence decreased? What if we started living longer and having access to more rest and better food? What if so many more people were living their lives without trauma, abuse, and gratuitous violence? What if we found a way to protect our communities without violence or threat? What if?

Embracing ugliness is choosing to be kind. It's deciding to opt out of practices and beliefs that harm or exclude other people, including people you don't know or people you don't believe deserve it. Kindness is not simply being nice to the people around you, practicing a religion, or treating others as you want them to treat you. Kindness is making sure that your city structure, office, restaurant, clothing store, car, bus, testing practice, interview and teaching style, and entertainment venue are welcoming and accessible to every single type of physical body that engages with them. Kindness is self-reflecting when someone told you that you harmed them—not because you are "wrong" but because you don't want to be a harmful or violent person so you want to know better. Kindness is choosing to surround yourself with people who make it easy for you to love yourself and no longer fear the cruel things people have said and done to you in the past. Kindness is being that person for someone else.

Refusing uglification makes it easier to be kind to yourself and others, to explore your joy and freedom, to center nonoppressive practices and traditions, and to exist in a way that is considerate to other people's freedom, joy, and kindness as well. All this together breeds the sort of creativity that is brilliant and sustainable enough to diffuse the patriarchy, like a tiny tea light in the monsoon of a new beginning. A peaceful beginning. A pleasurable beginning. A regenerative and safe beginning. A beginning that serves *everyone's* well-being.

It is our job to listen, to understand, to embrace, center, choose, and (if you are currently in a position of power due to the uglification and suppression of others) submit to the better and the difference that happens when we reallocate power from the people and practices that have always facilitated what hurt us. We don't have to do it in the way that Pat Riarchy does it. We don't have to initiate violence, threaten, or intimidate people, become tough guys, or uglify people into doing what we want and not trusting their own intuition. We don't have to watch our children die in the streets or be zip-tied and tear-gassed by police officers in the middle of a war or protest.

We don't have to fight the patriarchy. We can outsmart it and heal from it. We can say NO MORE to patriarchy. We can usurp its power by protecting and respecting each other's freedom and body. We can create something more liberating, freeing, and compelling. We can reclaim our power, imagination, and regenerated capacity by choosing to no longer fear the patriarchy's disapproval or submit to the patriarchy's authority. We can exchange resources, opt out of oppressive institutions, and transform culture without patriarchy even catching on to what we're doing. We can choose solidarity in the intersectional, collaborative, liberatory, and visionary leadership that blossoms when our roots are rid of the traumatizing nips of uglification and patriarchy.

When we do that and do it together, we can blow patriarchy's power, violence, and influence out like a tea light trapped in the middle of a faerie monsoon of transformative imagination and loving possibility. We can change the world. We can save our own damn lives. We can reclaim ugly.

## The Language of Uglification

Uglification consists of personal and cultural beliefs, behaviors, practices, and laws that dehumanize people as ugly, undesirable, immoral, and unworthy. It feeds, maintains, and depends on oppressions such as lookism, racism, ableism, sexism, homophobia, transphobia, fatphobia, and xenophobia. Unchecked, it facilitates, normalizes, and validates hatred, childhood bullying, workplace exclusion, criminalization, medical neglect, violence, exploitation, and more.

Uglification is used to segregate and oppress. We uglify people to exclude them from spaces, economic resources, opportunities, leadership, equity, safety, and other forms of systemic and cultural infrastructures. Uglification is used to justify why some people have second-class experiences or why it's okay to think lesser of a group or individual. We see this happen when we make up reasons for why some people experience difficulties that we do not (such as higher rates of incarceration, murder, abuse, and sickness) instead of looking at the external and historical circumstances that facilitate their experience, especially if those circumstances don't impact us the same or lead to our increased wealth and power.

Uglification is used to loot and control. We uglify people, groups, and locations to gain, take, maintain, and protect some element of power, wealth, and privilege at their expense. We use uglification strategies to justify why people don't deserve protection, safety, or the wealth/resource that was originally theirs, and then to validate why we should have it instead. Governments uglify Indigenous groups to co-opt their land. Formerly incarcerated people are uglified out of the right to vote. Poor people are uglified as less capable parents, and their children are looted from them by a government that refuses to effectively support them.

Uglification is used to indoctrinate and propagandize. Uglification is used to convince oppressed, exploited, and violated people that the violence and neglect they experience is just the way things are or their fault altogether. It coerces people to be complicit in, and complacent with, their own oppression—and to glorify, respect, and aspire to emulate the people who steward and benefit from their oppression. We can become so uglified that we stop liking and trusting ourselves, that we protect the people and institutions that harm us, that we become weapons against our own healing and safety.

Uglification is used to coerce and dominate. Uglification is used to protect the power that privileged groups are afforded at the expense of marginalized groups. People, especially oppressed people, who speak up, organize, and protest other people's mistreatment are uglified as irrational, bad, or a threat to safety to discredit them and coerce other people into seeing them as dangerous. Domination happens when people's voices are suppressed, and uglification is a suppressant.

Uglification is used to dehumanize and disconnect. Uglification is used to discourage different groups of people from having empathy for each other, compassion for each other's experience, and solidarity with each other's liberation. It slowly convinces us that other people don't need or deserve the same care, opportunities, softness, protection, or resources that help make our lives so wonderful. When we choose not to trust groups or individuals based on the messages we've been told about them or about what is right, believe that uglified groups get what they deserve for not doing what they're told, and disconnect our humanity from theirs, uglification wins.

# uglification
## noun

a social weapon that mobilizes people to fear, detest, support the oppression and marginalization of, or feel superior toward other people, beliefs, locations, causes, behaviors, desires, objects, or a specific individual

> Example: *Early fisheries and canning companies contributed to the uglification of natural waterway behaviors, like flooding and shifting river routes, to justify creating dams and other industrial manipulations of the land. We have since learned just how harmful most man-made dams are for the environment and the creatures who call those locations home.*

a tool, ideology, and type of oppression that designates some bodies as more or less worthy of love, respect, access, and dignity

> Example: *I see how much it hurts my partner every time her mother tells her that if she truly loved herself, she would do everything possible to lose weight and take better care of her body—even though she knows that it's just her mother's own internalized uglification talking.*

# uglify
## verb

to stigmatize a person, group, location, or trait as undesirable, unattractive, immoral, unwanted, unlovable, wrong/bad, or monstrous because of prejudice, fear, ignorance, anger, malice, or social conditioning

> Example: *Marsha's father recognized his butch daughter's gender queer tendencies early on and made a point to uglify every LGBTQIA+ person they encountered as sick in order to coerce her into performing heterosexuality and terrify her of being her true self.*

to ridicule, target, abuse, bully, or spread disinformation about an individual or group for an intended purpose or outcome

> Example: *Famous comedians love to claim that nothing should be off the table for them, and that "liberals" are too sensitive after people angrily hold them accountable for uglifying already marginalized and targeted groups of people for laughs.*

to validate, justify, or otherwise excuse, sustain, or deny the oppression of a group or individual to protect wealth, power, a status quo, or harmful system

> Example: *When women and other marginalized genders who work in the tech industry spoke up about being discriminated against and paid significantly less than their male colleagues, many men in the industry further uglified them by arguing that women's brains are less hardwired for the competitiveness of tech fields than men's.*

to diminish the worth, value, or esteem of a person or group because of perceived differences

> Example: *Consuelo and her son Rodrigo, both immigrant rights and racial justice advocates, stopped talking to each other after Rodrigo uglified Consuelo's choice to vote as being complacent with an oppressive two-party system and Consuelo uglified Rodrigo and his peers' choice to not vote as naïve and counterrevolutionary.*

to socially punish or ostracize an individual or group because of their unwillingness to acquiesce to the expected behaviors, appearances, and beliefs of those in positions of influence

> Example: *Every single time we organize a Black Lives Matter protest or any other public racial justice movement, the local news media uglifies us as potentially violent looters and encourages local business owners to board up their windows as if our goal is to smash glass or something. I don't understand why they don't understand that saying our lives matter is the opposite of violence.*

to critically perceive of oneself, a portion of oneself, or someone else through the lens of oppression

> Example: *Starting right now, I am going to stop uglifying myself by telling myself that I would be cuter if I had clearer skin. Skin is skin, damn it, and mine is just as wonderful as anyone else's.*

to create social hierarchies and/or decide the treatment of an individual or group based solely on systems of oppression and societal attitudes

> Example: *The casting agents of the film* Straight Outta Compton—*like most Hollywood endeavors—created a deeply racist and misogynist looks-based casting system that uglified dark-skinned, fat, kinky-haired, African-featured, and economically poor Black women. They labeled these women as D-girls in the casting call. A-girls were described as "the hottest of the hottest. Models ... real hair—no extensions, very classy looking, great bodies ... black, white, Asian, Hispanic, Middle Eastern, or mixed race."[3]*

to limit, assume, or impose upon the direction of an individual's life based on oppressive societal beliefs about some aspect of that person's body, appearance, disability, identity, belief system, or personal history

> Example: *After Aditi's interview, one member of the hiring team asked, "Are they really someone we want at the front desk? All that stuff about pronouns, and their facial hair, and—" But fortunately the manager quickly shut them down with a snarky remark: "I'd rather hire Aditi to greet everyone who visits our front desk than continue to employ someone who feels okay uglifying folks who embracing their gender and body. Take the rest of the day off and expect an email from Human Resources in the morning."*

to stigmatize bodies, appearances, desires, and beliefs as wrong, bad, ugly, immoral, and acultural

> Example: *I finally came out to my little brother about being a sex worker and told him about how much I enjoyed my job, and the first thing he did was uglify me by telling me that I was an embarrassment to decent, self-respecting Black women.*

to create systems, physical structures, or programming that is intentionally or unintentionally inaccessible to an already targeted, disenfranchised, excluded, or otherwise marginalized group

> Example: *"You know when I first realized I could fall in love with you," Ibrahim signed to Liyana. "It was when I realized that you call ahead to every venue we visit to make sure there are seats large enough to comfortably accommodate me and enough space to accommodate my scooter. I know that I won't have to feel uglified due to inaccessibility when I'm around you. That's just one of the reasons why I want to spend the rest of my life with you." Liyana, who broke into tears in the middle of Ibrahim's speech, signed back, "I want to spend the rest of my life with you too, noori. I will love and cherish you forever."*

to render a group or location as less worthy of safety and protection, cleanliness, support, love, equality, leadership, justice, autonomy, or sovereignty

> Example: *"When we asked you, the board, to hire therapists, restorative justice counselors, and more teachers so that our predominantly Black and Native students could have a better chance at learning, matriculating, and escaping the school-to-prison pipeline, you, the school board, wrote back and said that our students were performing normally for where our school was located. We cannot allow you to continue uglifying our children, our community, and our parents.*

# uglified
## adjective/description

a body, body part, individual, group, object, belief, desire, behavior, experience, or location rendered as undesirable or immoral by others or oneself

> Example: *The unhoused, impoverished, and socially uglified people of this community refuse to allow the police to continue trashing our encampments when we sleep. This is why we are asking those of you who are economically privileged to stand by and with us in resistance. We need housing. We need protection!"*

---

## SELF-REFLECTION, EMBODIMENT, AND SOMATICS CHALLENGE

Let's get vulnerable, baby! Each of those definition examples reflects my personal experiences, my inner world, and the communities I navigate. For this exercise, I want you to make them personal.

Your Self-Reflection Challenge is to write at least one personal example using the word *uglification*, *uglify*, or *uglified* that speaks to relationships, communities, and spaces that you navigate in your own life. In this context, spaces may include your profession or field of study, your hobbies or online communities, your political groups or movement/activism spaces, your spiritual practice or religious values, the city or town you live in, and what sort of access to power or influence you have in the friend, family, professional, political, and economic circles you navigate. (You can make it a Super Self-Reflection Challenge by writing the sentences and then giving yourself three to five more minutes to journal about the different ways you've experienced, witnessed, and even expressed this type of uglification.) Try not to shame yourself. This is an educational and healing experience where you get to learn from your greatest teacher, yourself.

Your Embodiment and Somatics Exercise is to explore how these words and examples feel in your body when you try them out. Give yourself the opportunity to speak them out loud or sign them boldly, then ask yourself these reflection questions:

If you sign: How does it feel in the palms of your hands or the slide of your fingers as you sign each word? What feels so right that you start to speak it with your entire body? What feels uncomfortable, confusing, or not right?

If you speak and/or hear: How does the breath feel as it dances up your throat and against your tongue when you speak the words aloud? Do you pause or interrupt yourself with physical expressions of discomfort? Are there sentences that flow so smoothly it's clear your body is recognizing them as true for you? How does it feel to hear these words out loud, outside your body? Does it feel honest to you? Are there parts you might want to modify or reflect on longer?

For everyone: How do these words feel in your body as you process and receive them? Are you aware of yourself processing emotion? Do you feel movement, energy, or knots in your belly? If so, where? Is there a tensing in your neck and shoulders, or are you physically relaxed? Are you breathing as you normally do, or have you paused breathing at any point? Has a part of your body started moving repeatedly without you thinking much about it? Are you resistant? Or is your body tensing with excitement at any point? Do you recognize previous physical embodiments (like scrunching up your lips, making side-eye, or rolling your eyes) or emotions like guilt or hurt or familiarity or validation when you speak or sign the words?

Are there moments when you want to stop speaking or signing these words? Moments when you want to change a word? Moments when you decide to rewrite the sentence? Moments when you pause and realize something new about your feelings or situation that is helpful to you?

From this exercise you can learn so much about your feelings and experiences, locate so much in your body, discover so many clues about what you need from yourself and the people around you to access peace, and gain so much direction about which practices and behaviors you respect and want to keep and which are no longer serving you that you may be ready to release. But you can only really notice and recognize these things if you allow yourself the patience, open-hearted curiosity, and space that you feel safe enough in to really try.

This activity allows you to practice being present with your body and to learn to recognize places of joy, stress, ease, and release through mindfulness. You can use that information to make choices to facilitate release, increase joy and peace, and decrease stress. You will have more emotional access to reclaiming a loving and compassionate relationship with parts of yourself that have been uglified. You will find more tools and opportunities to recognize ways to make choices more rooted in empathy for other people's need to also feel good, to have time to rest and process their feelings, and to get the resources they need to stay alive and well.

This sort of care and intention for oneself and others, regardless of how small or grand it may be perceived to be, is the sort of healing that facilitates liberation—the eradication of oppressive structures and the healing of what oppression has done. You will be a freedom fighter, starting with your own freedom and extending outward to the freedom of the people you love, the people you work with, and even the people you share a city with and don't know, don't think about, and were even taught to hate. If you are an artist, writer, or performer, someone who creates emotional experiences for other people, this exercise will enhance your attention to detail, which will, in turn, widen your creative palette and exponentially expand your range. Regardless of who you are and what you do, this exercise will help you separate the socialization of uglification from your own truths, perspectives, and standards for how you want to treat people and be treated.

# Uglification and Other Forms of Oppression

## Fatphobia

When I was growing up, both of my parents were fat. They were chubby, big-boned, full-figured, pleasantly plump, and whatever other language around size and bodies you like to use. My favorite term is *lush bodied* because it speaks to the decadence and sensuousness of having a fat body. And I loved my parents' fat, lush, decadent bodies.

I liked that they were soft and comfortable to cuddle with, that I could lean deep into the malleable warmth of their arms and drift off into a magical and comforting slumber. I loved that they looked big and power-ful. It made me feel safe when I was around them, like there was plenty of them for me to hold on to or hide behind if the reason ever arose. But more than anything, I just loved them and the warm fuzziness I felt in my heart every time I laid my eyes on them. They were gorgeous, graceful, snazzy, and glorious. They danced like rhythm was designed specifically for their bodies. They were my parents, and as a tiny human who loved them, every tiny bit of fat, hair, scar, and skin on their body was my absolute favorite thing to look at and touch. I never wanted to let go. When they decided it was time for me to sleep alone and explore my independence, I resisted. I fought it like I was fighting for my life and my happiness. All I wanted was to wrap my arms around their thighs or hold their hands and go everywhere they went—unless I was reading a book. If I was reading a book, I wanted to be alone. But otherwise, my parents were my Black Adonises and most opulent beloveds.

It wasn't clear to me, however, whether they felt the same way about themselves. They were always dieting, negatively commenting on their bodies' sizes, picking apart each other's weight and health practices, and judging and shaming each other for what they ate. I know, from my own adult relationships and health struggles, that most of the time interactions like those come from a place of intended love, care, and solidarity. To be clear, while these critical strategies may lead some people to center weight loss, they never work to facilitate wellness, much less loving intimacy within a relationship. Instead, they create a culture of shame, resentment, insecurity, and the belief that our bodies, health, and beauty belong to other people. They lead people to eat privately, have ungrounded and unpleasurable relationships with food, and feel guilty for their desires.

When we don't have a disability justice praxis, our desire for our partners to be well, feel good, and live long lives with us manifests itself as fatphobia, which is the systemic, interpersonal, and internalized oppression, targeting, abuse, and exclusion of fat people. My parents were fatphobic. As such, they often neglected to be present for each other's evolving beauty as they aged. They didn't recognize that their body image comments taught my siblings and me to judge other people's bodies and make unfair assumptions about people's characteristics based on appearance. I know that I am not the only person who grew up watching their parents direct fatphobia toward themselves and each other, and I also know that my parents are not the only fatphobic people out there. As much as I am embarrassed to admit this while existing within my own

300-pound body and being passionately in love with other fat people and the ideals of fat liberation, I too am fatphobic.

It is so hard not to blame, shame, and uglify my fat when I have health struggles or cannot do what other people around me do. When my loved ones or collaborators take me on a hiking trail or some other adventure that is inaccessible or difficult for me to equitably participate in, I immediately feel self-conscious about my body, size, and ability. I spiral through the many memories of being unable to keep up and feeling like I don't belong. I get caught up in a trigger that makes it hard for me to communicate my needs because I'm so ashamed of them and because I blame myself for not making the choices to be physically fit. But that is one of the many ways that uglification works—it teaches us to place the full weight of accountability on ourselves for roadblocks and disenfranchisements that could be easily removed or avoided.

This is why I so appreciate the essay "Access Intimacy: The Missing Link," by disability justice advocate and writer Mia Mingus.[1] Access intimacy, as Mingus describes, is the warm safety and inclusion you feel when other people get, honor, and consider your access needs. It's what happens when people check in to make sure trails and adventures are accessible to everyone attending, so that everyone can enjoy the experience and each other's company. Access intimacy happens when events have seating that is comfortable for everyone's bodies, when we remember not to wear perfumes and scented products in case someone around is allergic or has multiple chemical sensitivity. It's when we decide to create a world that is safe and welcoming for ourselves and each other, instead of ridiculing, excluding, or asking people to change themselves to fit in. We are brilliant and creative enough to imagine systems and projects that fit everyone—when we choose to.

Thinking through concepts like access intimacy and fat liberation—the creation of practices, systems, and values that support the lives, welfare, and inclusion of fat people as they are—has given me the tools to better teach people how to treat me with love and respect, as well as advocate for my needs when fatphobia is at play. It also helps me navigate my internalized fatphobia, and the fatphobia I direct toward others.

Internalized fatphobia is not a personal failing or wrongdoing. It is born from a desire to have a good life, and the quality of our lives is often determined by how the people around us treat us, the resources and opportunities available to us, and how the world and its systems create space for us. The world does not create space for fat people, especially supersized fat people, nor does it make any effort to protect us. That lack of care leads us to be casualties to systems of oppression, uglification, and the injustice of buildings, office spaces, transportation systems, and medical practices that were not designed with care or consideration for our bodies and spirits. When those structures so easily exclude us, it teaches us, and the thinner people around us, that our needs, lives, and involvement are unnecessary.

Internalized fatphobia is a desire to prove oneself necessary. Fat liberation is the political strategy to demand and create systems that protect our lives. Access intimacy is the people around us making choices and environments that enable us to have a good quality of life, as we are, in the moment. To survive this changing world, we need to belong to our communities, but that belonging can only happen when our communities do the work to be loving and accessible.

Fatphobia exists because of the way we uglify fat people, disabled people, people who aren't easily exploited by capitalism, and people not deemed desirable by cis, straight men in positions of power (as well as the people who protect those cis straight men's power). For the rest of this chapter, discussions about fatphobia will be integrated into all other conversations about accessibility and justice.

## Lookism and Beauty Standards

In my childhood home was a cup that my father received from Kaiser. It said, "Nothing tastes as good as being thin feels." That cup would haunt me every time I thirstily entered the kitchen. I couldn't touch it, much less drink out of it. It felt toxic to me, like a taunting reflection of the discomfort I felt in every aspect of my life. I did not feel good. I did not exactly enjoy my life. And food was one of the few pleasures and coping skills that was available to me. I loved the flavored sensations of eating, the creaminess of casseroles, the refreshing sweetness of fruit and juice, the fun crunch of cereal, the tang of a well-seasoned meat or vegetable dish, the absolute yumminess of dessert. Mealtime, whether I was alone or with others, was a sacred and treasured ritual that helped me move through my day.

That cup's message not only made me negatively question my love for food and eating, but it also made me feel like I would enjoy my life more if I gave that love up. That was hard for me as a child because I didn't yet have the emotional and psychological insight to concretely articulate what I was feeling at the time: It's not my fatness that makes me feel bad, it's the way people treat me because I'm fat. It was the all-day name calling I experienced at school that made me not enjoy my life. It was the kids who put their hands on me or who made up games and jokes about me that made me not enjoy my life. It was the loneliness, exhaustion, and anxiety I had from so much relentless bullying I felt that made me question whether I wanted to exist. It wasn't food, eating, or being fat. Those things, especially as a child, didn't impact my life at all until someone turned me into a joke or a punching bag.

If I could re-create that cup, it would say, "Nothing feels better than being treated with kindness and respect by the people around you."

Many people who fat-shame argue that they are concerned with other people's health, but the truth is that we live in a world that positions fat bodies, and many other types of bodies, as ugly, undesirable, unattractive, and consequently unnecessary to be kind toward. When I was a tiny girl crying because of how children talked about my body, the adults around me told me to lose weight so that kids wouldn't have anything to talk about. They did not tell me that what those children were saying was wrong, ask me what I needed to feel better and safe, or try to talk to the kids who harassed me about why they felt like it was okay to bully people for being fat. This is because the adults around me, mostly, were complacent and in alignment with the ideas that some bodies, thinner bodies, were beautiful and optimal, and that fatter bodies should lose weight to look like thinner bodies. This is not the privileging of health; it is the centering of hand-me-down aesthetics.

There are particular appearances, faces, and bodies that are universally lifted as ideals and #goals. We see these aesthetics on magazine covers, as news anchors and television hosts, as models and leading actors, as Fortune 500 CEOs and self-help gurus, as the faces of different activism movements and nonprofit organizations, and as the cool kids on campus. While there are outliers that we have glamorized and glorified as beautiful, and some that we have just simply fetishized and sexualized, our contemporary standards of beauty have been made immediately recognizable and unquestionable. When a writer describes a character as beautiful, they usually don't have to do much other than describe their hair and eye color, maybe height. Otherwise, our imaginations do all the work based off the visuals of beauty that have been spoon-fed to us throughout the years via myth, media, religion, and politics—as well as the images and personas that have been painted as ugly, laughable, and monstrous.

People who fit into Westernized standards of beauty, regardless of gender and sometimes ethnicity, tend to be slimmer with defined muscles and curves. If they are curvy, their arms, waists, faces, and ankles tend to be small. Their hair is full, straight, and long. If they are Black and have natural hair, it's loose curls, the kind of locks many of us heard referred to as "good hair" back in the day. They have larger eyes with visible eyelids, thick eyebrows, smaller noses, and small but pouty lips. Their skin is smooth and creamy, unmarked by pimples, bumps, burns, scars, and color variations. They wear fashionable, expensive-looking clothes that fit their bodies well. Their hair and nails are consistently manicured and designed. Their teeth are perfectly white and straight. Their skin is also white, or if they are people of color, it is on the lighter side. The few dark-skinned people who fit into "classical" beauty standards tend to have European facial features.

Sometimes when people are preparing for economic or professional advancement, they are told to "look the part." The previous description is the look they are told to aspire toward. These are the traits we have collectively, and coercively, accepted as universally and classically beautiful. Because of lookism (prejudice or discrimination against someone for not meeting social ideals of beauty) and beauty privilege, people who fit into these standards are regarded as more trustworthy, more intelligent, more capable, and more qualified to be in exclusive leadership positions—solely on the basis of their appearance. They are offered access to uniquely special treatments and opportunities because of social stratifications and attitudes that privilege, prefer, and glorify their bodies and presentations, and we are all taught to aspire toward them so that we, too, can access that same special treatment.

I believe that we should all have access to the same kindness, welcome, and opportunities regardless of what we look like. Our faces, bodies, wardrobes, genders, ethnicities, sizes, and other appearance factors have absolutely nothing to do with the way that we think, our ability to synopsize and articulate information, our inclination to be kind and honest people, how we determine integrity, and whether we can be insightful and compassionate leaders. Lookism and beauty privilege teach us to categorize people based on a snap judgment made within a few seconds of meeting them, but they don't teach us to get to know people, care about people who don't fit into those standards, or be curious about everyday people's lives, accomplishments, and struggles. Lookism prevents wholeness and denies people the opportunity to explore their whole potential.

Because of lookism, many of us are cruel to ourselves for not fitting into standardized beauty. We only see what other people think is wrong with us, and we use that information to justify why we can't access our desires and needs. Makeup, plastic surgery, clothing, skin bleaching, and weight loss commercials tease us about the lives we could potentially live, the opportunities that would become available, the love that is waiting for us once we make the choice to change our lives and bodies and become desirable. Those same industries have become obscenely wealthy by exploiting the ways we worship and privilege some bodies while ignoring, belittling, uglifying, and shaming other bodies. No one wants to feel shamed and be mistreated all the time. So we strive to be what others would call beautiful—instead of rejecting the systems and attitudes that teach us to treat ourselves and others this way.

We are trained by our culture to treat those we find beautiful with extra kindness, politeness, and attention. We are equally conditioned to glance over or direct ungenerous criticisms toward people we deem ugly, lacking, or even simply regular. People who are perceived as ugly are treated as failures, and people perceived as regular are ignored or treated as works in process. We assume that they want to fit into standards of beauty and just haven't gotten there yet.

Lookism is the reason why we discriminate against people we perceive as ugly *and* the people we think others will perceive as ugly. It's why some people find jobs, lovers, friends, and homes with ease, and others have a very difficult time being heard and getting their basic needs met. It's why some children get bullied and why other children do the bullying. It's why some people are loved and celebrated in public, while others are fucked in secret. It's why some people put themselves in dangerous positions for love and affection.

Just as there are widely accepted standards of beauty, there are also standards of ugliness. These are not named or analyzed like beauty standards traditionally are, but we are intimately aware of them. These standards change based on time, location, and who has the gaze; but they are also universal in some ways. We are aware of the parts of ourselves that society has conditioned us to believe are unappealing. We are aware of the uglified characteristics that we don't have, the ones we strive not to have, and the ones we work hard to change.

Although we rarely speak them, we know the standards of ugliness: We acknowledge the fears of our flesh expanding and changing, our skin aging and drooping, our hair graying and becoming sparse, and our face blemishing and pimpling. We think about a part of our body being the reason why someone else might judge us, reject us, or exclude us. We think about who has the least access to economic resources and systemic power while also being the most likely to be incarcerated, homeless, deported, physically or sexually assaulted, and turned into the butt of the joke on television. We look at other people and catch ourselves thinking those creepy, sometimes unwanted thoughts about how they can change something about themselves.

Even if we think people should have tougher skin and higher self-esteem, even if we agree with the standards of ugliness and depend on them to feel good about ourselves, even if we think "that's just the way things are" or subscribe to some survival-of-the-fittest mentality, we know what the standards of ugliness are and we know that when we direct them at others they can lead to great harm and pain. We also know how much it hurts when other people believe that we are ugly and respond to us accordingly.

Being perceived as ugly is not only dangerous to our emotional and psychological well-being, but it also impacts how we experience the world and how others treat us. We are treated as spectacle and public property. In fact, most MaGe bodies are treated as such; the tone and behaviors just look quite different based on the person's appearance.

"I don't care what anyone tells you, you are beautiful," I sometimes hear from strangers who roll their windows down to talk to me as I casually walk down the street minding my own business.

"Wow, I hope you know how gorgeous you are," a stranger once gushed in excited surprise after sitting next to me at a café. "You're not my normal type, so don't think I wouldn't have noticed if I didn't look so closely."

While those folks may have had good intentions, their opinions were offered without invitation and were far more a reflection of how well they understand ugliness, uglification, and beauty standards than an appreciation of my beauty.

One spring, while crossing the street in crowded downtown Oakland, a man stopped, stared at me, and told me I was beautiful.

"Thanks," I said and kept walking.

"Can I talk to you?"

"No, thank you."

"Why not?" he questioned.

"I'm sorry, sir. I'm busy. Please have a nice day."

"But I want to talk to you, pretty. Don't you want to talk to me?" he said, trailing me so close I could feel his breath on the back of my neck.

Nervous, I walked into the nearby Walgreens hoping that he would leave me alone. He followed me into the store, still talking to me, his comments becoming increasingly lewd.

"Leave me alone," I shouted, searching for the security guard who usually stood in the front of the store.

The security noticed my panicked stare, looked at the man follow-ing me, and then looked away. I looked at the long line of customers. A few folks were watching, a few looking at their phones, but no one said anything.

"Leave me alone, sir," I repeated.

Then, out of nowhere, the man lunged at me, screaming, "Fuck you, you Black bitch. Don't nobody want yo' ugly, fat ass anyway."

Terrified, I screamed and ran to the back of the store. Fortunately, the man didn't follow me, and he eventually left on his own accord. He wasn't asked to leave by the security guard or anyone who worked at the store. Nor did any of the people in the line intervene. No one stopped to ask me if I was okay or if I needed anything, though when I finally got in line, a woman told me, "Yikes. I saw what happened. That was crazy."

I don't think what happened to me was crazy, as that is a generic and ableist term meant to describe all sorts of random things and traits. I think what happened to me was violence, and the fact that no one attempted to intervene felt even more violent than the attempted attack. I was unsafe because the people around me didn't see me, or someone who looks like me, as someone worthy of protection.

A few minutes after leaving the store, I found myself walking to the bus stop behind a white woman who did fit into normative beauty stan-dards. She could not walk five feet without one man or the next catcalling her. At one point, a man in a business suit ran across the street to ask her if she was lost.

Annoyed, she said, "Nope, just walking to the bus."

"A woman as beautiful as you should never have to ride the bus," he said, pulling out his car keys and pressing the button to unlock the doors of a gleaming and fancy-looking car a few spots away. "Where are you headed? I don't mind giving you a ride."

"Um, no thanks," she said, looking just as panicked as I felt in the store.

"Are you sure? Maybe I can buy you a nice dinner."

Though our experiences were different, they were both harassment and they both spelled out the potential of danger. I did not ask to be followed into Walgreens, and she did not ask to be catcalled or have men try to convince her to get into their cars. Both men we interacted with ignored our no and felt entitled to our time, our space, and our attention. Beauty and ugliness are used to validate so much inexcusable, patriarchal abuse.

My friend and former mentee Travis Alabanza, a Black and Filipino playwright and performer from the UK, had a similar experience. One day when they were walking down the street in all their nonbinary, trans, high femme glory, someone had the audacity to roll down their window and throw a hamburger at them. This happened because their attacker was transphobic. It also happened because the world is transphobic, misogynist, and has not illustrated that it will take the steps to protect women and other marginalized genders, especially trans and nonbinary people of color. But Travis, being the phenomenal femme that they are, used that opportunity to reclaim their power and narrative from the impact of someone else's hatred: they wrote and starred in the award-winning, sold-out performance *Burgerz*. *Burgerz* opened so many hearts all over Europe, and likely saved the lives of more young trans and nonbinary folks than we know. Travis may have started out as one of my students, but today they are one of my femme superheroes.

It took me much longer to reclaim my power from the consequences and impacts of lookism and uglification. I spent years of my life trying to validate that I was beautiful, rather than rejecting the limiting narrative of beauty and ugliness that was projected onto me. I'd write poems glorifying the specific parts of me that others noted as beautiful. I'd awkwardly ask my friends and siblings if they thought I was cute or ugly, praying that they would say cute. I'd compare myself to other kids that were called ugly, examining the differences and similarities between our features, and using the criticisms lodged at them to justify my beauty and social value.

When I became an employed adult, I went from trying to hide my face and body to avoid negative attention to spending tens of thousands of dollars on clothes, hair, and makeup in hopes that people would pay me positive attention. While it is fun to play with style, and adornment is definitely a part of my femme gender expression, I did not treat the experience like it was something pleasurable. Instead, I shopped from a place of shame and desperation. I shopped so that other people would want me around, see me as attractive, not ignore and stereotype me when I went into a shop or to work, and not point or laugh at me as I walked down the street or rode public transportation. I was trying to buy acceptance because I didn't believe and hadn't experienced it being innately extended to me (often).

I've tried to purchase love and acceptance in so many ways over the years. When I was a little girl, I saved up the dollars my parents would give me as an allowance to buy other children candy and ice cream, hoping the gifts would compel them to include me in their games. It always did, until the treats and money ran out. As an adult, I dated very abusive and controlling people, conflating their violence and nonconsensual dominance with passion. Telling myself that my partners' jealous violence and control was an indication that I was beautiful and precious to them, I allowed my body and safety to be the currency.

When I finally stopped dating people who used their hands and words to manipulate me, I began dating cunning people who exploited my insecurity, generosity, and desperation for love to get their needs met: money, free housing, emotional labor, and other resources. Sometimes I would offer these things before they even asked because I thought that would make them see me as valuable enough to love me and commit to me regardless of what I looked like. I couldn't imagine being in a relationship with someone who simply liked me for me (even though many people did) because the world, television, romance novels, music, my loved ones, my classmates, weight loss ads, random strangers, and so many of my past experiences told me, over and over again, that no one wanted to date a fat, dark-skinned girl.

I swallowed those messages whole, not because I was weak or plagued with self-hatred, but because I was young, traumatized from a lifetime of living in a body that was read as ugly and undesirable, and hadn't yet been exposed to images of people who looked like me being loved and treated well.

Dating violence, childhood bullying, and overspending weren't the only consequences of how I internalized lookism and experienced uglification. When I was eighteen years old, a few of my super close friends and I went to the movies to watch Eminem's *8 Mile*. My friends sat in the seats to the right of me, and the seat on my left was empty. Shortly after the movie started, a white man in his late forties or fifties sat in the seat beside me. A little bit later, I felt his finger on my thigh and stopped breathing.

"Surely this man isn't caressing my thigh," I thought to myself. "I must be making it up."

A few seconds passed and his finger didn't move, so I released my breath, shifted my leg, and assumed that his finger landed on me because he didn't have enough space. His hand fell away, and I made myself just a little bit smaller, more invested in his comfort than my own, certain that his finger on my thigh was my fault. Then, after a couple of moments, his hand was back on my thigh.

My heart started racing. I didn't, couldn't move. I just sat there, frozen, unsure of what I should do. A part of me thought of loudly yelling, "Please stop touching me, sir." Another part of me considered asking my friends to move a seat down so I could manually put space between us. But there was a another voice in my head as well, a terrified, lonely, and insecure voice that said, "Vanessa, it's finally happening. Someone is finally touching you. Like that."

The voices in my head argued with each other, chasing after my morals, my desires, and my sexual thirstiness in unrelenting circles of confusion.

"Don't let this man molest you."

"Is it molestation if I want it?"

"You don't want it like this."

"This is probably the only way I'm going to get it. No one else has ever tried to touch me like this before."

"No, this is terrifying and unsafe. You don't know this man."

"Maybe that is what will make it hot. Surrender."

I heard my mother's voice in my head, asking me, "Vanessa, baby, if you want someone to love you and make love to you good, you need to lose weight." I flashed back to my father telling me that no man would want to hire someone who was fat and dark skinned. They will always hire someone who they like looking at." I remembered all the times one of my crushes told me, "No offense, you're not my type," and ended up crushing or dating someone who looked nothing like me. I visualized the many occasions boys and men approached my friends on campus, at amusement parks, at parties, at the mall, and ignored me, closed the door on me, and even cracked jokes about me being the ugly friend.

"This man chose you," I thought to myself. "Someone actually wants you, and you are horny. You have been horny for so long. Maybe you'll finally experience what an orgasm feels like. Let it happen."

So I sat there, and from a place of loneliness, scarcity, and hopelessness, I let this strange man, who hadn't yet said a word to me, who I had no attraction or desire toward, who I felt angered and repulsed by, rub my thigh and then the inside of my thigh. I shamed myself, shouted at myself, and questioned myself while his fingers inched closer and closer to my genitals. When he grabbed my hand and put it on his erection, I finally lost it. My stomach dropped. My throat gagged.

I whispered, "No," told my friends that the man next to me was touching me inappropriately, and asked them to move down a seat. I spent the rest of the movie disgusted and ashamed of myself for allowing something that felt so scary and wrong to happen, but I was also wondering if I made a huge mistake, if anyone would ever want to touch me again, if I would be lonely and horny for the rest of my life, if I was just being a frigid baby, if I was slut-shaming or limiting myself.

After the movie ended and I told my buddies what happened, a few of them asked me why I would allow that man to touch me like that, and one of them, the only boy in our group, told me he didn't believe me. I didn't know how to tell them that I let him touch me because I was horny and I didn't think anyone else would ever want me, that I was so grateful to know that at least someone did want me—even if it was a creepy stranger—and that our male friend's belief that I was lying confirmed the fact that people who weren't creepy old men in the movie theaters wouldn't want me.

Of course I was wrong. Uglification and lookism had colonized my imagination so intensely that I only believed the worst about myself and the worst about everyone else. I believed with my whole heart that everyone thought I was ugly, that no one would want me, that my friends only liked me because I was smart, silly, and generous. When I fantasized and masturbated, I always imagined myself in the future, finally thin, finally desirable. I thought that safe, consensual sex would only happen when I finally had a body that people wanted to have sex with.

What I didn't know, didn't yet have the capacity to imagine, was that one of the people who was there with me at the movie theater, the one I called my best friend, had a crush on me for years. Because I couldn't see my beauty and was very aware of hers, I didn't see the desire, admiration, and love reflected in her gaze whenever she looked at me. I couldn't recognize the bashfulness in her giggle whenever I directed positive attention toward her. I didn't consider the fact that she was always inviting me over because she really loved my company.

It wasn't until I was twenty-one that I finally got it.

I had just moved to San Francisco from Los Angeles a few months ago and immediately started visiting queer burlesque performances. There I saw women and femmes who were my size, even larger, dancing and stripping like the hot fire of Sapphic Eros on stage. I saw fat move like succulent bodies of ocean. I saw people in the audience fanning themselves, yelling affirmations, putting money in garters, or throwing it on the stage. I found the people dancing on stage to be so sexy, and wondered what it meant to be attracted to people I thought the folks I grew up with would call ugly or gross.

As I pondered that question, I thought, If I'm attracted to these performers who look so much like me, and if I am not questioning their beauty or erotic, why can't I decide to not question my own? Why can't I find myself just as beautiful? Why can't I believe that other queer people will believe that I'm just as hot as the people we were collectively lusting after on stage?

I started moving through the world just a little bit differently. I wasn't yet at a place where I recognized physical human beauty to be irrelevant, but I was starting to accept the fact that beauty, desire, and sexiness were objective qualities, that different people were attracted to different things, and that there was the potential for people to be attracted to me.

So my walk changed. My strut became pronounced. My hips started to swing. I smiled more instead of staring at the ground. I started wearing more colors than black. My clothes got a little bit tighter. My skirts a bit shorter. I laughed louder. I made eye contact with people.

Suddenly, folks were approaching me just to say hi and introduce themselves after class. My roommates wanted me to go to parties and bars with them. Strangers would stop me on campus or at a café to tell me that they liked my smile or that I had pretty skin, sexy eyes, or a thick booty. When people told me I was beautiful, I agreed with them. I saw my beauty as well.

And when I talked to my best friend, I finally started to notice that she, too, saw my beauty. That she wanted me. That she had been trying to hint at it to me for years. She and I ended up dating for four and a half years, and eventually became engaged. Earlier into our relationship, she told me that she perceived my lack of response as a lack of interest and that she never thought someone as sexy and confident as me would be attracted to her.

Uglification and lookism don't just inform how we experience the world or how we're treated by the world, they also inform how we see the world and how we perceive of ourselves. It took me years to stop seeing myself through the lens of oppression and colonization and to reclaim myself as whole instead of remaining an outsider or a victim. I don't judge myself for this. Instead, I understand myself to be a survivor of what lookism does. Lookism is connected to every form of oppression.

Just like my male friend thought no strange man would grope or molest me, most survivors—especially fat survivors, disabled survivors, and survivors with uglified bodies and facial features—are not believed. Though I wish the story about my best friend turned girlfriend had a happy ending, it didn't. The more confident and outgoing I became, the more other people began expressing their diverse attractions toward and appreciations for me, the more controlling and abusive she became.

Eventually that abuse became physical and sexual. When I exercised or tried to eat less junk food, she would complain that I was trying to lose weight so I could date someone more attractive than her. When I tried to break up with her, she'd tell me that no one else would be attracted to someone who looked like me. And when I finally told other people that I was being abused by her, people who didn't witness the abuse didn't believe me. They told me that they couldn't believe someone so much smaller than me could hurt me, or that someone who could date anyone they wanted would be abusive and controlling toward me. Some people directly told me that she was out of my league and I should be grateful.

Lookism protects violence and uglifies victims and survivors. We assume that most rapists, traffickers, and possessive partners target people who are traditionally desirable. The people they target are those of us who are most vulnerable to neglect and uglification, those of us the rest of the world claims are undesirable, those of us who are traumatized from bullying, exclusion, and previous experiences of neglect.

Lookism is a prejudice that exists solely because of who we uglify, and we only uglify people for a reason. We dominate, suppress, and oppress to privilege ourselves. People bully so that they aren't bullied. Racist people describe colonized and oppressed groups as ugly, unhuman, animalistic. Those words were used to uglify Africans and validate slavery. The same words were used to spur and justify the horrific colonial assaults on Indigenous people by European countries, militaries, and migrants around the world. Even in the twenty-first century, scientists have strived to prove that Black women and other darker-skinned people are uglier than women of lighter-skinned ethnicities for years.[2]

Lookism is a widely accepted form of hatred that must be addressed and interrupted. We cannot repeat the sticks-and-stones or self-esteem arguments any longer. It is time for us to start speaking up for people, standing up for each other's safety, and protecting each other's lives. We can do this by talking about lookism the same way we talk about racism and homophobia, by holding filmmakers and television showrunners accountable for how they talk about bodies and the types of bodies they feature, by refusing to listen to musicians who refer to people as ugly in their songs, and by refusing to conflate the trauma of uglification with insecurity.

While insecurity may surely play a role in why some of us strive to fit into beauty standards, I believe that underneath the surface, beauty is not our goal. I believe that what we really want is to experience peace, safety, love, and getting our needs met. Beauty is just a vehicle. Those needs are all urgent. They are not a luxury to be reserved for the few. We are all inherently worthy, and it's our collective duty to create a world that honors that truth.

## REFLECTION

- What did it feel like the first time someone called you ugly or insinuated that there was something wrong with the way you looked?

- What did it feel like the first time you heard someone call another person ugly?

- Can you remember the first time you called another person ugly? Why did you do it?

- Can you remember the first time you believed that you, or some part you, was ugly? Why did you feel that way about yourself?

- Can you remember the first time you made a decision on the basis of not wanting to appear ugly to someone else? What were you afraid of?

- Can you remember the first time you chose to treat someone poorly because you thought they were ugly or because other people thought they were ugly? How did that violence feel in your body? Why did you do it?

- Can you remember the first time you made a choice that felt like you were betraying or silencing a part of your truth in order to be accepted or liked by someone else? How did that make you feel about yourself?

- Can you remember the first time you thought another person was too beautiful or attractive to want to be your friend, date you, or take you seriously? Where did you learn to think that way?

- Can you remember the first time you were nervous about going to a party, a job interview, an audition, a doctor's appointment, or a home showing because you were afraid of being rejected based on your appearance, body, disability, size, gender expression, or other aspect of your appearance?

- Can you remember the first time you looked at another person and felt grateful that you did not look like them?

- Can you remember the first time you had to justify your attraction or desire for another person because your loved ones judged their appearance, heritage, education, disability, size, or economic background? What did that do to you emotionally? How did it make you feel about your own desires or the person you desired?

## Criminalization

Criminalization happens when laws, policies, and unwritten rules are implemented to mass-incarcerate specific groups of people and strip them of their rights, freedom, and ability to mobilize for change. It is an exploitation and abuse of legislative power meant to protect and center the desires of some groups of privileged and prioritized people at the expense of those who are criminalized, to control the masses through techniques of fear, abuse, and domination, and to maintain a social structure that reserves wealth and power for a small few. Criminalization works hand in hand with uglification, lookism, and many other forms of oppression to do this work in multiple ways.

We criminalize, uglify, punish, and prosecute social justice activists for participating in public protests when we don't understand their purpose or aren't impacted by the struggles they face. When protestors and organizers gather to make a public request for social or systemic change, such as Black Lives Matter, anti-deportation groups, and the Occupy movement, they are responded to with the same public animosity and scrutiny that was used for the witch hunts in European and early American history. Though some news media sources are empathetic and report on what's happening with compassionate solidarity, protestors who gather in large groups to speak up against the horrible conditions of their lives are frequently named *rioters, mobs, terrorists*, and *criminals* by news reporters, large business owners, and police and government groups.[3] They are decried for the potential of broken windows and doors, but not asked about the loved ones they have lost or the times they have suffered due to poverty, abuse, and state violence. In many children's stories and films, we're taught to protect the people who experience the most harm and disenfranchisement, even if it's from a nefarious government, leader, or business owner (just think about *Snow White, The Lion King, Robin Hood, Dumbo*, and more). In real life, we treat harmed people asking for change as if they are threats and risks, not the heroes who deserve our empathy, care, or protection.

This is the strategy of uglification. People are uglified as bad, dangerous, or wrong so that we don't have to care about what happens to them or we can feel justified in hurting them. Because protestors have been painted as monsters for disrupting the day-to-day ease of people who are less impacted by the violence and injustice that facilitated the protest movement in the first place, and the public accepts and complies with their uglification, they become easy and vulnerable targets for the terrifying impacts of criminalization. Police officers, sheriffs, the National

Guard, and private security groups are hired to suppress them. They shoot people, indiscriminately, with painful rubber bullets, life-threatening tasers, and pepper spray. They throw gas canisters. They beat people with their fists, their shoes, and their batons.[4] If they are camped out, like many of the Occupy groups were, they are raided in the middle of the night—their tents, structures, and belongings either set on fire or ripped off them as they sleep and thrown in the trash.[5] Members of law enforcement and other hired groups infiltrate the protestors and initiate infighting or window breaking to justify police violence and incarceration. And they arrest people. They yell at, intimidate, and handcuff peaceful protestors; force them into tiny, dark, solitary confinements built into two large police trucks; and then take them to jail where they are submitted to strip and cavity searches before being put in another cage.[6] When and if the protestors are released, they are fined an exorbitant amount of money and risk job loss and other threats.[7]

Sometimes protestors are murdered for protesting. In many countries, they are killed by the police and military.[8] But in the United States, most protestors are killed by lone vigilantes and counter protestors.[9] These types of killers perceive themselves to be heroes and are mobilized and terrified by how the media and conservative groups uglify social- and racial-justice protestors, as well as portray the causes being advocating for as bad, dangerous, and a disruption of the peace. In reality, they are working to sustain and protect a system that unnecessarily destroys lives, rips apart families, and teaches us to hate each other. Criminalization not only teaches us to hate, but it also teaches us who to hate: people who speak up about suffering, not those who cause the suffering, which is why this sort of criminalization and uglification is directly related to lookism.

When the media, vigilantes, police officers, and anti-protestors direct their gaze at a protestor, they don't see a complicated and nuanced human being who feels so passionately about their cause that they would put themselves in such a dangerous position, they only see what they choose to see and what they've been conditioned to believe about people who look or behave a certain way: bad, wrong, ugly, dangerous. They profile and stereotype based on how people look, their facial expressions, their body language, their outfits, their skin color, and who they are surrounded by. They make decisions about how some communities, venues, and actions should look, and they uglify disruptions as wrong. This is like how racial and citizenship profiling, another type of lookism and correlation, works. On the basis of race or how someone of a certain race appears, police officers and citizens of other ethnicities profile that person as undocumented, a thief, dishonest, or aggressive and dangerous. Similar to and in collaboration with what happens to protestors, people are arrested, incarcerated, deported, and murdered based on how someone else judges their appearance.

One day, while sitting in a café in downtown Oakland grading papers, my ex-partner and I watched a young, dark-skinned, Black man with locs, a grill in his mouth, and sagging skinny jeans, get randomly apprehended by an officer while casually walking down the street by himself. We quickly walked outside to videotape the interaction (this is called cop-watching). When the officer wasn't yelling at us to stop recording the scene and disrespecting his authority, he was putting handcuffs on the young man, touching every part of his body as if he were looking for something, and exerting his power and dominance by antagonizing him and then threatening him with arrest and prison violence every time he responded. The officer detained him for over twenty minutes while he ran a report on him. The report came back empty, to the officer's angered surprise.

Eventually he let the young man go *after* writing him a ticket for spitting on the sidewalk. Who knew that spitting was illegal? I have spit on many sidewalks and have never been questioned about it once, but I am not a young Black man with locs and a grill. At night I look like a weird, artsy book fairy, and in daylight a very jolly Sunday school teacher. The world marks me as safe and unthreatening, until they hear me speak, and I consequently don't experience the same sort of criminalization and lookism. Each time I have been pulled over or apprehended by the police, I was in a car with younger Black and Latinx masculine-presenting nonbinary folks, men, and butch women. Despite my being a dark-skinned Black woman, the police have mostly been friendly to me when they encounter me alone, even going as far as to offer me protection and resources when I've been threatened. I know that this can change at any moment—no Black, Brown, or Indigenous person is fully safe in America—but some of us do experience more intersections of privilege than other people of color.

When the young man who my partner and I were cop-watching for asked why he was pulled over, the officer told him that he looked like trouble, so he better stay out of trouble. He was apprehended, harassed, fined, and dominated because a man decided that he looked like trouble. That is the terrifying power of uglification. That is lookism working on a systemic level. That is a person using their privilege and power to profile, target, metaphorically step on someone who doesn't have the same access or support to safely protect themselves. The police officer effectively let the other man know that he was not safe, that he would never be safe, and that there was nothing he could do about it. I'm sure that the young man knew, just like my partner and I knew, that he was fodder for criminalization and assault before the officer even saw his face.

Usually when we talk about criminalization, we focus on race, class, or immigration. But there is another group of people in the United States of America who have been criminalized in the most contemptible and under-discussed of ways: disabled people, and in particularly, disabled people who are also old, people of color, poor and houseless, and/or don't exist within the gender binary—and yes, it has everything to do with how disabled people are looked upon by others. The people who experience the most uglification are those who have the most intersections of identities.

## Ableism

Unfortunately, the majority of us live among and depend on social structures that were not built to consider and support the diverse ways all our bodies and intelligences function, much less provide for the different things different people need to learn, to be, and to do to navigate these streets. Ableism happens when we center, hire, and privilege people who can access systems and structures as they are, at the expense and exclusion of those who cannot. On a meta level, this practice segregates people who have some disabilities from people who don't have those disabilities. It segregates classrooms, cities, amusement parks and other pleasure venues, schools, places of employment, doctors' offices, and any other part of the public sector. This segregation means that some people get access to having their needs met, some people have a lot of hoops to jump through, and some folks don't get their needs met at all.

For example, if I, an arts organizer, host a performance or training without hiring culturally appropriate ASL interpreters and Deaf performers/facilitators, I'm participating in ableism by excluding Deaf and some hard-of-hearing people by only catering to people who can hear. I'm also contributing to the supremacist and oppressive history of entertainment where only certain bodies could get access to a stage and an audience, leading artistic brilliance to be easily associated with those particular body types. Erasure and exclusion in the arts and entertainment realm inherently uglify and other those who are unseen and whose stories are untold.

As an arts organizer, I have a powerful capacity to curate spaces where historically excluded voices are shared, where uglified bodies are portrayed as art, and where narrative gets to expand with the complexity of all different human experiences. If my event, class, or building is not mobility-device accessible, including an ADA-compliant bathroom, my offerings exclude and deny people who rely on mobility devices to frequent venues, which perpetuates the violence and exclusion disabled people continue to experience.

For example, the erasure of Deaf and other disabled people from the media and leadership means that organizations and groups often forget about disabled people when creating cultural competency and human resource trainings. That forgetting leaves service workers, like police officers, social workers, school faculty, and security guards, unprepared to support, communicate with, and protect disabled folks in need. It's why police officers killed Magdiel Sanchez and Daniel Harris, two Deaf men who were attempting to tell the officers that they were Deaf while in the process of being shot.[10] Because of their invisibility and the police's lack of training—the result of exclusion and uglification—officers did not even consider the men's Deafness as an option for their lack of requested response. They just saw them as a threat, someone who refused to fall in line, someone to be afraid of, and hence someone to be eliminated just in case their own lives were at risk. These Deaf men would still be alive if Deaf lives were valued enough to be protected by officers and other folks in positions of leadership to implement the structures needed to save their lives, such as Deaf cultural competency trainings by Deaf activists, increased Deaf officers of peace (please notice I said *peace* and not *law*), and creating more space for Deaf leadership at the table.

Disabled people, especially poor, homeless, and BIPOC disabled people, have been treated as social threats and criminalized throughout history, simply for existing. In the late nineteenth century, different cities began implementing policies and laws currently known as ugly laws. In 1881 the Chicago city council ordained a law that stated anyone who was "diseased, maimed, mutilated, or in any way deformed, so as to be an unsightly or disgusting object" should not only be banned from view, but they could also be fined or sent to the county poor house or asylum.[11] People were arrested and fined for being disabled, sick, poor, old, or having survived physical trauma. People were criminalized solely for existing in a body that someone else could report as ugly.

The first ugly law was passed in 1867 in San Francisco.[12] This law, like all the others, had several purposes and groups it was targeting. Many poor white people from the Midwest and American South traveled to California in the mid to late nineteenth century hoping to find gold in the mining industry and strike it rich after the Civil War. In the process, a significant number of those people became disabled, sick, addicted, and took to panhandling for food and money. Similarly, more and more Chinese migrants were being recruited, and exploited, to do the harrowing, body-destroying work of building railroads. Those who survived that work ended up in the bustling and growing city to find work. There were also many other people arriving in San Francisco every day, usually old people and migrants, all disabled, who were increasingly visible and asking for help and support. As the affluent residents complained about unsightly sick and disabled people in the streets, lawmakers and newspapers were concerned about the city becoming a place of refuge.

The ugly laws were created because of lookism, classism, and ableism. Wealthy, able-bodied, privileged people wanted to enjoy their creature comforts without watching people suffer. But instead of addressing the systems and circumstances that led so many people to be in the streets asking for help, the city used its resources to create almshouses. Almshouses were positioned as charitable living situations for people unable to pay rent due to age or disability, but they were state-run buildings that people were forced into by officers, judges, and court systems. They were not safe spaces for rest. Residents were abused, dehumanized, forced to work there to pay their way, and put in dangerous situations. Most almshouses shared land and facilities with asylum hospitals, also state-run institutions (though some were private) that incarcerated disabled people, MaGes, and poor people.

For over 100 years of American history, people could legally be sent to jail, fined, or forced into a hospital just because they were disabled and poor in public. Laws were created to hurt and target them because they existed within a culture that only valued bodies deemed as healthy, beautiful, and capable of working. Though ugly laws no longer exist on the books, our culture has not changed nor has our legal system. Almost everyone in prison has at least one chronic illness or disability, and over 60 percent of incarcerated MaGes are recognized as disabled.[13]

## Internalized Ableism and Capitalism

In 2 Thessalonians 3:10 (King James Version) it says, "This we commanded you: that if any would not work, neither should he eat." Throughout history, this verse has been used to exploit the destitute for free labor in the form of slavery and serfdom. It was used to silence and shame the very human need for rest, regeneration, and pleasure. And it protected a hierarchical power dynamic between the workers and the individuals who profited from their labor, thus allowing one class of people to decide what work was and who got to eat.

Those of us who subscribe to contemporary, intersectional Black feminism have reclaimed what labor means and who gets to decide what labor is recognized. Emotional labor, whether it's unpacking systems of oppression, healing yourself from the trauma that comes with generations of oppression and violence, holding yourself back from snapping at a demeaning employer, raising children, or supporting others through their own healing and self-reckoning process, is labor. Being an adorable sunshine Care Bear and providing entertainment, joy, and positive energy to the people around you is labor. Writing poetry, dancing, or singing is labor. Existing in a city or rural infrastructure that refuses to accommodate bodies like yours, whether by racism, lack of disability access, or transphobia, is labor. Deciding to not allow stress to bear the axe on your spirit is labor. To be clear, *you* are the executive of your brain and the consequent executive of the labor you share with yourself and the world, and all of it is critical.

If your labor has been traditionally recognized—midwifing, farming, programming computers, teaching, healing, caring for elders, clerking, banking—but you are only able to contribute a few hours a week or a day, that labor is still valid, and you deserve to eat. We were not born to be consumed by a machine that is only in service to someone else's wealth or a system that harms us. That is not the human purpose. The human purpose is to experience the great majesty of this earth with our whole bodies; to pollinate both plants: art and intellect; and to love and nurture each other's wellness and freedom. I believe our purpose is to experience as much joy and pleasure as possible, and for some of us, that is very much recognizable work.

I love to teach, to facilitate healing and intimacy spaces, to steward people along their journey of self-actualization and collective liberation. I love to laugh, to help people feel comfortable and welcome, to celebrate the shish kabob out of other artists and healers. I am so blessed to live in a temporal and physical location where this is recognized and honored as labor. I understand that, given my body and social positioning, I would not have had the same access a hundred years ago, possibly not even fifty years ago. My career is a privilege of the time, the educational experience my parents were able to provide for me, and the labor to which so many Black, fat, and/or queer feminists (and many other social justice superheroes) have devoted their lives. I am so grateful.

But for most people in the United States, and the various countries it's imperialized, the archaic pastime of people dehumanizing and oppressing other people is still very much alive and unchallenged in its attachment to morality and which bodies and personas we hold cherished and dear. We see this in the abysmal minimum wage that leaves people spending their entire lives doing tedious labor until stress and exhaustion kill them. We breathe it in when we walk or ride by the stench of human release on the streets, because we're so attached to the value that only certain types of labor result in survival resources that we refuse to house people *despite* the number of vacant abodes available. For example, in 2020 San Francisco had 11,760 empty homes, and Oakland had 5,898— and this doesn't include empty office buildings and other constructs with roofs, walls, and bathrooms. Yet in the middle of a pandemic that was killing thousands of people every day, Oakland had 4,071 unhoused people and San Francisco had 8,000.[14]

This ideological practice that prioritizes constructs of earning one's way into food and shelter and protecting symbols of wealth over the actual well-being of people is a manifestation of uglification. This type of status-quo uglification exists and depends on us uglifying poor and impoverished people so that the rest of us can validate and self-soothe ourselves from participating in the injustice of it all. It's easier to say "I work hard for what I have" than it is to say "I don't care about the struggles of people I don't know. I'd rather spend *my* money on the things that I've been convinced I need for pleasure or even pay taxes on properties I own that no one lives in, than I would invest my resources so that we all have everything we need to thrive and be well."

Capitalism tells us to think only of ourselves and our families, and even then, to assess who is worthy of our generosity. This, the idea that some people are worthy of something that others are not worthy of due to some assessment, is supremacist. So is the idea of laziness. And the Bible has taught us to use the imaginary construct of laziness to validate that supremacy and therefore decide which types of labor, what quantity of work, and which experiences of people make them worthy of receiving what they need to live.

Laziness is a figment of our colonized and desperate imagination. It is not real. A culture, government, and employment system that refuses to recognize and adjust itself to the diverse ways our brains and bodies function is real. Digging in our heels about practices that are not sustainable and hence leaving whole bodies and families out of participating is real. Discriminatory hiring practices are real. Office buildings that cannot not be navigated by people with large bodies, disabilities, and children without childcare are real. Exhaustion, depression, and standards around mistreatment are real. But laziness is not real. What we have been taught to perceive as laziness is a phenomenal intelligence and perseverance.

For many years, I thought that I was lazy because I could not do what I felt was expected of me to earn the money I needed to live and the respect I needed to advance in my career. As a child, I thought I was lazy because I couldn't focus on anything long enough to accomplish a goal without adult supervision and inevitable punishment. I now recognize that my "laziness" is my body's investment in its survival, its hard boundaries against exploitation, and a misunderstanding of work effort that doesn't account for learning differences and neurodivergence.

I spent more than seven years of my life working for a small community college as an English instructor. I taught three to four classes a semester, which meant that I taught four to five days a week. Each class had thirty-plus people. Grading a five-to-seven-page paper, as our students were required to write, usually took me twenty to forty minutes (and that's if I wanted to genuinely offer feedback and support my students' growth). Including all the meetings I was required to attend and the office hours I volunteered, my part-time job was about forty hours a week if not more.

I never made more than $20,000 to $25,000 annually teaching at college level. As hard as I was working, as tired as I was, I had convinced myself that if I took on more work, did a better job, I could have a living wage. So I worked more, taught at other colleges, taught theatre and writing to youth, took on side gigs. When I was finally making a semi-sustainable living (a little under $50,000 annually), I was working closer to eighty to ninety hours a week. I had no time left to live my life the way I wanted, which included going on vacations and taking time to care for my body the way I wanted to, and I donated a good portion of my income to other people whose marginalization meant they couldn't do the work I was doing.

I later learned that the chancellor of the college district I worked for had a starting salary of $260,000 annually, plus perks, and worked closer to forty-five to fifty-five hours a week. Like the chancellor, I had an advanced degree. But something in the system we navigated decided that his work was more valuable than mine and consequently more deserving of money and time for rest. And because money and rest inform the quality of life we live, this same system decided that his life was more valuable than mine, and that my life is more valuable than people who don't have degrees, don't speak English, and cannot navigate white-supremacist professionalism the way I had learned from my parents.

Internalizing meritocratic beliefs, like working hard gets you far in life, damn near cheated me out of the pleasure of this beautiful planet we live on. This is systemic and class-based uglification. Through the privileging and prioritizing of some lives, we uglify others out of wellness and access and then convince them it's their fault because they are "lazy." Regardless of whether uglification shows up as mental breaks, cancer, horrific accidents, heart attacks, fear- and competition-related violence, suicide, or our bodies just stopping with exhaustion, it literally kills us.

This murder that our system perpetrates against us is unnecessary. If the empty houses to houselessness statistics don't touch your heart, think about this: according to the USDA, a minimum of 133 billion pounds of food is thrown away every year, while 35 million people in the US struggle with hunger and 14 million households are food insecure, per 2019 data.[15] It's criminal when food is thrown away, for any reason other than it being toxic/poisonous, when millions of people are hungry.

This is a nation and culture that would rather see people starve or die from exhaustion than feed them. Honoring the sentiment of 2 Thessalonians 3:10 is completely irrational. If we have enough food to throw away, and more empty homes than homeless people, there is absolutely no logical reason for us to decide that people who don't work, or who don't do enough of a certain type of work, shouldn't be housed and fed. Some people might say that if we just gave free food and homes away, no one would work. That is not true. People might rest more, as they should. People might spend more time indulging in pleasure, which keeps us alive and peaceful. But people would work... they would just do the work that *they* wanted to do rather than submit to the expectations of people in positions of economic power and control.

People love to garden when they aren't slaves or exploited migrant labor. Being on the earth, watching plants grow, eating the herbs you picked and the meat you cured is pure pleasure for so many people. We could create extraordinary and artistic systems to curate our lives together. We could become our masters. We could take care of ourselves, trade, and buy our wares from our friends and neighbors instead of the multibillion-dollar corporations that only care for a few people. We would dream up ways to be that truly stewarded liberated lives, joy, and ease.

When people say that folks would stop working, what they really mean is that they would stop tolerating their oppression and refuse to work for groups that didn't care about them. This lie about people not working is a strategy of uglification to gaslight us into complacency and out of our creativity, imagination, and human potential for extravagance.

This lie is an example of us valuing ancient ideas, commerce, and wealth over actual people; it is the result of centuries of nations and groups uglifying the poor, the sick and disabled, the neurodivergent, our elders, and other groups of people at the bottom of the economic totem pole. It's a legalized murder. And friends, family, you deserve so much better.

Just like we created the system we currently live in, just like we created serfdom, chattel slavery, sharecropping, billionairism, Wall Street, and conglomerations, we can also create systems that work for the health and sustainability of all human beings, all human bodies, and the earth that holds us all. Reclaiming the parts of us that have been uglified means reclaiming our imaginations from the cyclical and reproductive humdrum of oppressive uglification. It means interrupting these systems when and where we can, and it starts with simply choosing to not accept them as the only logical option. When we open our hearts to something different, our behaviors change, and eventually our realities and the realities of those around us change. We can do better. We deserve better. We can create better for ourselves and the people around us. We can save lives simply by rejecting the status quo.

This is not just affirmation for those of us affected by uglification. It's also information for people who steward these systems, who have the power and wisdom to challenge and divest from them. Brilliant people of the world, unfurl those gorgeous brains of yours. Roll up your sleeves. And let's use our own lives to practice a liberation that other people can taste as well.

---

## LOVING REMINDER: YOU ARE NOT LAZY!

The concept of laziness was created to manipulate us into invalidating our very real needs, our bodily intelligence, our autonomy and freedom, and our senses of self-worth and self-awareness. *Laziness* is a subjective word that, especially in work and intimate realms, depends on us dangerously comparing ourselves to others and inherently creating harmful binaries.

You are a precious and magical person, not a puppet to be manipulated through judgment, shame, or the threat of loss/exclusion/invalidation. You deserve to know what your body (brain and spirit) needs and to honor it.

- If you are fatigued (physically or mentally), you deserve as much time to rest as you need.

- If you are wary, you deserve the opportunity to reflect, process, and honor your intuition.

- If you feel exhausted, you deserve occasions to play, vacation, dream, and regenerate creative energy.

- If you are hopeless, you deserve the support to help you laugh and nurture your heart and imagination.

- If you are distracted, you deserve the stimulation and solace to refocus.

- If you are unhappy, you deserve the chance to imitate change and pursue joy.

- If you are frustrated and resentful, you deserve the time to understand your needs and figure out the boundaries that support you.

And you do not have to validate any of this to anyone.

But you are not lazy, and your worth is not dependent on or defined by someone else's standards of usefulness.

Being unhappy, exhausted, sick, overwhelmed, or pleasure/joy/fun-deprived is not a sign of a poor work ethic or a lack of integrity. That's left over from social hierarchies that arbitrarily deem some people laborers and other delegators, some people owners and others property, some people royalty and others serfs, some lives important and other lives disposable.

Pleasure and joy are not just for the economically, racially, physically, or even locationally privileged. These things are critical to all our survival, sustainability, creativity, purpose, and well-being.

What if instead of assessing individuals based on how hard they work or how productive they are, we asked these questions?

- How joyful are you when you work/serve/give?

- Does your work/work environment stimulate, invigorate, or creatively/intellectually challenge you in ways that feel empowering?

- Do you have the opportunities, support, and resources you need to regenerate and restore your energy and creativity?

- Do you feel welcomed, centered, and included when you work with your team or the people you serve?

- How often do you take the opportunity to check in with your body and spirit, to assess your needs and desires, and to share honestly and vulnerably with your team?

- Do you feel cared about as an individual with flesh, family, dreams, and desires outside your ability to contribute to a team or project at work?

---

## Misogynoir

When I was a little girl, I was drawn to my father, attracted by his youthful charisma and the exciting energy that he and his friends would drum up. They would smoke cigarettes, drink Hennessy, play spades and dominoes for hours, talk all sorts of delicious and competitive shit about each other, and politick hard. Around them, I felt my brain bump and prickle with curiosity and desperately wanted to be a part of whatever it was they were doing. But alas, although I could occasionally entertain them with recitations of poetry and Bible verses, I was not invited into the conversations, and I was usually ignored and unseen by them when they really went in. My brother, on the other hand, was sought out and welcomed with rigor, whether he wanted to be with them or not.

One day while my brother and I were playing, one of my father's friends, who was a bit tipsy at the time, led the crew over to us to bring my brother into their conversation about the importance of keeping a "fat bitch" around. The crew did not notice or acknowledge my presence. While they were laughing and one-upping each other as they often did during an especially rambunctious game of spades, the man who approached us asked my brother if he knew why all men should have a fat bitch. When my brother laughed, in his tiny performance of baby boy coolness, and said no, the men began to unpack the resourcefulness of dating fat woman in the most objectifying and dehumanizing way. I heard things like:

"Keep a fat bitch for when you need emergency bail or something nice for court."

"When you're running low on funds, call your fat bitch."

"You like this watch? My fat bitch bought it for me."

"Visit your fat bitch before a job interview. She'll buy you a new suit, hype you up, feed you good the next morning, and not expect nothing back when you start getting paid."

"You're missing out if you don't keep a fat bitch on call. They will be so appreciative that you want to fuck them that they will put in extra work."

"I only fuck with fat bitches because they easy and I ain't trying to get in no relationship."

"Fat bitches are sweet and submissive because they know that you could leave them for someone cute at any time."

Eventually my father noticed how uncomfortable my brother and I were becoming and told his friends to knock off all the cussing around his kids. But that conversation became one of many that led to the formation of my own feminism and queerness. To be clear, I have been queer and sexually amorous for as long as I can remember, even as early as kindergarten. I remember my young and evolving sexuality as being lush, abundant, and appreciative of so many genders, bodies, and expressions; of craving touch and connection; of practically purring underneath the soft and occasional caress of a compliment from one of my classmates.

But that conversation taught me early on to be afraid of the cis boys and men who wanted to pursue or have sex with me. Though I didn't have the language or courage to speak up at the time, I knew that what those men I called father, uncle, cousin, grown-up were saying was wrong and abusive, dangerous, perhaps just as dangerous as the bullets I was taught to drop and hide from, and I felt infuriated to witness these men I trusted pass the pistol to my younger sibling. If I had had the words *uglification*

or *oppression* in my repertoire at that point, I would have recognized my
father's friends' language and actions as weapons of both concepts.

To be sure, these men were deeply demeaning and uglifying fatness,
autonomously. But they were also cis, Black, middle-class men who were
dating, married to, or otherwise engaged with Black women—some of
whom, including my own mother, were fat. Whether they recognized it
or not, they were specifically uglifying the fat Black women in my life,
the adult women who were constantly telling me how beautiful I was;
who held me when I cried, taught me to love books, and kissed me up a
thunderstorm when I got A's or wrote a new poem; the women who were
always cooking for, serving, washing dishes, ironing suits, and cleaning
up after those men; women dressing up extra cute when they were out
in the world, who wore expensive perfumes and spoke softer than usual
when greeting their friends and colleagues. Fat Black women, goddesses
worthy of worship and adornment, butter-soft beings deserving kitten
kisses and protection, precious beings who should be protected at all
costs, were turned into jokes and commodities by these men, and to an
extent, I hated them for it. Whether they acknowledged it or not, those
men spoke with such robust confidence and navigated their own realm
of Black masculinity with an astuteness that made it clear to me that they
knew the power dynamics at play. They knew that fat Black women were
a group of people they could exploit and manipulate, and their completely unrepressed and unrepentant sense of entitlement to our bodies,
resources, and exploitation is no different than a dog's entitlement to a
bone, a raccoon's entitlement to a chicken, a hunter's entitlement to a
deer, and a slaver's entitlement to our ancestors.

While they may not have been exposed to language like *fatphobia* or
*misogynoir* (the unique and specific ways racism and misogyny intersect in
the oppression and mistreatment of Black women, within and outside the
Black community), they were conscious of the fact that fat Black women
experience a lot in life that makes us easier to target in such a way, and
they felt so entitled to how this status quo privileged them that they felt
it was okay to teach this vicious privilege to a little boy, my brother, and
to do so in front of a chubby little girl, me. My father and his friends were

subscribing to, validating, and educating my brother and me on how ugli-fication and oppression categorize people into hierarchies of social value. "Fat bitches," or the Black women around me, were in a category that was okay to exploit because these were women deemed unworthy of being protected or cherished. And the fact that they had been doing this meant that, indeed, the fat Black women in their lives were not being protected from them, much less from people with desires and beliefs more mali-cious than theirs.

Regardless of the uglification, my father and I had a strong and beau-tiful relationship during my early childhood. One of my favorite parts of that relationship was the time we spent reading and analyzing Afro-centric literature together. He taught me language like *diaspora, coloniza-tion,* and *revolution.* We unpacked the South African liberation movement against Apartheid together. He talked to me about the American Jim Crow South. He celebrated movement leaders like Malcolm X, Huey P. Newton, and Muhammad Ali, showing me videotapes and playing cas-sette recordings of their speeches.

He talked me through his own experiences with white supremacy as a young Black man, how he was arrested as a basketball-playing college student in the South after he and his team passed through a *sundown town* after curfew (sundown towns were Jim Crow–era municipalities that had laws in place allowing their police to criminalize and incarcer-ate Black people in their jurisdiction after sunset, or whose local white supremacist / KKK gangs harassed or tortured the Black people who wan-dered through their towns until they left or were killed), or about being put into a police car as a small child after one of his friends threw a rock back at a group of white children who were throwing rocks at them and the other Black kids walking home from school. He unpacked the Civil Rights Movement for me, told me about Emmett Till, helped me under-stand why the Los Angeles riots of my childhood were happening and why the Watts riots of his childhood happened.

My father, and other Black men of his generation, understood the mechanics of racism and white supremacy with expertise. But the ugli-fication of fatness and womanhood combined was so seductive and entrenched in their imagination and socialization as cis, straight men that they could not see the parallels between how the state, the police, and their employers oppressed and targeted them as Black men and how they as Black men targeted and oppressed fat Black women.

It is the combination of white supremacy and misogyny that has created the circumstances that leave some Black women more susceptible to exploitation. And the men, including men who also experience racist oppression, who feel entitled to benefiting from that exploitation, become tools, weapons, and perpetrators of racism. My father's friends weren't just exploiting Black women, they were also exploiting the structures and histories of white supremacy that have left so many Black people, and especially Black women marginalized by fatphobia, colorism, ableism, classism, lookism, and transphobia, to experience an intersection of oppression and destitution that leaves so many of us hurting, broken, and traumatized.

Within marginalized and uglified groups, sometimes we don't like to recognize the way we harm each other or the fact that we have different experiences of oppression. I have been in many predominantly or solely Black spaces where the conversation of oppression cannot push past the generalization of racism or white supremacy. When colorism or other forms of oppression are brought up, more systemically privileged members immediately argue that we all experience the same racism and that speaking about the intersections of oppression and inequity solely works to divide us.

But consider the fact that fat women were singled out and specified. By singling out fat women, or fat bitches as they called us, those men made it clear that thinner women were not targets of this sort of exploitation. Thin Black women, at least among these men, sat higher on the social hierarchy and were consequently safer and more protected from their exploitation. They created an unspoken binary between "thin bitches" and "fat bitches." While I don't know if I feel comfortable saying that thin Black women have the luxury of being universally or even predominantly cherished or protected by heterosexual Black men, or any other men, for that matter, the role that the patriarchy has designated for them establishes a different standard and treatment. If the uglifying qualifications for the exploitation that my father and his friends discussed were fatness and womanhood, it meant that people who didn't exist within those intersections were privileged and protected at the expense of people who did fit into those standards.

Regardless, the men designating and recognizing themselves as the assessors of which "bitches" get exploited and which do not are acknowledging their overriding privilege and dominion. They did not name each other as people to exploit, have, consume, or assess—only women—and the deciding factor of what that exploitation looked like was who they deemed to be universally attractive. I frequently listened to who they thought was attractive or not, and all their examples were Black women who were thin, light skinned, and had a certain hair quality. Repeatedly. The same type of Black women I most frequently saw in the *Jet* model of the week, on MTV and BET music videos, and on Black TV shows and movies. There was a clear correlation between who was designated as beautiful, worthy of visibility and representation, and archival in the Black patriarchal imagination versus who was unseen, easily targeted, and construed as ugly and resourceless; that perspective, and its disregard, is very much aligned with the white-supremacist lens of standardized beauty and value.

To be clear, valuing MaGes because of sexual desire, perceived beauty, or where one thinks they fit within the binary categorical hierarchies created by uglification and oppression is objective and violent, period. Even MaGes who are perceived as more beautiful and desirable within these standards are objectified, labeled, assessed, and consequently dominated by the gaze and power of those privileged by the patriarchy. The patriarchy and systems of uglification teach cis men that they get to designate beauty and worth and that they are entitled to consume and enjoy that beauty, that those women were designed for their desire and consequent possession.

Uglification is death to the imagination. I decided early, after listening to that initial conversation about fat bitches, that I did not want to be a part of a world like that. I did not want to be assessed, consumed, or exploited by any man; no man would ever feel entitled to control or dominate me. My fatness, my Blackness, and my body would never be theirs. But as much as I wanted to, I could never fully excuse myself from the uglifying gaze of the patriarchy.

The uglification that Black women experience surrounds us and infiltrates nearly every part of our cultural experience (outside of the sacred spaces only a few of us have created for ourselves); it empowers the systemic and social neglect, the violence and poverty, and the trauma and stress that kill us. That is because uglification is a form, tool, and weapon of oppression, a sophisticated hatred so clever it even turns our babies and siblings against us. And, as difficult as it is, I empathize deeply with all of them. They are the victims of America, white supremacy, the patriarchy, and uglification themselves—and that is a stressful trauma.

Although these Black men and children who direct misogynist hatred toward Black women may be unwittingly taking their pain, anger, insecurity out on external people and images, they are also beating up themselves. By attacking each other, they also attack the Black people who lay together to create them and the six million Africans who were kidnapped, enslaved, and colonized into acquiescence to their oppression and into further agonizing submission.

Their taunts and memes are extensions of our shared colonization, leftover whip lashes lodged deep in our subconscious, the epitome of how uglification and internalized racism work together to sustain the white-supremacist status quo, whether white people are around or not.

Here, members of an oppressed group use the preestablished societal hierarchies and traumas around race, skin color, gender, beauty, and desirability to degrade a member of a similarly oppressed group (or the same oppressed group) to distance themselves from the psychological torture of oppression, hence positioning themselves closer to the perceived safety of a more privileged and systemically empowered group. This is internalized uglification and sustained oppression. Black people ridiculing other Black people for having darker skin or more African features than themselves is a short-term coping mechanism and faux survival tool for navigating the devastating emotionality, hopelessness, and pervasive disenfranchisement of white supremacy.

The psychology is this: "I may have this unwanted trait, but I am recused of the abuse because I don't have it as much as this other person," or "If I direct attention to this person who has more unwanted traits than me, my oppressors will see that I am more like them compared to the person I have targeted, which will protect me from the abuse," or "I am not what the stereotype says, so I should finally get equal treatment." Uglification distorts our sense of selves and others. It conditions us to conflate destroying others, or perpetuating other people's suffering, with our own safety. Instead of striving for our collective liberation, we celebrate and commemorate ourselves for not experiencing the oppression or harm that others experience.

Although it is easy to be angry at these specific individuals who steward and perpetuate a violence that hurts us all, it's important to realize that they, like me, like you, are also victims of this violence and are attempting to survive it. I will repeat over and over in this book that most people who uglify others are also people who have been uglified. Uglification is an oppression-survival strategy and a tool of oppression at the same time. It is pervasive and insidious in the nuanced and sophisticated ways it affects and challenges us.

# 4

# Dangerous Uglification

The attitudes that my father, his friends, and so many other men hold about Black women and other uglified individuals don't just affect our feelings and self-esteem, they steal lives. They are why more than 40 percent of Black women will experience intimate partner violence in their lives, compared to 31.5 percent of women in general.[1] Those attitudes are the reason why Black women are 2.5 times more likely to be killed by men than white women, why 92 percent of murdered Black women were killed by Black men, and why 56 percent of those murderers were their current or former lovers.[2]

Uglification is much more than bullying, internalized oppression, abusive interpersonal dynamics, and intimate partner violence, as gruesome and painful as those are. It is a structural practice and ideology that sustains the foundation of every system of oppression. It is complicit with white supremacy in American colonial and genocidal projects like slavery and the prison-industrial complex. And it is as old as misogyny. As uncomfortable as this is to say, the group of people who are the most dangerous and the most protected perpetuators of uglification—regardless of ethnicity, class, location, body size, and level of education—are cis, heterosexual men. I don't like targeting a specific group or casting blame in this way, but I believe we need to acknowledge this in order to explore what is needed to create change.

In 2013 a United Nations study revealed that 96 percent of homicide perpetrators were men.[3] If you put 100 people who've killed other people in a room, only 4 of them would be a gender other than male. More than 90 percent of incarcerated women have been battered by their male partners.[4] They are caged and sometimes slaughtered by the state for saving their own lives from a man who likely would have killed them if they didn't—because no one else protects them. The current "preferred" solution is leaving the abuser, which places the blame on women and other genders for not leaving, which simply protects abusive men's ability to continue to be violent and kill. It is a systematic gaslighting that covers up the fact that survivors are unprotected and further justifies the patriarchy's existence.

One in seven women are stalked by an intimate partner.[5] Victims of murder-suicides are 94 percent women.[6] Of women killed by men they know, 63 percent are killed by a current or ex-partner.[7] Over 70 percent of women killed in domestic violence disputes are killed by their abusive ex within the first few weeks after leaving them.[8]

Murderous uglification is especially tied to misogynoir. The men who made those posts that uglified me (and so many other Black MaGes) and who kill their Black female sexual partners are victims of the same belief systems that render Black women three to four times more likely to die of a pregnancy-related cause than white women when treated by white doctors;[9] the same belief systems that leave Black girls nearly six times more likely to be given out-of-school suspensions than their white counterparts, and more likely to be incarcerated than any other ethnic group of girls;[10] the same belief systems that have positioned 41 percent of Black trans people to experience homelessness (five times the nation's general homelessness rate) and 34 percent to live in households with incomes under $10,000 (which is twice the rate of non-Black trans people at 15 percent and four times the rate of Black cis people at 9 percent);[11] and the same belief systems that have led Black women between the ages of forty-nine and fifty-five to be 7.5 percent biologically older than white women of the same age (our internal organs age faster due to higher stress levels).[12]

MaGes are punished with death for deviating from the expectations of piety and submission placed on us. Such was the experience of famed Pakistani social media content creator Fouzia Azeem, also known by the moniker Qandeel Baloch. Qandeel Baloch was an entertainer who first began to shine among the masses after participating in *Pakistan Idol*. After leaving the competition, she made many humorous, musical, artful, and eventually political social media and YouTube posts—specifically advocating for more equitable rights for Pakistani women. Within a week of releasing a music video called "Ban" with artist Aryan Khan about the unjust restrictions on women in her country, in which she was dressed in a manner that some would consider scantily clad, she was murdered by her brother. Upon arrest, he told police, "She was bringing disrepute to our family's honor and I could not tolerate it any further."[13] Baloch was uglified by many more conservative and religious leaders, in addition to a conservative population, for having a platform, for speaking up against the cultural norms, and for celebrating her body and freedom, and that uglification led to her vicious and intimate murder.

Many American readers may argue that this sort of murderous patriarchal system is limited to non-Western countries, but the uglification of MaGes is very much a part of our cultural and structural landscape as well. Those of us who engage in sexual freedom, pleasure, and expression—as well as those who engage from a place of intimidation, coercion, and trafficking—are named sluts, thots, insecure, desperate, and other derisive terms, and then are treated as if we are inferior and abominable. We are openly berated and objectified in song lyrics, stand-up comedy and talk shows, religious ministries, and even by members of the American government. For example, consider Donald Trump's well-documented attacks and sexual assaults on so many women, Bill Clinton's merciless degradation of Monica Lewinsky to protect his presidency, Joe Biden's callous and misogynistic handling of the Anita Hill vs. Clarence Thomas case, and the 2018 confirmation of Brett Kavanaugh as Supreme Court Justice, despite being accused of sexual assault by multiple women.[14]

We saw the same abuse of power enabled by the vilification of individuals uglified by their lifestyle or source of income in the case of Jasmine Abuslin, also known as Celeste Guap, a teenager who was trafficked by and among Oakland and Richmond police officers in exchange for not being arrested for sex work.[15] The intersections of her gender, race, economic background, and participation in sex work led police to render her as someone to be exploited and consumed rather than protected. They knew that in the grand social hierarchy, the same systems that uglified her out of her safety and care would privilege them with protection—and it did. For years, Jasmine was exploited and then blamed for her exploitation, though with the support of community and advocates, she has since emerged as a badass activist herself.

I also witnessed this dynamic with one of the formerly incarcerated women I have had the pleasure of serving. She was facing a life sentence in prison for killing the man who abused her and her children, which included raping one of her daughters. Prosecutors repeatedly attempted to use her own sexually liberated history and profession to invalidate her fierce determination to protect her children. I believe that if she were a man, she would be lauded as a hero for attacking her daughter's rapist.

We live in a culture where men are celebrated for protecting the chastity of women and girls. The prevalence of purity balls and Daddy-Daughter chastity clubs continues to promote the existence of female sexuality as wrong, women as incapable of navigating their own sexuality, and men as their captors who deal with them as sexual commodities to be given someday to another man. The coercion of women into such groups is a form of violence, which leaves them susceptible to further abuse by the patriarchy.[16]

One interviewee told me of one such experience, exemplifying the misogynistic beliefs propagated by purity balls and chastity clubs, which are still so prominent in our society. She told me that after he walked in on her making out with her boyfriend when she was twelve, her father spanked her every day for a week and did not let her leave her bedroom for almost a month—he even explained her absence in school by telling her teachers that she was recovering from an illness.

"One day," she told me, "he walked in and just stared at me and cried. Then he said, 'My mother would turn in her grave if she found out that I raised you to be a whore.'"

The word *whore* (and *ho*) is commonly and historically used as an uglifying term for female sex workers, those who do the work by choice and those who don't. It is used to strip people of their full humanity and identity by referring to them solely by their role, also signifying a separation between them and other MaGes who do such work. Though there are many men who offer sex work services as well, they rarely experience the malicious social ramifications of this word or experience the violence that this word often justifies in the patriarchal imagination. While many have reclaimed both versions of the word to embrace career and/ or desire choices—including me—it is still used by stewards of oppression to validate the desecration of our sexual agency and embodied personhood.[17]

Recently, my beloved—a nonbinary and gender queer person who was assigned female at birth and reads as a masculine-of-center woman by most people—and I were blessed enough to be nude models for a feminist drawing party. As we were sensuously posing, one participant argued that if we were heterosexual, our position would be perceived as porn. Her argument relied on the uglification of pornography creators, many of whom take pride and agency in creating consensual erotic images for the enjoyment and wellness of their viewers (though, of course, this industry is also saturated with exploiters, like many industries), but also then went on to use that uglification to denounce the beauty, magic, and sacredness of my and my partner's bodies, modeling, and sensual expression. Her assessment was centered in the idea that sexual and sensual expression, when not confined to privacy, is immoral and that certain bodies and behaviors cannot be perceived as art. Just as in the experience of my interviewee being labeled a whore for expressing her desire, this participant was wielding the oppressive values of the cishetero patriarchy in an attempt to whorify our experience.

Sexual expression amid MaGes has been so uglified by history, religion, and misogyny that a feminist art space couldn't fully hold my and my partner's fat and queer erotic expressions as art (though art has depicted the erotic for centuries), and, as I described earlier, a father could use his prejudice-based fear to transcend love and condone holding his pre-teenaged child captive. He was so angry at her behaving in a way he was taught to perceive as ugly that he beat her and imprisoned her in her own home. So unfamiliar with bodies like mine and my partner's as being held sacred, the feminist drawing participant could not see us outside of the patriarchal lens of the profane. The father's imagination, his values, and his ability to love were thus tainted by uglification, as was the drawing participant's ability to archive and recognize beauty. Neither of their actions was unique, but the father's was extreme and violent. Both people learned this fear and condemnation from the world that bred them. Their solution to the sexual violence and oppression MaGes face was to tell us to perform respectably or be shamed and punished and accept that any horrible things that happen to us are our faults, brought on by our disregard of the accepted guidelines that make anything we do, in our bodies that have been deemed ugly, also ugly and deserving of harm. These restrictive and shaming norms will continue to be our solutions until we're able to see the detriment of the current systems that shape our ideas of what is considered ugly and who is considered worthy of a whole (sexuality, sensuality and eroticism included) self.

We see this same strain of structural uglification in the 64,000 and counting missing Black women and girls who make up over 10 percent of the US's missing people list—even though we are less than 7 percent of the population.[18] Black MaGes, like many other MaGes of color in this country, are hypersexualized and fetishized in the racist and patriarchal imagination of cis-male supremacy. Hypersexualization and fetishization are forms of uglification that limit our ability to see a whole person outside of our own sexual morality and fantasy. When we allow ourselves to uglify people in this way, we allow our imaginations to strip people of their feelings, their histories, their dreams and desires, their future, their agency, their softness—and we replace their delicate humanities with our sex-negative prejudice, our desire for conquest, and our investment in punitive forms of correction. This sexualized disregard for life, and especially Black life, has a deep history in the United States, which has informed the behavior of so many uglifiers and their enablers.

## The Ugliness of Gendered and Sexual Violence

During the US slavery era, and especially after the trafficking of Africans from Africa became illegal (this was not the end of slavery on US occupied land, however), rape breeding became a regular practice on plantations and was offered as a commercial service by some enslavers to other enslavers.[19] Black men with physical traits valued by the slavery economic system were treated as bulls and forced to rape Black women repeatedly until they became pregnant, leading to the birthing of another enslaved person. Though we're taught to perceive rape as something that one person does to another, in this situation, both Black men and women were raped by the institution of slavery and capitalism as they were both denied the opportunity to consent or have sexual agency over their bodies.

Uglification and oppression stole sex, a beauteous act that should only be used for pleasure, intimacy, and/or consensual child creation, from so many of our ancestors and sullied them with a violence and trauma that still lingers today. This was legal because enslaved Black people were lawfully recognized as the chattel property of their enslavers. The government was so complicit in the prosperity of slavery that enslavers paid yearly state taxes on the people they kidnapped and exploited, taxes on people they trafficked (who the government referred to as "imports" at the time), and occasional federal taxes, depending on the year and political need. For example, during times of extreme poverty or during wars, the slave property tax would be more significantly enforced than at other times.[20] Some abolitionist politicians in Congress believed that taxing enslavers for each person they enslaved would decrease or depopularize slavery, but it never did, and the tax was rarely sufficiently enforced except when the federal economy needed the revenue from it.[21]

I believe that the trauma of the forced breeding of enslaved people, which existed for hundreds of years in this land, is one of the reasons why our earlier interviewee's father reacted by beating, imprisoning, and labeling as a whore his own daughter, for making out with her boyfriend. His response, though in no way acceptable, is trauma retention, the result of what was done to his ancestors and how they learned to survive, and his reaction was an attempt to keep that uglification outside his family and away from his daughter.

Regardless of how hard abolitionists attempted to curtail slavery by uglifying, shaming, and punishing enslavers, they were unsuccessful. Enforced illegalization of it barely made any impact. So many white people in the South and other parts of the country still cling hard to their Confederate roots and the ideological entitlement of enslaving and oppressing humans that came along with it, despite the death, bloodshed, and shame slaves experienced. One might argue that the practice and psycho-emotional impact of uglification is fueling some whites' romanticization of their oppression and oppressive ancestors. The praxis of uglification is the same in both Southern whites embracing their ancestors' enslaver statuses and the father shaming and punishing his daughter for her desire to explore her own sexuality and pleasure. There is the same ignorance of, or unwillingness to look at, how uglification is motivating their actions. The father did not remotely dampen his daughter's desires, just as the denial of harm caused by enslaving people does not in any way erase or lessen the lived reality and trauma of those who were forced into slavery, or their descendants who carry that pain, knowledge, and trauma too. In both cases, there were resentment, distress, and a still-to-be-healed rift. In both examples, there were people being torn apart, whereas dialogue and compassion could have brought them closer.

To fight the legacy and impact of structural uglification, it's important to understand why we choose to uglify ourselves and each other. Where does this instinct come from historically, how does it manifest today, and where does it live in our own energetic and physical bodies, including in the DNA we receive from our parents and ancestors? For instance, sexual chastity was, for many years, a privilege that only belonged to free white women, and specifically to those who were of economic affluence. People who did not, or whose ancestors did not, receive that privilege might feel a powerful need to claim it for themselves and loved ones, and to protect it by any means necessary—including violence.

In this situation, I use the term *privilege* lightly, given that chastity shouldn't be a privilege, it should be a choice. Even those women who were allotted the right to not be sexually assaulted, exploited, or raped didn't have agency over their bodies. Historically, most of their marriages—from who they married to when they married to what that marriage looked like—were decided by cis men. Though I am discussing this through an Americanized lens, it is not just an American phenomenon. We see this practiced throughout history, across cultures, and it is referenced or mandated in all religious texts. Consequently, I believe that cis men's sense of entitlement to MaGes' bodies has become genetic and ingrained in our human consciousness and imagination.

It is not just a thing that we MaGes and our allies need to fight against; it is something that people of all genders need to recognize, heal from, and use to explore how to reclaim our agency and relationships to each other across gender. I believe that understanding how the gender binary system was created in our ancestral and diasporic cultural histories— which feminist historians, like Aurora Levins Morales, who wrote *The Historian as Curandera* and *Medicine Stories: History, Culture, and the Politics of Integrity*, do so well through their life-saving texts—will help us learn how to reclaim our bodies, minds, and relationships from our colonized and intersectionally oppressed histories. White MaGes—you also deserve to heal from the viciousness that the patriarchy visited on your ancestors, and reading authors like Dorothy Allison, who wrote *Bastard out of Carolina* and *Skin: Talking about Sex, Class, and Literature*, will support you with that healing.

Though conversations around uglification and white-supremacist and patriarchal beauty standards (which are also upheld by people of color) should include desirability politics and how people discern who they pursue as partners versus who they sexually exploit, we must also discuss how marriage is an institution that consecrated the oppression, subjugation, exploitation, abuse, and rape of MaGes by cis men. Even MaGes privileged by other MaGes' uglification and oppression were oppressed—which is why I am discerning when discussing *privilege* and the concept of *beauty privilege* while unpacking healing, justice, liberation, and the reclamation of what uglification has stolen from us.

It wasn't until 1976 that Nebraska became the first state to outlaw marital rape,[22] and states are still creating laws to protect married women from the violence of their spouses. Even today, while marital rape is federally outlawed, some states have different laws or stipulations around prosecuting people who rape their spouses versus people who rape people they aren't married to. In Michigan a person can only be legally accused of rape if their spouse can prove that they were not "mentally incapable" or "incapacitated" at the time of rape, meaning it is currently legal to drug and rape your spouse in the state.[23] Many religious texts, including the Bible, position MaGes/women so they are the property of their husbands and are responsible for adhering to sex at his desire. So even though white women of all economic backgrounds, but especially wealthy white women closely protected by law, had access to resources, and men who raped other women, including their slaves and indentured servants, did not experience the constant and unrelenting intersection of structural and interpersonal uglification that Black, Indigenous, and migrant women of color experienced, they very much knew and suffered under the violent dominion of the patriarchy. Women who weren't protected by men or wealth, or who didn't acquiesce to the chastity and piety laws or conditions of their time and location, regardless of ethnicity, were also unprotected by their governments and religions for most of Western history. They were instead uglified by state and religious leaders, and in turn, through the behaviors of the communities they resided in. Historically, and in the present day, women who fight back are further uglified and persecuted.

## A Fear of Self-Actualization

One of the most empowering and resilient stories of a person surviving the horrors of structural uglification to create something transformatively healing for a wide range of people belongs to CeCe McDonald.

McDonald, like so many other MaGes, is a living testimony of what it means to be violated by the uglification of the patriarchy and then punished for protecting what systemic oppression refused to safeguard and rendered invaluable: her life.

On the evening of June 5, 2011, McDonald, a queer transgender Black woman, and a few of her friends, other queer and trans Black people, walked down the street toward McDonald's home carrying groceries they had just purchased. They passed a mixed-gender group of intoxicated white people standing outside a bar. Members of this group began to yell racist and transphobic remarks toward them. After they spoke up for themselves, one woman, Molly Flaherty, charged at McDonald with a glass of alcohol, smashed it against her face, and left her with a bleeding six-inch gash that required eleven stitches. McDonald fought back until people from the attacker's group pulled the women apart.[24]

As McDonald and her friends attempted to walk away, a cis heterosexual white man named Dean Schmitz, high on alcohol, cocaine, and methamphetamine, continued to aggressively follow and harass the friends, including charging and grabbing at McDonald and others. Terrified for their lives, a member of the group stabbed Schmitz in the chest. Some of the group ran off, while McDonald and another friend ran back to the grocery store they had come from, found a police officer, and told them what happened. McDonald took the blame for the stabbing and was arrested for protecting her life. Though McDonald is a woman, she was put into the jail cell for men because the prison-industrial complex, like so many other systems of oppression and constructs of uglification, is steeped in transphobia and its stewards and workers refused to recognize her womanhood, much less protect her from the dangers of being a woman in a jail for men. Later, after her sentencing, her life would once again be jeopardized when they put her in two consecutive male prisons.

During McDonald's trial, she confessed that she did not stab Schmitz, who died as result of the stabbing, but the court refused to believe her testimony, instead honoring the stories of the more socially privileged, less structurally uglified members of case. As the court case proceeded, the judge and jury continued to protect McDonald's attackers instead of her and her friends. Schmitz—who was once part of a white-supremacist group, had a swastika tattooed on his body, was, according to the autopsy, amped up on multiple drugs at the time of the incident, and had a long history of over two dozen criminal court cases, including three for assault—was intensely protected and advocated for by the proceeding's judge, Judge Daniel Moreno. Prosecutors working against McDonald argued that Schmitz's swastika could not be admitted as evidence as it would cause unfair bias, and Judge Moreno declared that the swastika as well as Schmitz's former assault convictions were inadmissible as evidence of his violent disposition. But Judge Moreno did permit statements McDonald previously wrote on blogs and Facebook statuses to be used as evidence against her. He also permitted a motion to impeach her testimony, which had the effect of completely silencing her voice and refuting her story, because she had previously been convicted of writing a bad check. This court was interested in performing justice for a white man who had been arrested multiple times for beating women, rather than speaking up for the safety and protection of a Black MaGe and her friends, who were just trying to go home peacefully after grocery shopping.

Moreno said that it could not be proven that the meth, alcohol, and cocaine in Schmitz's blood had led to violence, so the toxicologist was not allowed to testify as to how those substances may have influenced Schmitz's actions that evening, which again protected him, posthumously, over the lives he threatened in the incident with McDonald. And in addition to refuting that someone convicted of violence, white supremacy, and more could potentially be a violent threat to yet another woman, Moreno also would not allow experts to testify about why experiencing racist, transphobic threats from Schmitz might make McDonald fear for her life.

McDonald's story epitomizes how structural and interpersonal uglification work to dehumanize marginalized people, enforce our oppression and uglification, punish us for fighting back, use the laws and other tools of the state to suppress our self-advocacy, and uphold the status-quo social hierarchies of who gets protected and who doesn't. McDonald was uglified for her transness, her Blackness, and her refusal to allow the white-supremacist patriarchy to stomp and spit all over her. She was punished for prioritizing her survival over the life of a white man who was assaulting her and may well have killed her—like so many other Black MaGes in history. When we enforce the gender binary on our children, when we refuse to protect trans children and MaGes, when we use religion and the Bible to decide whose bodies and desires are right and wrong, we support men like Schmitz and Judge Moreno. And we put more and more people like McDonald and her friends in dangerous, unjust, and life-threatening situations.

Although she did not have to serve the full sentence that horrific judge bestowed upon her, McDonald still faced the trauma of nineteen months in jail after fighting for her life—as she likely had many times and in many different ways before those people attacked her and her friends. It is because of how insidious and compulsive uglification is that I'm even writing this statement, but McDonald was blessed in a way that so many Black women assaulted by the cis white (or even Black) patriarchy are not. Queer and trans Black communities, alongside non-Black queer and trans allies, were ready to fight for her. McDonald got to experience what it feels like to have a community care about you and advocate for you in the name of justice, which is why her story is one of my favorite narratives of resilience and resisting uglification.

McDonald, alongside activists, writers, filmmakers, lawyers, and more, decided that they were not going to let white supremacy and transphobia discard another life, and collaboratively they set McDonald free from her state captors.[25] This is important to me because McDonald was consistently involved in her advocacy and the direction of her life. She set the tone. She spoke her truth. And when she was able to return home and heal, despite being on probation for years afterward, she dedicated her power, her energy, her brilliance, and her love to other trans people, including youth and captives of the state. McDonald has spoken on numerous television shows, on college campuses, at protests, and has written articles and essays about her experience. She has created curricula and, while I was writing this book, served as a fellow at Barnard Center for Research on Women.[26]

McDonald and the people who have supported her epitomize what it means to (U)plift, (G)lorify, and (L)ove (Y)ourself and create a world where others can as well. McDonald grew powerful sunflowers of healing and pathways to liberation for so many people out of the seeds of her injustice and oppression. She, like other trans and nonbinary people, refuses to submit to the uglification of cis heteronormativity by allowing herself to be who she is despite external attitudes, by forging a life for herself and embracing a community that loves her, and by using her resources and platforms to advocate for the safety and wellness of so many other people.

But, like I said, her experience is still tragic, and her blessings are comparatively rare. Many people do not get the support and protection she did from structural uglification.

Many people, like Gwen Araujo, who would be just a year younger than me if she were still alive today, have had their lives stolen because of uglification. Araujo was murdered over the course of many hours by boys in her neighborhood, two of whom she had had sex with previously, and in front of a party full of people—none of whom reported her murder to the police.[27] Hers is an agonizing story of uglification at its peak. I was fortunate to listen to Gwen's mother speak when I was in my late teens. I got to witness a young trans girl be loved and grieved for deeply by her mother, and to see her mother use her pain as a source of healing for so many other people.

We should not have to be so strong and generous with our pain. We should not have to grow beanstalks with our suffering. But because uglification leads to us being unprotected, right now those of us who experience the most villainization and disenfranchisement in this system are forced to be each other's heroes. Trans women of color will always be my heroes because I think being trans in such an oppressive society is the ultimate and most courageous act of choosing self-actualization and liberation over the threat and violence of uglification. I want to exist in a world where being trans is no longer a courageous or radical existence and is instead an embraced and beloved expression of humanity and freedom.

It is because of legacies like the ones I've mentioned that I understand why my earlier interviewee's father feared his daughter's sexual actualization. I understand why someone would perceive sexual expression as dangerous, bad, immoral, and something their child needed protection from. As much as I dislike his behavior and absolutely hate that his child had to endure it, I do not want to uglify this man for responding to a terrifying-to-him situation with what may have been the best parenting skills and emotional resources he had at the time. It is the same reason why so many parents spank their children even as we learn that spanking causes more harm and facilitates feelings of shame, fear, and social hierarchy instead of critical thinking.

Although this father's belt and ire landed on the flesh of his daughter, I read in its ferocity the unhealed weeping of his ancestors paired with his desire to have control over protecting his family from what he likely perceived to be the greater harm that systems of oppression and uglification would perpetuate. I also understand why some parents might consider their daughter kissing her boyfriend at home as disrespectful, but I believe that, too, is a result of how our sexualities and desires have been uglified by oppression and history.

Kissing and sex are only noted as disrespectful because we don't respect them as actual parts of human development and we don't respect the self-determination of MaGes and most children. If female sexuality, or Black MaGes in general, wasn't uglified and didn't carry the embodied, intergenerational trauma of sexual violence and slavery, this father may have just recognized his daughter as a young person exploring her sexuality, attraction, and desire with a person she trusted in a place where she felt safe and protected. Or perhaps he would have used the incident as an opportunity to discuss safe and consensual sex practices as well as boundaries and expectations.

That his terrified response showed up instead is why an in-depth, healing-based social reform led by MaGes of color is so critical to the eradication of uglification. We all need to reclaim our imaginations and understand how we contextualize and perceive, from historical and contemporary perspectives, the violence that uglification produces within our communities and families, and within ourselves. The legacy is thick, and merely continuing to survive, or even figuring out how to thrive in this system, is not enough to heal what has been done to us.

## Uglification Protects Abusers

Uglifications like those you have read about in this chapter so far are predominantly enacted by cis men—and by MaGes invested in morality hierarchies and conservatism to excuse cis men of rape, sexual assault, and other forms of degradation and exclusion. They allow people to think that we, survivors and victims of sexual abuse, harassment, assault, and attempted murder, deserve what we experience, and even worse, that we're asking for it when we allow ourselves to be our true selves. This uglification exists because of binary thinking around morality and the assumption that there is only one way of appropriately being sexual. It's similar to lines of questioning and blame employed by rape culture, such as, "Can you tell me what you were wearing when it happened?" or "Were you drinking?" or "Why would you choose to put yourself in that situation?"

The violence that comes from and is protected by this line of thinking will not stop until we begin to create a culture that embraces all bodies, desires, and sexual orientations—regardless of gender. When we stop repressing and fearing our sexualities, and when we stop shaming other people's, predators will have less power and access to exploiting that shame. Furthermore, by accepting our sexualities, we will allow people who may have otherwise grown into predators to access the resources and support they need to develop healthier desires, to respect boundaries, and to find safe ways to explore their sexualities without harming others.

The simplicity of outlawing and vilifying dangerous sexualities and fetishes does not prevent people from pursuing them at the expense of other people's lives and consent. But perhaps if we move away from uglification and accept humanity for what it is, we can use our brilliant minds and creative resourcefulness to embrace people in their wholeness, provide them with safe alternatives to harming people and themselves, and create a world where more people can live happy, joyful lives.

For instance, people tend to belittle others for enjoying kinks like furry play, age play, impact play, or dominance and submission, or for pursuing relationships with dolls, machines/robots, or virtual reality/computer characters. But I think that fantasy and technology are and can continue to be developed into incredible tools that can support the diversity of ways in which human sexuality manifests itself. And let's be real, some human desires are dangerous to others or might not be something others will consent to. Here, technology can be used to protect those who are most vulnerable while providing a harm-reduced outlet for people to explore, actualize, and understand themselves. Erotic play is an essential part of expression for so many people, and it can be a place of healing and social transformation.

As much as we may loathe rapists, necrophiliacs, statutory rapists, and people with other violent and dangerous cravings, their fantasies are a result of the world that humanity has created. They come from the uglification of non-hetero and non-reproductive sex, of queerness and transness, of femininity, and of desire. They come from a history of shaming and fearing what we don't understand while creating a culture that chastises people the moment they express an interest in something non-normative. They are born of the entitlement and violence that have long beset women, trans and nonbinary people, people of color, and fat and disabled people. Simply belittling, ignoring, or incarcerating people who ascribe to violent ideologies will not change the fact that somehow our society continues to produce people who are thus inclined. Reclaiming ugly means taking further steps to allow for real conversations that aren't rooted in shame and that are geared toward transformative solutions and finding the people capable of designing and implementing those solutions. If we do not take these steps, we will stay stuck in cycles of violence, and our imaginations will continue to be stimulated and repressed by the uglification of others.

It is these imaginations and repressive belief systems that create people like the well-known Ted Bundy and the lesser-known Samuel

Little, a serial killer who confessed to taking the lives of ninety-three women between 1970 and 2005.[28] Little said that he believed he would never be caught by police because people weren't interested in accounting for or protecting victims like his, predominantly Black cis and trans women with a sprinkling of non-Black Latinx and white women. Little surmised that lack of care accurately.

Little was eventually caught and incarcerated after police were able to connect three of the victims to him, but it was only after eighteen months of imprisonment that he spoke about the other ninety people he killed, many of whom weren't even on police radar as being missing or were listed as missing people or runaways—not potential murder or trafficking victims. Those who did have death certificates were all registered as overdoses, suicides, or accidental and undetermined deaths, even though Little strangled all his MaGe victims. He used crude items like pantyhose and ropes, which left easily recognizable marks.[29]

It is because of structural uglification and the social devaluing of MaGes that Little killed poor people, people of color, people struggling with addiction, homeless people, mentally ill people, disabled people, trans people, and sex workers; that coroners couldn't see the trauma done to their bodies underneath the social stigma associated with them; and that police detectives were unwilling to perceive their deaths as being important enough to understand and create cases for. This is how interpersonal uglification—attitudes about who is and isn't worthy of being treated with care, safety, and respect—informs who our systems serve and protect, and who they allow to be quietly slaughtered, dehumanized, and experimented on.

Little eventually died in prison of COVID-19, but neither death nor prison evokes justice for the people he and our societal attitudes killed, neglected, and abandoned. Nor did his death or imprisonment make the world safer. Incarcerating men like Little has not decreased the number of people who are assaulted, trafficked, killed, and stolen from their lives and loved ones every day. It just produces more stigma, more violence, and fewer opportunities to understand and prevent these circumstances from happening again. MaGes are still being targeted and killed by lovers, strangers, and even family members every day. Incarceration and policing have yet to shift that, so I can't help but question why policing and incarceration is our civic and cultural go-to.

People like Little and other serial rapist/murderers and perpetrators need help; they need protection from themselves and the world that enables their actions; and they need resources and alternatives that can support them to live good lives and positively contribute to their communities. That is the direction we must work toward to save lives, liberate people, and heal us of the harm we've already experienced. That is the power of radical imagination and reclaiming ugly. Although the many years of tragic violence that stole nearly one hundred MaGe lives is absolutely the result of Little's choices and actions, and although he deserved to be held accountable, the tone, timbre, and inclination of his violence are the result of religious moral dominion and oppression, patriarchal supremacy, capitalistic dehumanization, and the colonial history of legalized rape and sexual torture of Black women in the US.

During the same period of legal rape breedings that I mentioned earlier, doctors like James Marion Sims, who invented the speculum and various post-partum gynecological surgeries, were leasing enslaved Black women from their owners so they could practice surgery on their bodies.[30] Sims began his career by servicing enslaved people who were harmed while partaking in their forced and unpaid labor, but he later focused specifically on gynecological surgeries that would ensure that women could continue to produce children for the purpose of slavery if they had been injured giving birth in the past. He would practice the surgeries many times, night and day, often on the same person, until he had perfected it—all without using anesthesia. One young girl named Anarcha experienced over thirty surgeries from him before she reached the age of seventeen.[31] Once he felt secure enough with his success rate, he began to practice the surgeries on white women, *with* anesthesia. He argued that Black people are physically stronger than other races and do not experience pain the way that white people do—an idea that is still maintained to this day by some medical professionals.

A 2016 study found that only 57 percent of Black patients being treated for extremity fractures were likely to receive anesthesia in the emergency room, compared to 74 percent of white patients who expressed experiencing the same pain levels.[32] This study showed that Black patients, and other patients of color, were also significantly less likely to receive appropriate pain medications, such as opioids, during crises, including cancer and appendicitis.

This trend is one that was birthed from Sims's era of doctoring. His violent practices were not just limited to women's sexual health. He also believed that Black people were less intelligent than non-Black people and blamed this on the supposed rate of our skull growth. He tried to prove this theory by using crude nonsurgical tools, like the ones used to make shoes, to pry apart the bones of Black children and loosen their skulls. When those children and other patients died, he blamed "the sloth and ignorance of their mothers and the Black midwives who attended them" instead of his surgical techniques, an argument used similarly to attack Black mothers today for the way their children struggle to assimilate into the systems stewarded by white supremacy.[33]

Here Sims relied on the uglification of Black people as lazy—an argument similarly used by enslavers to claim that Black people were only good for slavery and were unable to be self-sufficient, as well as to justify the physical violence they used to mete out punishment for underproduction or resistance—to excuse himself from the devastating murders he facilitated. And even still, amid all this, he was named the "father of modern gynecology." This is a good time to note that he was named the father of modern gynecology (keep in mind, he only did this work for the purposes of sustaining slavery) because he was one of the few doctors willing to examine women's reproductive organs. Women's genitals and birthing processes have been uglified by scientists and philosophers for most of history and have been discussed as being more primitive than men's genitals.

The systemically internalized belief that Black people are stronger than other ethnic groups is the same one that motivates police officers and detectives not to see the distress of our dead bodies or search for our killers. It is what has them argue that Black MaGes who go missing are runaways who left home by choice instead of people in potential danger who need and deserve protection. The practice and ideologies of uglification work in collaboration to undermine our very existence, in life and in death. They protect our traffickers, abusers, and murderers, as well as the circumstances and beliefs that transform people who could be our allies into sources of danger, repeatedly.

Black MaGes are not the only ones suffering from systemic uglification in this way. In counties where they live alongside other nationalities of people, Native MaGes are sexually assaulted and raped at rates ten times the average of other MaGes. In some predominantly Native towns and communities, they are murdered at rates over ten times higher than the average among any other group.[34] As of 2016 there were over 5,700 missing Native American MaGes reported to the National Crime Information Center.[35]

This terrorizing pandemic of cruelty is another consequence of the hierarchies created by colonial white supremacy and its critical efforts to uglify and dehumanize Indigenous people to conquer their land—the land I am currently living on while writing this book. This injustice continues because of our courts' refusal to protect Indigenous people, and specifically Indigenous MaGes, from the sadistic and bloodthirsty impulses of men who take advantage of their privilege in the cis male supremacy. Sixty-seven percent of the reported assaults on Native women were perpetrated by non-Native men, specifically white men employed by the US government and oil companies to mine and create pipelines.[36]

Although many MaGes who are raped and sexually assaulted in the US are attacked by men they know, including relatives and former lovers, the majority of Native MaGes are attacked by strangers, men they have never met, who their families cannot point out in a lineup, and who are literally protected from any consequences by the United

States Constitution and, at the time this book was being written, its Republican Senate.[37]

Prior to 2013 neither tribes nor state governments had jurisdiction to prosecute non-Native people for murder or rape of Native people on their reservations.[38] Such cases could only be prosecuted by the federal government, which declined more than two-thirds of the cases sent to them.[39] It wasn't until the 2013 reinstatement of the Violence Against Women Act that tribes received the jurisdiction to prosecute Native and non-Native perpetrators of felony domestic violence.[40] Although the Act granted jurisdiction to use the court systems to protect Native MaGes from general assault, sexual assault, rape, sex trafficking, murder, and other violence, the Republican Senate stalled on reauthorizing it with these broader powers for several years, until it finally passed in 2022.[41]

As I have said earlier, I believe in the abolition of prisons. In particular, I do not believe that prisons are the solution for rapists. Prisons are not really used to pursue justice for rape victims. There are thousands of unprocessed rape kits across our country, tens of thousands of rapes that have not even been counted for a plethora of reasons related to structural uglification, and so many laws that have been designed to protect the perpetrators of assault against women. Over 50 percent of the rapes that happen to incarcerated people are perpetrated by prison staff.[42] Prison is not the solution to what uglification produces; it is just a container for it, a weapon of it, and a distraction from the solution to it.

Discussing the inequities of how the prison-industrial complex and court system are used to target, control, and suppress groups who have been historically uglified—and protect those who have been privileged by the legacies of systemic and interpersonal oppression—is critical to revealing just how prevalent and murderous uglification is, and how invested our government is in protecting and sustaining it. When we protect the privilege of sexually violent and murderous men and their ability to perpetrate oppression or other forms of harm without a consequential loss of power, we both overtly and inadvertently signify that their victims are less worthy of protection, less important in the optics of hierarchy, and less valuable members of society.

The Senate's reluctance to give tribes full jurisdiction over their land not only demonstrated how much they do not care about the lives, safety, and suffering of Indigenous MaGes, it also revealed the fact that they are still invested in protecting their ability to infantilize and dominate Native people. It's a living indication of their investment in white supremacy, colonization, and Indigenous holocaust. This is uglification, and it's an uglification with ramifications just as vile as the murder of Qandeel Baloch, the murders committed by Samuel Little and protected by police and forensic officers who deemed his victims not important enough to follow up on, the gruesome and murderous surgeries done to Black women's bodies, and the state's disgusting attempt to silence CeCe McDonald and punish her for protecting her right to live.

Yes, uglification is about how we perceive and treat each other, but those perceptions come from somewhere horrible, systemic, and historical. It was born long before the stealing of Native land to create the United States of America, and it was uniquely revamped and revolutionized to aid this nation's birth. Conquistadors, missionaries, frontier folks and cowboys, enslavers, and the Founding Fathers were its midwives, its surgeons, its Frankensteins that our school textbooks glorify, that our governing systems lift up, and that so many of us have been bamboozled into loving far more than we love our neighbors and ourselves.

Continuing to embrace, participate in, and accept these systems as immovable and necessary protects the horrors created by legacies of violence and oppression and damn near sanctifies the people who kill and exploit those of us who have been terrorized the longest and most formatively by said legacies. Doing so allows us to continue to be deceived into killing ourselves and centering the desires and dominance of people who don't care about our well-being and freedom. These systems teach people in various positions of power that their placement within hierarchies of uglification means that they are entitled to the bodies and lives of people more uglified and oppressed than them. And they teach the most intersectionally uglified and disenfranchised of us that we are not entitled to live freely, to stand up for ourselves within and outside the courts, to heal and rest so that we can reclaim our wholeness, to have our own autonomous desires and dreams and act on them, and to demand change from the individuals and structures that facilitate our harm. The values spouted by uglification (whether they come from the ministers at our church, our parents, the police and courts, corporate leaders, newscasters, elected officials, our crushes, or the occasionally angry and defeated voices in our head) gaslight and coerce us into believing that when we suffer from the systems that were crafted against our dignity, brilliance, and freedom, we are to blame, it is our fault, and there is no escape. This is internalized uglification.

# 5

# Future Histories of Reclaiming Ugly

We cannot unpack and dismantle uglification the way we unpack other forms of systemic oppression. As you learned in the previous chapter, it does not have any specific target or beneficiary group. Though some of us are more impacted by the violence and oppression that uglification spawns, we are all uglified, we are all inclined to uglify, and we are all repressed, in some way, by the cultural ramifications of uglification. We must think of it as a praxis that harms and privileges all of us depending on how, when, by whom, and where it is used—regardless of what the user looks like or has experienced. Uglification is a torture cage that can confine and contort everyone's personhood and imagination, regardless of their physical size, age, or proxy to what we call beautiful.

Uglification is something we all use, we're all exposed to, and we all suffer from. Our experience with uglification does not make us good, bad, righteous, or innocent people. It simply means we're alive.

Whether we are examining the ways we uglify ourselves and others or the ways we have experienced being uglified, our history of and inclination toward uglification cannot become an extended source of shame. We mustn't weaponize this language against ourselves or others. It is solely an invitation to understanding and transformation. It's important that we have remorse and compassion for ourselves and those we may have hurt (and are, possibly, still hurting). Guilt is not bad when we have done things that are not in alignment with our values or other people's right to safety and love. But shame and guilt become enemy to reclaiming your ugly when they become a prison, a sunken place, or a flagellation tool that interferes with your healing, growing, and facilitating change.

Guilt should be a launchpad into curiosity, listening, learning, and growing. Shame, when in an encouraging and loving environment, can transform into a portal of healing, releasing pain, exploring the potential pleasures of an open heart and a commitment to everyone living good lives, and swooning on down the pathway to your own increased freedom, joy, and liberation. Being willing to recognize that some belief or action of yours is wrong and allowing yourself to reform is the most beautiful thing ever.

That is reclaiming ugly. It is creating legacies of healing and freedom in the hearts of everyone around you. It is what saves other people's lives.

## Reclaiming Ugly Must Be a Cross-Issue, Intergenerational, Intercultural Movement

The first UGLY Conference brought so many different components and identities of community together. It took place at my residence of the time, an all queer and trans POC collective of artists, farmers, and activists who, together, ran a community garden and co-op. I relied on so many people to help make it happen, including the financial support of BGD Press.

With a crew of amazing visual artists, performers, cultural workers, organizers, and writers who identified as LGBTQIA+, BIPOC, fat, disabled, undocumented/immigrant, youth, elder, and one cis man, we transformed our storefront into a work of art and hosted a series of potent and vulnerable conversations, creative activities, embodiment and reclamation rituals, keynotes, panels, and performances—we even ended with an UGLY balloon drop and party. It was magical, but the true charm of our time together was less about the content I planned and more about the stories, experiences, voices, and camaraderie of the extraordinary people who chose to be in attendance.

People of so many different ethnic, racial, and cultural identities came. There were educators, doctors, performers, lawyers, sex workers, writers, unemployed folks, visual artists, community organizers, college students, cooks, and more. Our next-door neighbor, Peacock Rebellion, allowed us to use their ADA-accessible bathroom. The only thing the conference didn't have, which I truly regret and will hopefully never fall folly to again, was an ASL interpreter—the revolution needs funding, y'all. One participant said that the conference was, while not perfect, one of the most inclusive and accessibility-centered events they had ever been to.

We did embodiment activities that centered the joyful movement of all bodies, facilitated by Ifasina TaMeicka Clear of Get Embodied Soul Dance. We had an Elder, Activist, and Thought Warrior panel that was absolutely lit. We had small spirit circles where people were able to unpack their current and historical experiences with uglification, and we had breakout spaces for people less affected by ugliness as a disenfranchisement to explore their own histories with uglification. We had volunteer therapists there to support people if the dialogue got too tough. And we ended with a gorgeous and inspiring conversation about what healing feels like and what a world without ugliness as disenfranchisement looks like.

Because of who was in attendance, the conference became the epitome of what happens when cross-cultural, cross-issue, cross-movement, and cross-identity events go very well. We held each other in laughter and teary-eyed vulnerability, had vulnerable and hard conversations, and made long-term relationships. People of all age brackets, from teenagers to folks in their seventies, came and stayed the entire time. Super-fat disabled people and thin people cuddled on the same couches, flocked to be in groups together, and supported each other with food accessibility and space navigation. Black queer femmes, supported by our diverse friends and lovers, were in organizational leadership and felt safe, respected, and whole enough to honor our leadership.

It was in this conference that I first heard the word *uglification*. A participant who, according to the shallow and surface lens of white-supremacist beauty standards, may have loads of beauty privilege, broke down uglification from her experience. Even years later, what she said has stuck with me. I'll paraphrase it:

> *Uglification is about appearances and so much more. While I have pretty privilege on some levels, I live an uglified existence.*
>
> *I am trans, and society uglifies my gender, body, and existence because of transphobia. I have Tourette's syndrome, and people think my disorder, my outbursts, and the way my body moves is ugly. I can try to hide it, hide my ugly, so that I can fit in and make people comfortable, but it causes me to be sick with migraines and nausea for days afterward. Me being healthy is ugly to other people. I'm an anarchist, not a touchy-feely social justice warrior, and some people think my cynicism is ugly. There are so many reasons why people don't want me around that have nothing to do with the actual way I look.*

When she said those words, she changed my life and, in some ways, the direction of my work. Although I was already exploring and unpacking how diverse perceptions of ugliness, from body parts to desires to locations to lived experiences, lead to disenfranchisement, ailment, and trauma, I did not have language. My discussion of the topic was clumsy. This participant's generous share helped me realize just how important, slick, and intersectional uglification is. I realized that yes, people with faces, bodies, and identities perceived as physically or tangibly ugly *do* experience oppression based on beauty and respectability standards, but uglification is something much more—and I desperately needed to understand it and why human beings, of all identities, backgrounds, and exposures to the harm of injustice and oppression (including myself) seemed to partake in it with an almost compulsive ease.

## Uglification Teaches Us to Take Out Our Pain and Fear on Others

A month or so after the conference, I applied for Show Us Your Spines, a research and creative writing residency for queer and trans people of color at the San Francisco Public Library, which was funded and organized by Radar Productions. My focus was on the history and expressions of uglification. I read from books like *The Fat Studies Reader* edited by Esther Rothblum and Sondra Solovay, *Are All the Women Still White?* by Janell Hobson, *Thick* by Tressie McMillan Cottom, *Ugliness: A Cultural History* by Gretchen E. Henderson, *The Body Keeps the Score* by Bessel van der Kolk, *The Politics of Trauma* by Staci K. Haines, *Fearing the Black Body* by Sabrina Strings, and *Hunger* by Roxane Gay. I reread novels that explore different types of uglification like *The Color Purple* by Alice Walker, *The Bluest Eye* and *A Mercy* by Toni Morrison, *The Fold* by An Na, and *Bastard out of Carolina* by Dorothy Allison.

Through these readings I learned something important, something that maybe I already knew in my heart but had not fully internalized as clearly and concretely as I did until then. **Ugliness is not a state of being, a location, a trait, a quality.** Being ugly, or being perceived as ugly by others, is not a thing that needs to be fixed, modified, or removed. Ugly is not a thing we grow out of like some ugly-duckling-to-swan fairy tale. It is definitely not something that is worthy of shame or any other negative emotion. Being ugly has no concrete or identifiable meaning, but it's one of the most powerful words a person can use to hurt other people.

The only legacy or purpose behind the word *ugly* is the historic justification of separation, exclusion, and violence toward already marginalized and discriminated-against people, such as the sick, the disabled, and elders.

People tend to assume that we universally agree on what or who is and isn't ugly, that ugly is a bad or problematic thing to be, and that people can make choices to no longer become ugly. We also assume that we universally agree that a person being ugly is reason enough to exclude them from space—for example, consider who tends to be cast as leading romantic roles in film and television, who we watch in music videos, who serves us at the most expensive of restaurants and clothing stores, who tends to be promoted into visible leadership, and even who gets welcomed into different groups and cliques. The consistency and universality of these choices make ugly standards (like beauty standards) appear objective and natural.

When working under the assumption that anyone possessing traits, behaviors, and desires perceived as ugly would naturally want to fix them to become "beautiful" and beloved, people tend to pathologize those who don't strive toward those same beauty standards. These people treat uglified folks, disabled folks, fat folks, people who are aging without shame or modifications, hairy people, and those of us who suffer the ostracizing and impoverishing consequences of social bias, with disgust, pity, and justified exclusion/erasure. They don't think they are uglifying or hurting people; they simply think their beliefs are normal and reflective of what everyone else thinks, and their harmful beliefs are protected by crowd mentality and acceptance. This cycle is commonplace but it's also flimsy, because people who uglify certain traits on certain people will also love and celebrate other people with those same traits.

Regardless of how often anyone speaks uglification into the world or treats ugliness and beauty as if they were universal, they still tend to see so many different people and bodies as beautiful. **Even the biggest bully absolutely loves someone who has the traits that they criticize in others.** They might have a physically disabled or neurodivergent parent who they cherish, a queer or trans teacher who inspired and nurtured them, or a fat religious instructor who held them down through crisis. They might even have a secret crush or desire that they are repressing because of their own fear of being stigmatized the way they stigmatize others. We all, every single one of us, see beauty in bodies and ideas that other folks perceive as ugly, and we recognize nuance in situations that other folks attempt to make about good and bad. There is nothing objective or universal about ugliness. Every person has qualities that are ugly to one person, beautiful to another, and irrelevant to someone else.

But we don't see the expansiveness of who we know and love reflected in the television we watch, the books we read, and the musicians we jam out to. Depending on who we spend our time with, we may not even hear the diversity of beauty reflected by the giggles and gossip about attraction and desire that we share with our friends. Non-hegemonic desires are invisiblized, hidden, and under-discussed, which is why so many people, especially younger people, believe there is such a limited understanding of beauty. It's the same reason why people in some communities are afraid to speak up about how they want to live their lives or the parts of their lives that feel bad: they don't know that other people share their desires or sentiments. The power of uglification doesn't exist in another person's cruel or outspoken opinion; it exists within our fear that everyone else agrees with that person's gaze and that there is something wrong with us.

Our imagination about what would happen if others perceive us as wrong, bad, weird, different can be so severe that some of us dedicate our time, energy, and resources to being what we're told is good, right, and beautiful at the expense of our own joy. When we do this, we don't only modify our bodies, we also modify our dreams, potential, and creativity. Once we give so much up to not be uglified, it's difficult not to become invested in the expectation that other people make the same choices we've made, no matter how much it hurts us or them. That is why some folks feel rage and animosity when confronted with people who unapologetically embrace the parts of themselves that they've been coerced into changing, hating, or fearing.

By asking someone to be something they are not because you're afraid that the world won't like or respect them, you are also keeping them from building relationships with people who will love them for who they are, love them as they are, and think they are the epitome of beautiful and good. Similarly, people who may be judging you, your body, your desires are also not inherently right. Their perspective is not the most important perspective, nor is it a worthwhile one. They don't have to be the people or voices to determine which choices you make. Don't let uglification gaslight you into being something other than the magical and precious little butternut squash you are. Don't let it destroy the relationship you can have with your children and loved ones, your parents and neighbors, your siblings and colleagues. Unlike faces, bodies, and locations, ugliness is intangible. Choose human lives over ideologies.

It's important to recognize that although we, as individuals, absolutely have the power to eradicate uglification in our worlds, it is also global and structural. Ugliness is a point of view that births uglifying behavior. Uglifying behaviors are a series of choices that people make as a result of how they choose to perceive themselves or other people. Uglifying perceptions are the psychic values that one person or group imposes on another in order to validate or instigate a set of harmful actions. This cycle culminates in prejudice, ignorance, and malice that benefits a governing and corporate minority—not actual people, including the people participating in the uglifying behaviors and perception. "That's ugly" is a verb, and the speaker's voice (and what births from that voice) is the action. It is not a theoretical, academic word and we cannot limit it as such. Uglification is as real as life or death, and it's the most devastating when we do it to the people we love and ourselves.

Uglification is not just a result of hatred. It's also born from hopelessness and exhaustion. We uglify as a way to access a sense of agency or control when we need someone to blame for the horrible, deeply unjust, violent, or discriminatory things that happen to us, for the isolation, loneliness, insecurity, and lingering resentments we feel; and it conditions others to convince us to believe what we experience is our fault. Uglification is the ultimate gaslighting tool.

Naming it and recognizing when it is happening is the only way that we can protect ourselves from the very familiar descent of its claws. Understanding how and why it is being used can help us interrupt ourselves from wielding it against others and ourselves, while reclaiming the lush fullness of our gorgeous and most liberated imagination.

Uglification will no longer be effective once we reclaim our intellectual autonomy and ability to be creative and flamboyant in our truths. It will no longer steal our ability to appreciate or enjoy who we are and how we were made. It will stop bludgeoning our capacity to recognize the diverse and incredibly lush types of beauty that *all people, all bodies* possess in multitudes. And it will no longer squish our ability to empathize broadly and with nuance, to self-reflect without shame, and to dream without the juicy fullness of pleasurable possibility chopped up into tiny, hopeless, selfish pieces.

## Uglification Unjustly Puts the Onus of Healing on the Individual

While the first UGLY Conference was an intimate, day-long convening of dialogue, healing, and connection, putting it on was no easy feat. It brought up all my nerve-wracking insecurities and forced me to confront some serious trauma. Namely, I still felt lingering shame about how much my own experiences with childhood bullying still took up space in my consciousness. I hadn't yet divorced from the idea that I was bullied so consistently because I was ugly and unappealing to look at. I also was ashamed by how much I still suffered emotionally when thinking about childhood bullying.

I was afraid that by talking with others about those experiences, or ugliness in general, I would portray myself and other survivors of intense uglification, lookism, and bullying as people who haven't figured out how to heal. I didn't want people to think I have a victim complex, I wanted (and still want) to be read as powerful and confident. Today I realize that my fear of and concern about how others perceive me, and my quietness in the face of that fear, are critical to the insidious and covert way that uglification works.

**Uglification puts the onus of healing and survival on those of us who've experienced the harm, while pressuring us to act like we are imperviousness to the abuse, injustice, and pain we have experienced.** We are encouraged to be strong, to compassionately intellectualize why people are cruel, and to move past the impacts of that hurt while lifting ourselves up. We do this all even though we have learned to give up hope and expectation that perpetrators of uglification will change their behaviors, or that community members, school boards, and policy/law makers creating cultural and structural shifts will systemically facilitate those changes.

As a bullied or formerly bullied person, how many times have you heard "that's just the way things are, get over it" from a loved one, instead of them collaborating with you to find solutions for how to make it better, or them simply affirming the fact that you deserve better protection and better treatment? What about "you need to heal and move on with your life" without anyone actually supporting you through the process of healing in tangible and hands-on ways? Then there is my favorite, "ignore them, they are just jealous of you," in which a person subliminally asks you to prioritize compassion for the people who hurt you by imagining yourself as being better than them for not being jealous and having something they don't have. These folks are suggesting that you respond to uglification with further uglification, not offering you protection and healing from uglification.

When I was a bullied child, I rarely experienced my teachers or school counselors talking to my classmates about the bullying I was experiencing. Instead, I—a Black girl child in a world where Black children are frequently groomed for incarceration via the school-to-prison pipeline—was told to stand up for myself, to start fighting back, to stop being so sensitive, to not be such a crybaby. When adults tell tiny humans in need of protection to not be a crybaby, they train those tiny humans to not reach out for help, to be complacent, or to deal with their problems on their own. That teaches children to uglify their own emotions, their need to feel safe and protected, and their urge to express concern or distress, which sets people up to become both victims and perpetuators of violence. Although I'm sure it was not my teachers' intention to do that to me and my peers, it was a clear reflection of how they were trained and taught to respond to their own exposure to violence and harm. The adults who were supposed to protect me from abuse, who spent more time uglifying my responses to violence and encouraging me to get over it than they did addressing violence in the classroom, were likely just as unprotected growing up as I was.

We see something remarkably similar when it comes to more systemic examples of uglification. When a Black, Brown, or Indigenous person is unjustly killed by the police, a police-like racist (such as Trayvon Martin's murderer, George Zimmerman), or a racist militia, the first thing too many police spokespersons and news media reporters do is find ways to justify the murder and drive empathy for the murderer in the American consciousness. Victims are uglified as being dangerous. Their past school disciplinary issues and police interactions are dug up without holistic context; narratives of them resisting arrest or their suspicious and supposedly criminal behaviors are broadcast and analyzed; every single controversial image on their social media is dragged into every spotlight imaginable.

We are manipulated by police and media to empathize more with the individual's murder, their fear of Black and Indigenous people, and the system that enables such murders than with the actual family members and loved ones. When George Zimmerman killed Trayvon Martin, we heard so many stories of his fear of Martin and Martin's school troubles.[1] When Derek Chauvin kneeled on George Floyd's neck for over eight minutes, until he died, we were told stories about how he was afraid of the small crowd of community members who begged him to stop.[2] If you read the social media comments (*never read the social media comments*), you will find trains of regular, everyday people analyzing and validating such murders even more directly. This is what uglification enables.

When Black Lives Matter and other liberation-based organizing fronts, like Oakland's Black Seed and Black Brunch, began to host protests and demonstrations against the violent and homicidal injustice people of color perpetually experience at the hands of white-dominated courts and police groups, they were portrayed as terrorists, as dangerous, and as hell-bent on attacking police officers, business owners, and the safety of white and white-adjacent people (*white-adjacent* people, in this context, are folks of color who have subscribed to white-supremacist/ capitalist-meritocratic ideologies, desires, prejudices, and standards) instead of being seen as empathetic and care-deserving people who were speaking up about the pain and violence we just keep experiencing at the hands of law enforcement.[3]

Both lawmakers and groups privileged enough to not experience the same sorts of racial profiling, police abuse, poverty, and systemic violence that Black and Indigenous people experience chose to accuse us of wanting special treatment instead of listening to our request, much less caring about our experience. Similarly, when LGBTQIA+ people demand justice in the forms of equitable legal protections and media/political representation, the homophobic and transphobic majority accuse us of having a gay agenda as opposed to a desire to simply live safe, good, accessible lives. The continued validation of this gay agenda is what led to legislation like Florida's "Don't Say Gay" bill, which limits the schools from creating LGBTQIA+ safe spaces for their young people or teaching queer and gender justice education, among other things.[4] It is the uglification of queer and trans rights that enables Texas lawmakers to accuse parents who support their children's trans identities and allow them access to trans-affirming healthcare of punishable child abuse.[5]

When migrant families from Mexico and Central and South America risked their lives to travel to the US for the safety to raise their children and instead were separated from each other and placed into concentration camps, politicians worked hard to convince a concerned population that there needed to be consequences for breaking American laws and disrespecting the American process and Americans' safety by "illegally" crossing imaginary and colonially made borders.[6] This is, once again, uglification being wielded as a tool to intervene against empathy and human rights. We uglify people in search for safety, instead of imagining a world where we are all committed to and invested in each other's safety. What if hospitality and compassion were social and cultural norms?

Our system's infrastructure, cultural imagination, and societal values were designed to validate the oppression and violence that marginalized groups and individuals experience, shame them for their pain and outrage, and uglify and punish them for trying to pursue justice and a better quality of life. As a result, many of us have learned to ignore and uglify our own pain, acquiesce to the injustice by naming it as "just the way it is," and strive to do the best we can to achieve status and class mobility within it (or simply not succumb to it). And we expect the same "fake-it-'til-you-make-it, keep-your-head-down-shuck-and-jive" survival strategies from other people affected by oppression and uglification.

## Uglification Leads Us to Not Trust Our Own Truths

Once I started to trust myself and feel more grounded in the importance of publicly discussing bullying and ugliness, I began to think about how to frame the UGLY Conference to my community. I knew I wanted to collectively name the trauma and violence that come along with existing in a body or identity that others recognize and respond to as ugly; to explore the different and shared ways we've pursued healing and survival; and to create room for people who were still hurting from uglification and bullying to have a sacred and healing space amid beloved community. But I knew that I wanted it to be more than a venue to unpack personal pain or healing. I wanted something that would also facilitate both systemic and personal change. And then, one magical afternoon, while having tea with a fellow artist homie, I explained my quandary.

"Vanessa," the homie said, "We *absolutely* need to have a conference devoted to unpacking ugliness as disenfranchisement, and you are absolutely the person to facilitate it."

When they said the word *disenfranchisement*, my eyes started to water. I cried so hard because I felt seen, recognized, and so grateful and hopeful to finally have language that felt so daring and accurate. The truth is that people who are perceived as ugly by others absolutely experience disenfranchisement. We are disenfranchised out of our safety by bullies, abusers, police officers, judges, and juries who conflate innocence with white standards of beauty and professionalism.

We experience disenfranchisement by doctors, as Tressie McMillan Cottom explored in her essay "In the Name of Beauty." Cottom tells the story of going to the doctor, bleeding, pregnant, and terrified that something very wrong was happening to her baby and her body. Her doctor asserted that she was bleeding because she was fat and her pain was normal. Later that day, she began to have pain in her butt and lower back. She called the nurse and was told it was constipation. Seventy hours later, in even more pain, she went to the doctor again. The doctors told Cottom that it was probably a result of her eating something bad, but after more self-advocacy, they finally gave her an ultrasound. It was then that they not only learned she had two tumors larger than her fetus, but she had also been in labor for three days. She only found out she was in labor after a nurse chastised her for not telling them of her situation. When she was giving a painful birth to a baby who would pass after only a few breaths and crying out in agony, her doctor coldly threatened to leave and not give her pain relief.

Because of how her medical professionals were trained and socialized to perceive a fat, dark-skinned, pregnant Black body, they were unable and unwilling to give her the care and empathy she needed. Their internalization of which bodies to listen to and empathize with, and which they understood to be irrational and untrustworthy due to uglification, meant that they did not listen to her, they did not empathize with her, they did not take her seriously. They did not protect her life or the life of her child. Uglification, in the form of misogynoir and through the words and attitudes of people whose job was to care for her, took her child's life. This is the same medical disenfranchisement that led to the death of Dr. Susan Moore, a Black doctor who spoke out publicly, through her social media page, about the neglect and dismissal she experienced from her doctor just a few weeks before she died of COVID-19.[7] When people are uglified so much that others can't see their humanity or recognize that their body experiences the same amount of pain and needs the same amount (if not more) care than bodies privileged and protected by beauty/whiteness/ability/cisgender, it means their humanity is not protected.

We experience disenfranchisement when we go to job interviews and encounter employers more interested in attractive employees with stylish wardrobes and thin bodies than skilled and committed workers. We definitely experience disenfranchisement in academia, as illustrated by researchers at Duke Health in their 2019 study that found that fat people and individuals with facial features perceived as ugly were 50 percent less likely to receive an interview with seventy-four different faculty members at five different radiology departments.[8]

As much as we may want to simply state that everyone has different preferences, systemically and socially, people with features perceived of as ugly are absolutely disenfranchised and discriminated against when it comes to friendship, romantic relationships, and reciprocally pleasurable consensual sex. Even babies who are born without visible disabilities and with facial features that are perceived as more attractive are more likely to be looked at, held, and responded to by both nurses and parental caretakers. Children born with physical disabilities and faces perceived as less cute are more likely to develop behavioral and cognitive problems as they age.[9]

Talking about uglification, bullying, and how they impact our lives is not wallowing, trauma bonding, or self-victimization. It is the work needed to figure out what we want to heal, how we need to heal it, and how to create a world that doesn't produce so much of it—if any.

My homie's affirmation that ugliness is disenfranchisement, paired with the whole process of opening myself up to talk about uglification publicly, was healing. Incidents that I had previously tried to shoo away as not being a big deal came searing back to my consciousness, and I found myself able and willing to forgive myself for all the insecurity and shame I had internalized as weakness. Just like I have compassion for how we respond to traumas like sexual abuse and assault, racialized and gendered microaggressions, and parental abuse, I needed to have compassion for how I have learned to navigate a lifetime full of uglification in the form of bullying.

After that conversation with my homie, I was not only breathing easier, but I also finally felt free, ready, and excited to talk about the UGLY Conference with my community. I no longer felt fear that I was just organizing a trauma bonding session or another think tank that stopped at thinking. I knew that this would be the beginning of something critical and important.

## A REMINDER TO TRUST YOURSELF

Everyone will have a reaction, some sort of advice, and an analysis about you, your decisions, your behaviors, your situations, your appearance, your relationships, your body, your illness, your disability, and what you should and should not be doing with your time/talent/skill/heart, and more.

Remember that these people's opinions, feedback, perceptions, and advice—even drenched in love, compassion, empathy, and experience; even from people you admire or who admire you; even from people who have known you your entire life—are more about them and their experience of the world than about you.

This doesn't mean you should not be open to, curious about, or willing to learn something from the information folks who love you direct at you. We can all benefit from diverse perceptions, new information, and the expansion of ideas. But remember, you know you better than anyone else in the world—yes, even your momma, your partner, your teacher, and your doctor. You are an expert on you, your body, your needs. Not everything that someone else says to you is relevant to you, so don't let someone convince you of something about yourself that you know, deep down in your heart, is an untruth.

Don't let someone paint their trauma on your body. Don't let someone project their insecurities or fears on your choices. Don't let someone seed doubt into your wisdom or resilience. We've all got our own demons, and mine/theirs/others' really and truly don't need to be yours. Trust yourself and all that gorgeous brilliance of yours, boo. Honor yourself. And keep on flapping those bright, sparkly wings.

## Uglification Creates Unjust and Arbitrary Hierarchies

Not only does uglification manipulate us into distrusting ourselves and believing we are responsible for the impacts of the violence, abuse, and oppression we've experienced in our lives, it also aggressively coaches us to justify harmful ideologies about who other people are, how things must be done, and why some people deserve empathy when they struggle and others condemnation. Uglification enables and protects us from the accountability of changing or disrupting the oppressive project of how things are done—even when those projects obviously hurt or exclude us, the people we supposedly care about, and strangers alike.

Because we're socialized to trust systems and the people who successfully navigate those systems, we're likely to blame the people who can't navigate those systems for the devastation they experience, rather than being curious what led to and facilitated the devastation. For example, we are all identified by checkboxes and put into units, leagues, classes, races, statuses, ethnicities, and genders before we are even born. We have no say over these boxes and no opportunity to assert who we actually are and how we want to exist in the world before those categories are used to determine what sort of opportunities, resources, protections, stereotypes, blame, and investments we have available to us. And we're expected to accept that this is just the way things are, that these protocols protect culture, systems, and democracy, and that we are all powerless to shift them. This inevitably facilitates and sustains the legacies of power dynamics and hierarchies that have hurt humans for generations.

Most of the time these unjust power dynamics and hierarchies are not easily recognizable. For example, we may choose to hire/promote/elect people into positions of leadership based on how well they are able to practice the language and behaviors already standardized as professional, powerful, and even cutthroat or ruthless. However, most people who speak that language and engage in those forms of etiquette are able to because it was modeled for them, early on, by multiple people and interactions, such as their parents, friends' parents, neighbors, educators, and mentors. They are able to grow those skills through competition, nepotism, and at the expense of people who haven't had the same exposure and guidance. As such, many, many people allotted the opportunities that lead to influence, affluence, and power come from environments that culturally prepared them for their role and position and taught them they are better and more qualified than people who don't come from their background and cannot learn or compete with their etiquette. They did not have to unlearn their upbringing, assimilate into someone else's protocols, or practice a style of communication that is deemed superior to the ones they grew up learning. They were born into power and spawned into hierarchy. And if they happen to be cis, heterosexual, and nondisabled, they are likely easily able to stay at the top of that hierarchy without excess struggle.

They did not have to sacrifice their cultural tongue or instincts to perform the standard. They did not have to uglify and reject the spiritual and cultural wombs that birthed them. When those of us who aren't born into that realm attempt to push past our various glass ceilings in the race to survive capitalism and keep our heads above the waves of poverty that sustain capitalism, we have to psychically choose to dissociate from so much of what and who reared us. There is an inherent and horrific dependence on hierarchizing and uglifying in order to embrace that shift. And sometimes, because of the social consequences and mechanisms of uglification, such as poverty, systemic neglect, and societal antagonism, it's easy and even preferable to embrace the uglifying hierarchization and accompanying social modifications.

When we choose to opt out of a cultural or class group deemed subordinate or ugly to the hegemony, we're not just rejecting our families and upbringing, we're also rejecting how our families were treated. We're rejecting the poverty that people in positions of power have decided are acceptable for our families to experience. We're rejecting the lack of safety, rampant addiction, police profiling, educational and medical neglect, and exhaustion that we and our parents navigated. We're choosing to no longer be the butt of so many jokes and case studies of discrimination. We're fighting for our children to know the childhood resources, care, and ease that we and our ancestors deserved—such as access to clean and abundant drinking water, the ability to escape the environmental emergencies that are increasing due to global warming, urgent and equitable healthcare when our bodies start to fail us, safe and comfortable transportation, earth-based organic foods, and even the security to speak up about the injustices we encounter and to demand better. Choosing to not combat uglification and hierarchy is choosing to allow the premature and unnecessary deaths of many over the discomfort of systemic transformation, and it's also complicated for those of us who just want the opportunity to survive.

I've listed a few of the cultural experiences of being born into a group that's uglified and hierarchized as socially subordinate. But there are also more concrete examples of what it means to be born into a classed group that society, as it is, is invested in protecting versus invested in using and consuming. If you grew up in a neighborhood with well-paved, clean, and spacious streets, if there were sufficient and clearly placed traffic signs, if the architecture around you was both pretty and utilitarian, if the schools in your community were spacious and updated, if you could easily access a clean grocery store with a diversity of healthier foods, if you could visit top-grade libraries with regular community events, and if you could go play at clean playgrounds full of greenery, you grew up experiencing the abundance of someone born into a class of people protected and privileged by the uglification of people who grew up with none of that. That childhood experience is not the norm. Many of the people you may have academically and professionally competed with and soared past, including people you may supervise and expect to perform the same way you perform, did not grow up with any of those basic things you had access to. Struggling with other forms of trauma and exclusion due to queer- and transphobia, misogyny, ableism, bullying, and domestic violence does not level the emotional or psychological playing field, because people who grow up in communities without the luxuries you grew up with still experience that same violence and were raised, educated, and neighbors with people also surviving and succumbing to that violence. When you expect those people to be able to attain what you have attained or blame them for being unable to, you are upholding the social hierarchies that uglification creates and feeds off of.

While those of us most negatively impacted by uglification can choose to shift our belief systems, the way we navigate interpersonal relationships, the values with which we raise our children, the media and ideologies that influence us, and how we perceive ourselves, we don't have the same power and influence to shift systems as those people who are privileged by those systems. In fact, changing systemic uglification must be a charge led by people who are positioned as gatekeepers, leaders, enforcers, and beneficiaries. If you are someone who feels safely protected by the police, there is a huge chance that you are also someone who can shift police mentality, as well as the perspective of other people who are protected by the police, through the trustworthiness and insight that come with your social positioning.

Adopting the language and ire of the oppressed is not leveraging your privilege to create change. But by understanding yourself as someone who is an intellectual expert in the rhetoric and decorum of oppressorship, due to your upbringing and sense of safety navigating cis white-supremacist systems (even if those aren't your identities), you can then use that intelligence to effectively mobilize the heart- and mind-changes that will create systemic changes. You have the historical resource of an insider's advantage, being able to talk with peers in these systems about creating social change. This is a way to reclaim ugly as a person who is privileged by uglification.

Similarly, if you are tasked with hiring or supervising people, it is highly likely that you have the power to create a work environment that might be healing, liberating, and empowering for the people employed by your company. You, uniquely, have the ability to look at the systems that protect your power while diminishing other people's power, and to collaborate with those who feel less empowered to change them for the collective better. You get to examine the protocols that protect fear- and money-based hierarchies, then work with brilliant social architects to create protocols that recognize all community members as stakeholders. This is a risk for you. There are people who will lash out at you because they don't want to lose their privilege, just as people lash out at people of color when they demand equity or queer and trans people when they have the audacity to be their true self. Fighting uglification is audacious in a world that has co-opted those practices into religion, legislation, and cultural pastimes. Supporting the eradication of uglification takes courage, determination, and a sort of fierce righteousness. It requires extreme emotional and psychological fortitude, as uglification is absolutely abuse, and you need community support to hold and nurture you through the process. Taking on the challenge of reclaiming ugly as a person with privilege is choosing to fight for and alongside people with less privilege. You are choosing to be a warrior. You will need care.

Reclaiming ugly in your personal life, at work, and while serving and stewarding communities is an invitation to collaboratively dream and imagine the difference we all deserve. Framing it as systemic disruption is sexy for some people, but for me, it's about the beautiful power of creation. Those of us who care can absolutely create small economies where all workers are recognized to be partners and stakeholders. It means giving up traditional forms of power, but can you imagine how rewarding it would be to share and grow power together? We can visualize systems that support liberty, accessibility, and collective success as opposed to fear- and scarcity-based professional hierarchies that build wealth for some at the expense of others. What if we saw businesses as communities who collaborate on a project that sustains each other's well-being— from financial wellness to protecting the resource of brains and bodies from overconsumption and stress? What if exploitation was treated as a cultural and social taboo, as opposed to smart business and financial growth? What if we valued, uplifted, and paid people to help us figure out how to create a work environment that enables this, as opposed to investing in the programming that has yet to illustrate any sort of positive social change? Reclaiming ugly is audacious, but it's lifesaving.

Reclaiming ugly is choosing to love publicly, politically, and systemically. It's creating structures and processes that are rooted in love for the people you live and work with. What does it mean to design modes of transportation while thinking loving thoughts about disabled people, fat people, seniors, pregnant people, people with small children, poor people, and the people who work for the transportation systems? What does it mean to build city infrastructures, design hospital and medical policies, and participate in elections with that same effort of love? What if we recognized that love in this way requires a great deal of skill, logistics, and practice, so we trained and awarded people who are willing to devote their energy to thinking and scheming with love? What if love were the absolute baseline? There isn't much room for uglification and oppressive hierarchy when negotiating love and care for a person. You cannot just watch someone you value suffer without making any effort to support them or alleviate their pain. What if we felt the same way about Earth and all her inhabitants? Love is a serious, tactical, scientific strategy.

People and businesses fail because of lack of love, not lack of effort or desire to succeed. We succeed when we create spaces that allow us to be whole, feel invested in the community we collaborate with, heal from previous traumas and oppressive work/educational environments, say no to that which doesn't serve us, and know that we have everything we need to care for bodies, minds, and families. Reclaiming ugly is reclaiming how we access success and recognize successful people and practices. Success is not a location, an action, an amount of money, or an event. Success is a collection of experiences that allow us to collaborate toward the joyful and peaceful actualization of our shared vision and wellness. Success is always happening. It happens behind the scenes, in our bodies, our relationships, and through the accomplishments that folks we don't know may never see. Success happens in each life we've touched, and all the lives that those people touch.

We don't achieve success, we steward success, and we get to do it with love for ourselves, others, and the earth at the helm. But let's be real. There are so many gatekeepers who read ideas like this as naïve and ideological, as opposed to being curious and courageous about figuring out how to use them. For those of you who are committed to the figuring out how, I want you to know that it is NOT a thing that can be done alone or simply outsourced to social justice consultants. It is a psychological, cultural, and even spiritual resetting. Some gatekeepers will attack your ideas because they don't want to see changes to the systems that protect the hierarchies that serve them. They don't want to face the responsibility of recognizing a wrong. So if you are someone who is willing to reclaim ugly through systemic or structural change, you will need the support systems to build up and maintain the courage and determination to say no to injustice and uglification. We must be willing to risk and trust the unfamiliar, the gray that happens when you forgo black and white, the slow openheartedness of learning a new thing throughout the process of co-creating it. Fumbling in public is terrifying, but with supportive people, it's inherent self-discovery and exploration. In fact, fumbling is a beautiful part of growing and being. It illustrates our aliveness and our potential. When you are perfect, or are committed to being perceived as infallible or unquestionable, there is no potential. There is no life. There is no breath.

Hierarchies colonize our freedom and creativity, our ability to see possibility and healing, and our courage and determination to create change, and fighting hierarchies is a magic. You are infusing life and breath into the lungs of so many people who have had their chests stomped on by the fatigue of constant hate. Celebrating yourself and your collaborators is crucial, and you are absolutely worthy. There is a joke that I constantly see turned into memes about not giving allies cookies. I believe in abundance and the fact that we all need each other to make change, regardless of where we live on the privilege-oppression spectrum. We need to work with each other, across difference, across identity, across privilege. We need to celebrate each other for the courage to speak up and keep speaking up. We need to feed each other as often as possible. We need to keep going. Whether you are infiltrating the top to create changes or revolutionizing and healing the people pushed to the bottom, I want you to have your cookies.

# 6

# Surviving Uglification

I spent a portion of my childhood self-identifying as a suicide activist. This was long before I heard of the medically facilitated suicide that some nations allow for people who believe their illnesses do not let them have a worthwhile quality of life. Later on in life, I realize that I wanted the right to escape from the agony of uglificaton and hopelessness, not from life.

My parents might tell you that I was boisterous, excited about learning, friendship, bugs, art, performance, and love. A kid who needed to greet every stranger at a restaurant or who couldn't resist picking things up off the grocery floor store and joyfully putting them in my mouth. My friends from back then, especially those I'm still in touch with, might tell you that all I wanted was to love and be loved, and that most of our classmates weren't yet ready for a person like me. A lifelong friend recently reflected back to me, "Vanessa, you were the future." Baby me would have told you that I was the weirdest, perkiest little bit of starshine who was desperate to be a famous actress, preacher, author, and rock 'n' roll singer. To be fair, all that was true. But also I was so sad, for such a long time, that by the time I reached eighth grade, I felt completely desolate.

Around fifth grade, I started constructing long fantasies about my death. To soothe myself during moments of extreme bullying or loneliness, I'd dream about the different ways that I could die. Sometimes it would be in class, in the middle of a lesson or assignment, after yet another classmate threw an eraser or rubber band at me or passed me a note explaining that I was ugly, that they hated me, that I should kill myself, and that they were going to beat me up after class. Other times it would be on the walk or ride home from school after I was surrounded by a group of swinging and kicking ten-year-olds who were spewing insult after detailed insult about all the ways my face, body, and existence were ugly. And almost every evening, just after praying with my mother and siblings and listening to my mother's sweet, beautiful voice read us stories or sing us songs, I'd slip back on down to my knees and beg God to rescue me from my life, to take me home to heaven where I would be safe, to never wake me up.

Though those prayers were utterances of desperation and despondency and always accompanied by body-shaking sobs, they were also some of the softest parts of my day. Because as soon as I fell asleep afterward, I'd have the snuggliest dreams about being in heaven, sitting on God's massive lap (of course he was a massive white man), and listening to him tell me all the ways that he loved me, saw my specialness, and would keep me safe. In those dreams I was not sad or defeated. I was hopeful about what my life in heaven could be like and all the things I could imagine and create while existing in a world where no one wanted to hurt me and people other than my family loved me. My sleepy imaginings of God was my safe place. Fantasizing about death was an escape from systems and ideologies that taught my peers it was okay to bully me and that convinced me to devalue my own life. Uglification thrives because of how well its seeds can root in our individual and collective imagination.

One of the most heart-wrenching and moving scenes I have ever encountered was in Octavia Butler's novel *Kindred*. *Kindred* is a story about a Black woman named Dana from the twenty-first century who is repeatedly magically summoned to a slave plantation in the antebellum South by her young ancestor Rufus, the white child of the plantation's very violent master. During one of the trips back, Dana encounters a group of Black children who, still too young to be put to work by the plantation's overseer, are playing auction block games, pretending to examine, sell, and trade each other, bickering over who is worth the most money. They are performing their colonization and oppression, acting out the only world they know. So were the children who bullied me.

The kids at my school who relentlessly made fun of my appearance did not create their insults out of thin air. They were not bad eggs randomly in possession of some cruel spirit or sadistic desire to hurt my feelings for no reason. Their tiny voices were regurgitations of what they heard in the world, what had been said to them and in front of them, how they heard their loved ones talk about each other and themselves, what they listened to on television, and more. Just like those fictionalized enslaved Black babies, the Black babies I grew up with were learning and processing the values of the society that birthed them early on. And unfortunately those values taught us that the darker our skin is, the fatter our body, the more ethnic our facial features, the kinkier our hair, the uglier and less valued we are. Though it wasn't overt at the time, we were taught to hate ourselves, to find the bodies that birthed us as inferior and problematic in the realm of beauty, and to know it was more than okay to be cruel to the people we disliked or found ugly.

Today I weep, grieve, and applaud the child version of me who identified as a suicide activist. My activism and research were a result of a hopelessness so deep that I could imagine only death as a solution to escape the pain I was in and the uglification and bullying I was experiencing. But it also illustrates the fact that itty-bitty teeny-tiny me knew that my experiences were not just, the uglification of my body and personhood was not true or accurate, and I did not deserve it. I understood that there was a better, and I wanted that better.

I, like many other bullied, abused, and uglified people, have been told by many, as a child and as an adult, that I need to increase my self-esteem and learn not to care about what other people have to say about me. I have realized that when we tell a person struggling with bullying, exclusion, and the punitive palm of uglification to develop their self-esteem, self-love, or self-worth, we are making them responsible for the violence they experience. We are asking them to change, instead of advocating for them, rallying around them, protecting them, nurturing them with softness, and asking the world to make better choices that would serve and save us all. Resorting to a conversation about self-esteem does not save lives or empower people on its own. It is not much-needed tough love or wisdom. Putting the critical onus on the individual is an unimaginative, gaslit utterance that protects the cultural practices and ideologies that consistently whip the esteem out of us.

People, and especially children, suffering from the impacts of uglification need warriors who will surround them with loving care and fight on their behalf. In the book *Beloved* by Toni Morrison, a Black woman named Sethe escapes slavery only to be hunted down by slave catchers. In an act of terrified desperation to protect her children from a life of slavery, she kills her infant daughter and almost kills her other children. The majority of the book is a ghost story, however, that explores what happens when the murdered daughter, Beloved, comes back to haunt her mother for the loving childhood she never received. Toward the end of the book, there is this incredible scene where the church ladies, mostly elders, surround Sethe's house and sing, cry, wail, stomp, and dance in grief for Beloved's spirit and Sethe's trauma. They grieved for hours and hours until Beloved is able to get the loving acknowledgment and grief ritual she desperately needed and then move on to whatever happens after death. I cried so hard when I read that scene, and then I read it over and over, absorbing all the love and possibility from it I could. Those wailing, crying, screaming, dancing women were warriors of love and healing. They let both Sethe and Beloved know that they were worthy of time, attention, and care; that what happened to both of them was atrocious and sat heavy in all their bodies; and that they were not alone. It is this level of ferocity and visibility that we uglified people, and especially the babies, need from the community who loves and protects us—especially from the adults. And honestly, the people who do the uglifying and bullying also need this same type of care, nurture, and support.

Bullying is not a natural thing that all children do. Nor is it a thing that we grow out of as adults. Bullying is the slaughterous violence that uglification births and manifests through the words and fists of our young, and many of us continue to do it as adults. As an adult woman who studies ugliness and the ways people uglify themselves and each other, why we do it, and the impacts of uglification through the lens of power, privilege, liberation, oppression, and healing, I now have so much compassion and grace for us all. I have compassion for the uglifiers and the uglified, the bullied and the bullies, the abusers and the abusees, including the people who have hurt me the most consistently and aggressively.

I have separated bullies into two general categories. The first are those who truly benefit from and facilitate oppression with their bullying. They are the Donald Trumps, the corporate CEOs, media powerhouses, and other powerful leaders who strive to control the world. They have race, class, and systemic privilege and use their privilege to steal resources and hog power at the expense of others while belittling anyone who gets in their way. They organize to suppress the liberation and equality of the people whose oppression they benefit from. These people punch down.

The second category of bully includes the rest of us, the people working hard to survive oppression and uglification by stewarding their own and others' uglification. Because they have been so uglified that survival has become a chore rather than a prize of possibility and exploration (and after watching the adults before them struggle to survive as well), these people have internalized the practices and ideologies that validate social hierarchies, exclusion, and punishment for being other. And they have learned to utilize and weaponize those ideologies for their rescue. Rather than seeking collective belonging and solidarity, they aspire to have the privileges of their oppressors and to perpetuate the violent behaviors of oppression. They cling to, depend on, and enforce different types of disenfranchising and hierarchizing of respectability and beauty politics for their own validation, protection, and ascension. These people punch inward, laterally, downward, and diagonally.

To be clear, I believe that we are all these people. Most of us do this to ourselves and each other. People of color project racist ideas and assumptions that validate and protect white supremacy onto people of their own ethnic and cultural background, and they do it to other people of color as well. I will never forget the disappointing agony I felt when I brought my friend who has a Black father and an Indigenous Mexican mother to a Black lesbian retreat I frequently attend. A group of us were sharing breakfast, and a few women started making very xenophobic generalizations about Mexican people. They used those stereotypes to create a Black versus non-Black Mexican binary that uglified Mexicans and made them feel better about their Blackness. And though they didn't realize my friend was Mexican and thought they could safely make their comments because all the other people around them were Black, my friend was very hurt by what was said. I, too, was hurt. Because uglification, and any form of oppression, hurts my feelings. Because I care about my friend. Because I resonate with the feeling of ostracization. I know that those women wouldn't have made the statements they made if they, too, weren't hurt by the oppression they've experienced, including anti-Blackness from other non-Black people of color.

Oppressed people perpetuate oppression against each other because they are all looking to belong. Just as I desperately wanted to feel welcomed and included among my peers as a child, the people who bullied me and lauded my uglification were also trying to feel accepted—only they were doing it at my expense. As survivors of extreme and generational racialized violence, trauma, oppression, and abuse, we have been conditioned to pursue a sense of worth and validation by assimilating and proving that the stereotypes constructed against us are untrue, that we are just as capable and powerful as our oppressors. And we do this by unconsciously glorifying and ascribing to the ideals of uglification and oppression that bullies perpetuate to protect their own power and keep us from creating the much-needed change to their structures, systems, and ability to govern. We use the weapons they wield against us to inform our behaviors, values, and standards.

The concept that a fat body is bad, unattractive, and unhealthy is an uglification and ideal of the misogynist, anti-Black patriarchy that is weaponized against us and that we weaponize against ourselves and our loved ones. Similarly, the concept that thin or fit thick is the standard for attractiveness and desirability and the assumed goal of all MaGes is also an ideal that we weaponize against ourselves. These ideals allow us to decide who is bad/unattractive and who is beautiful/preferable; we then use that information to determine who we align ourselves with, idolize, and express empathy toward versus who we segregate and target.

We use these ideals to create an in-group and an out-group within our shared spaces; we hold a sense of sacred identity and exclusive belonging versus others, folks who we have decided don't make the cut, who aren't pretty enough, aren't in shape enough, aren't educated enough, don't use the correct social-justice language, aren't woke enough, and more. We bully, perpetuate uglification, and discriminate against people we place in that out-group, and we create standards and challenges that threaten members of the current in-group to go along with the hegemonic flow. Folks who reject or interrupt the hegemonic ideal, even if they fit into it, run the risk of ostracization because their choices break the machine and spotlight the fact that uglification is a choice. Because those members have borne witness to how othered and outcast people are treated, abused, targeted, and bullied, they usually stay silent, acquiesce to the status quo, or enact the violence—all to protect and maintain that sense of belonging and the specialness that comes with being among the top tier of their social hierarchy.

On the surface, people who move like this appear to be moving from a place of power. They seem to have an experience of safety and community while they hurt, antagonize, and exclude others from that safety and community. But it is a performance, a psychological coercion that this system has done to them. And it is all about fear. Their choices and actions result from the force, fear, violence, and horror of how we privilege and oppress different people on the basis of trivial standards of structural and cultural uglification and a yet-to-be-developed ability of how to think, dream, and imagine difference with creativity and liberation. Oppression and uglification leave us traumatized. These traumas and the anxiety that comes from them suppress our neural pathways, our ability to find logic outside of fear and survival, and our access to empathy.[1] Most of us don't heal from the bullying we experience in childhood or afterward—capitalism, adult responsibilities, and other oppressions don't provide us with the time and space, much less resources and support, we need to heal (seeing a therapist once a week is not enough when you live in this world twenty-four hours a day, seven days a week). Instead of healing, we learn to tolerate a normative cyclic uglification, validate it, and perpetuate it against each other. We learn to turn the other way and mind our own business and be happy that we're safe when we see it happening to others.

This is not an empowered action. It is what happens when our only source and model for identity and safety comes from the very people who violate us the most and get away with it because they are protected by the projects born of uglification and oppression. Bullying and uglifying others, especially when you are an uglified person, is what unactualized power and suppressed imagination looks, smells, tastes, and feels like when it is being punched into your head. It is a painful, regurgitating symptom of what was done to our ancestors and what is still being done today. It is sad and *just* as murderous as our oppressors are. It is what happens when we unconsciously become our master's tools and our oppressor's weapons.

This malicious and disempowered manifestation of uglified trauma and undeveloped survival skills works to suppress our liberation and imagination. *Liberation* is the ability to be free to safely enjoy our lives, live in our truths, access the resources we need to eat and sleep well, and to love ourselves and each other wholly—without state and interpersonal oppression clouding the way. It is choosing to (U)plift, (G)lorify, and (L)ove (Y)ourself *while creating a world where others can as well.* It is impossible to be about liberation and love while antagonizing, discriminating against, molesting, abusing, bullying, or uglifying any other person—including trans and nonbinary people, queer people, fat people, cis women, sick and disabled people, autistic people, sex workers, formerly incarcerated people, people with HIV, single parents, people struggling with substance abuse, and people that you, for whatever reason, perceive as ugly and unlikeable.

We must learn to be in solidarity and collaboration with each other, to truly have each other's backs, if we want to save our lives from what histories and legacies of uglification have done to us. And we need to put as many resources and as much education as possible into teaching our children this. Young bullies usually grow up to be adult bullies. As adult bullies, we take out our patterns of oppression and uglification on our children and limit their freedom and unique expressions because we fear them experiencing what we experienced or what we did to other kids. Some of us become comedians, teachers, policymakers, or employers and force our unhealed traumas and uglification defense mechanisms onto everyone we have some power over. Some of us become homicidal or suicidal because of them, and we die or kill before we get the opportunity to heal.

It is this type of uglification that led to the suicide of young Amanda Todd, a girl who was harassed, stalked, forced to move to multiple schools, cyber and in-person bullied, and then beat up by multiple children.[2] Todd met a man on the internet, entered a flirtationship, and sent him a topless photo at his bequest. This man then cyber-stalked her, and when she refused to "put on a show for him," he sent the topless photo of her to everyone in her contacts as revenge. The fact that her stalker knew how MaGes are uglified and dehumanized for their bodies and sexualities put Todd's stalker in a gruesome position of power, and he exploited people's bias for vengeance and domination. Todd's classmates responded the way misogyny and the patriarchy have socialized people into responding to sexualized and molested children: they turned into a mob and tortured her, throwing insults at her every day in class, drowning her social media presence with cruelty, following her from school to school and around her neighborhood with fists and threats; they made sure that she knew just how inferior and unworthy of kindness or peace she was in their eyes. They felt entitled to harass and abuse her solely because she made a choice that broke the oppressive and restrictive moral obligations that society enforces on MaGes, especially girls, and it was their harassment that killed her. It was unchecked and unprocessed uglification that killed her.

Childhood bullying that results from the uglification of our bodies, faces, and desires is also what killed McKenzie Adams (at age nine), Rosalie Avila (thirteen), Kyler Prescott (fourteen), Leelah Alcorn (seventeen), Blake Brockington (eighteen), and so many other children.[3] Adams and Avila, the youngest of this group, both wrote their parents apology letters for being so ugly just before they ended their lives. These tiny children were tortured because other children thought they were ugly and felt entitled to relentlessly entertain themselves at these kids' expense.

When my partner and I are done with work, chores, and adventures for the day, we love watching quirky comedic television shows like *The Big Bang Theory* and *Half & Half*. But like in many television sitcoms, the writers of these shows evoke humor by making the characters relentlessly crack jokes about each other's appearances and bodies. These are the parts of TV sitcoms that I hate, but this is a practice that is almost impossible to avoid if you enjoy narrative plots that aren't thrillers, mysteries, or full of violence and war. These shows normalize making fun of each other and teach us that it's okay to constantly rib people because of their qualities that society deems unattractive or unacceptable and that the victims of the bullying should be able to get over it.

But unlike the characters on television who have friends and support, the children who get bullied the most are often lonely and alone in their experience because other kids don't want to be associated with them and risk getting bullied as well. This loneliness and isolation, paired with the constant attack against their personhood, facilitates a depression that kills. It was the world that reared the children who went to school with Todd, Adams, and Avila. The bullying Todd experienced was slut-shaming and misogyny. Adams, a Black child, and Avila, a Latina child, experienced bullying that was loaded and spliced with racism. Because of how different racial identities are uglified and policed, by their own people and by different ethnicities, these small girls had a wide lexicon of assault and uglification placed onto their tiny bodies.

Similarly, Prescott, Alcorn, and Brockington, all trans youth, had to navigate vicious intersections of uglification during their young lives. Before their deaths, all three youth spoke vehemently about the bullying, attacks, and isolation they experienced because of people's response to them attempting to live their beautiful, precious, trans lives. Prescott wasn't just uglified at school; he also was uglified at the hospital that was supposed to save his life when his nurses and doctors refused to address him by his chosen pronouns and acknowledge the truth of his identity.[4] The structures of oppression that masquerade as places of help and safety are not safe nor helpful for people with identities excluded and uglified by the religious majority and status quo.

Alcorn experienced an even more terrifying and violent uglification from these institutions. Not just bullied by her classmates and online, she was also bullied and uglified by her parents, who went as far as sending her to a Christian conversion program. They attempted to psychologically torture the transness out of her instead of just loving and learning about their sweet baby. These parents' choices were a result of generations and generations of religiously and scientifically standardized binaries of what is right and what is wrong, what is healthy and what is sick, who is demonic and who is angelic. They chose to view their child through this lens, not through a lens of love or care. It was the white-supremacist and misogynistic early psychological community, which listed queerness and transsexuality (which we now call transgender) as a mental disorder that needed to be fixed, paired with the patriarchal male supremacist views about gender, bodies, and sexuality of the Christian church that birthed the sort of institutions that Alcorn's parents sent her to. Alcorn's life and death illustrate that uglification can make it so that a targeted person is not safe anywhere, not at home, not at school, not out in the streets.

Her parents strongly contributed to her death, but our nation continues to allow and protect religious groups' practices and pedagogies of hate and uglification that try to push a moralistic platform into our consciousness. Although there are many lush places of worship that preach true love and care for all humans, too many others hold on to supremacist ideals that teach us to protect and value some lives (cis, straight, white, "attractive," thin, pious, not disabled or sick, young, legal citizens, Christian) and slaughter those who don't fit into those categories.

Brockington was blessed with a degree of protection and support that other youth weren't, due to being a visible and known advocate for the rights of LGBTQIA+ youth, but he also fit into so many of these less valued categories—Black, trans, AFAB (assigned female at birth), queer, poor, and neurodivergent. While advocating for the safety and self-worth of other trans youth, he also spoke vulnerably about the depression he was navigating, the constant online and in-person bullying he was facing, and the angst of his identity and wholeness being rejected by his terrified parents. He succumbed to the consequences of an uglification that had been clawing at him for far too long in his young life.

The practices and principles of uglification, internalized and inter-personal, start early on. Even if we live in families that strive hard to teach us self-love, worth, and compassion, even if people eventually start to see how magical we are and love us, those practices are so tangible in our communities and schools that it is so easy to believe there is no escaping them. This is why teaching your children or yourself fierce self-love is so important, this is why standing up for bullied people is critical, and this is why neither of these is anywhere near sufficient on its own.

I believe we have to help ourselves and our loved ones understand how uglification works, how they can recognize it, and how they can practice not internalizing it, while surrounding themselves, ourselves, and each other with our versions of Toni Morrison's love warriors from *Beloved* as frequently as possible. We must collaborate with the people in our communities, our places of work, and our families to create struc-tures and practices that help liberate us from the impacts of uglification instead of closing our eyes and tolerating them.

We must decide that we care more about the healing, survival, joy, and wellness of our most intersectionally uglified and excluded people (no matter how much our own conditioning by systems of uglification coerces us into blaming others for their oppressions or thinking we've made better choices or worked harder) than we do about fitting into and benefitting from the familiar and glorified traditions of the status quo. It is then, and only then, that violence will end.

## A Critical Reminder for Those Struggling to Stay Alive after Being Uglified and Mistreated by the World

I love you. I want you here. I want to see who you become when you're finally free from the people who don't know how to recognize and appreciate your beauty. The way they treat you is about what oppression has done to their brains. This has nothing to do with you, and you will not always be treated this way. You will meet people who see you, who love you, and who want to appreciate, protect, and care for you. They exist, but you have to be willing to find them. That means taking the risk of leaving behind those people who don't know how to stop uglifying you.

You can love and care for people from a distance. Setting yourself free is not abandoning the people you love. They abandon you with each uglification, each refusal to love and embrace you at your most whole and happy. Setting yourself free from that reflects your choice to stay alive and live a life you feel joy and pleasure living. You deserve to be happy. I need for you to choose and embrace happiness as frequently as possible. Because that is the place where you will begin healing, reclaiming your imagination from uglification, and joining me in the creating a world where no one gets treated the way you and I have been treated. I believe in you. I believe in us. We're going to save lives, together.

Now, please enjoy the next few affirmations. I wrote some for people I witnessed suffering from uglification, myself included, and some for people who experience the fat, Black, dark-skinned, queer, femme intersections that I do.

- Though you are utterly perfect in this moment as well as the next, perfection as we're taught to perceive it is not real. It's a

tool created to make us doubt ourselves, limit our opportunities, curtail our potential, and exist in the constant psychological skirmishes of competition and juxtaposition.

- You *are* perfect, and your perfection doesn't have anything to do with anyone else.

- Your perfection exists when you trust your feelings and intuition and honor them with action, decision, boundaries, and gratitude.

- Your perfection exists when you allow yourself to lean into your weirdness, your creativity, and your wildness and explore every corner of your personhood.

- Your perfection exists when you are unapologetic about your worth, your needs, your dreams, your desires, and your boundaries with yourself and the people you love.

- Your perfection exists when you let someone know they have crossed your boundaries and you inform them of how to honor their mistake and move forward appropriately.

- Your perfection exists in the self-love and collective care that coats your no.

- Your perfection exists when you open your heart wide and tell the universe yes.

- Your perfection exists when you can throw your head back, laugh, and think of nothing but the joy and bliss of the moment.

- Your perfection exists in the lessons you learn and the compassionate space you allot for the awkward trial and error of implementing those lessons.

- Your perfection exists when you can let someone else lavish your body with pleasure, care, and sensuality in a way that you both enjoy and consent to.

- Your perfection exists when you decide to create a lifestyle that centers deep, soulful moments of pleasure and joyful connection with yourself, the earth, and other people.

- Your perfection exists when you do something that feels important to you, and you allow yourself to sit in the joy, pride, and gratitude of that experience.

- Your perfection exists in the moments when you allow yourself to be still and guilt free.

- Your perfection exists when you let your body move the way it wants to, whether it's languid and slow, angled and jerky, focused and sharp, gentle and timid, wild and free, or delectably still.

- Your perfection exists in the movement of your voice or hands over language, thought, and expression.

- Your perfection exists in your kindness and care that you reciprocate for the people who treat you with love, who nurture you, and who respect you, all of which inspires your magic.

- Your perfection exists in those tiny conversations you have with yourself as you move through the day, the affirmations and reminders of all that you are and all that is possible.

- Your perfection exists in the choices you make to heal from what has been done to you, from the hierarchies and oppressive ideals you've been taught to adhere to, and from the privileges you've swallowed with a misled entitlement for far too long.

- Your perfection exists when you release your heart from and rinse it of the bitterness and resentment that may color your perspective with internalized uglification.

- Your perfection exists when you're able to lean into the compassion that allows you to recognize the humanity of the people who have harmed you and the violent systems that constructed them and nurture yourself enough to release their hold on your heart and set yourself free.

- Your perfection exists when you make the choice to uplift, glorify, and love yourself and create a world where others can do the same with more passion, devotion, and determination than any perpetrator of uglification will ever have.

- You, beloved starlight, are perfect in your existence, in your curiosity, in your self-efficacy and self-determination, in your connection with other beautiful beloveds, in your values and politics, in your growth and healing, in your compassion and willingness to try again, in your forgiveness and your righteousness, and in your willingness to let you be you.

- You don't need to do anything but continue honoring when you feel the best, when you enjoy your life the best, and when you experience the most ease and well-being and learn from those instances. There is so much wisdom in joy, so much intelligence in the pleasure of knowing you. The answers are there. You got this! I love you and I am cheering you on.

# 7

# Love and Family as Tools against Uglification

Whenever I give talks about interrupting uglification, one of the first things people ask is what kind of advice can I offer parents and caretakers. This question brings up so many feelings of overwhelming passion and simultaneous hesitation for me. All people, even those who commit the greatest atrocities against other humans and the earth, were once small children, and because the folks who birthed them, raised them, and played a role in their character development were also once small children, the relationship between child and adult is one of the most crucial and potentially gentle places to focus long-term harm prevention and liberation building.

This question also brings up some very personal feelings about my own upbringing and family that I want to treat with care and intentionality. In writing this chapter, I took time to reflect on how my parents raised me; how the complicated, human quality of their lives and histories contributed to my quest to reclaim ugly; and how I learned ugliness in the first place.

Parenthood can be difficult and so very traumatic—especially for Black and Brown parents; houseless, incarcerated, poor, systems-impacted, and working-class parents; undocumented and documented immigrant parents; sick, disabled, neurodivergent, and mentally ill parents; orphaned, abandoned, familyless, and single parents; queer and trans parents; and folks who became parents in their teen years or late in life. In a world with a gaze narrowed by uglification and false paintings of normality, these are the invisible warriors who get the least support, encounter the most violence and antagonistic setbacks, and suffer the heaviest, hottest load of blame when things go wrong. These are the people who tend to be most isolated and affected by intrusive and suffocating capitalism, a community or nation that doesn't care about their well-being, personal histories of harm and uglification, and other oppressive and difficult forces rooted in systemic oppression.

As we discuss family and parenting in this chapter, I want to hold our entire and whole truths with a ripe softness that can foster healing, grow liberation, and seed more intimate and generative connections. Our families are sacred.

## Fighting Uglification Is a Family Affair

Although I'm sure it's rarely their intention, our parents are our first teachers of uglification and our first, and most effective, uglifiers. Some of our parents are outright bullies. It is our parents who tell us what to strive for, what is right or moral, what is beautiful even. Similarly, they are also the ones who teach us what is wrong, what is ugly, what is disgusting, and what is worthy of punishment. Sometimes the traits and behaviors they perceive as wrong, ugly, and immoral are who we, their children, are when we can lean into our most free and joyful selves.

As I was editing this chapter, my own father told me that I was disgraceful. He looked me in the face, rage in his eyes, and said, "Vanessa, you shame me. You shame our ancestors. I would hate for my [dead] mother to see the disgusting shit you post on social media."

He was responding to me expressing my queerness, sexuality, and gender-queerness online. My social media page is where I feel the most free expressing my truths and exploring my desires. I often feel a great deal of joy when I share my writing and photos with my online community; I experience an acceptance, validation, and connection with like-minded people that I wish I experienced with my actual family. Though my father has been uglifying my body, personality, neurodivergence, gender expression, and queerness for as long as I can remember, his words still hurt. I know that I am not the only adult who suffers as a result of parental rejection and uglification. As hard as we may work to love ourselves for who we are, there is very little pain like the kind that comes from being rejected and maligned by the people we come from. Words like this hurt, but what hurts more is the fact that it's my joy and liberation that disgusts him. Uglification teaches us to value the hegemonic opinions of others, including people we don't know, over the well-being and joy of the people we supposedly care about. Uglification chooses ideals over relationships, and that is both dangerous and common.

The West Coast has seen several seasons of intense wildfires over recent years. Some of those fires resulted from "gender-reveal" parties gone very wrong. Just as these elaborate bombs of pink and blue scorch our earth and burn down our trees, leaving ugly scars of death and loss in their wake, when parents enforce cisgendered absolutes on their children, they can cause similar harm to the heart, spirit, and body of their child. Teaching and forcing children to adhere to cis-heteronormative and binary gender roles, before giving them the space to learn and choose who they authentically are, often leads to many arduous years of unwrapping damaging and inaccurate psychological packaging. Punishing or chastising children for exploring their truths causes even more damage and strife. It is not just uglification, it is bullying people into being at odds with who they are. This sort of formative bullying can produce shame and hatred in the uglified child—both toward the uglified and unfulfilled parts of their self, and toward people who have chosen to embrace the truths that they themselves have been bullied for.

When a parent recognizes that their child's essence and behavior spills outside the traditional gender roles they were raised to see as normal, and then they try to pressure that child into a container in which they don't and can't fit—by giving them inappropriately gendered clothing, forcing them into gendered activities they are not interested in, or by even giving them shameful critiques—that parent is actively uglifying their child. They are teaching their child that they must change who they are and how they show up to be accepted by their family and receive safety and love. Even if that parent believes they love their child with their entire heart, their actions teach their precious baby that love and approval are dependent on the child's willingness to acquiesce to standards that are at odds with their truth. They are teaching their baby to modify and hide who they are, not only for acceptance by bigoted and transphobic people but for the peace and safety of not constantly receiving critical attention. Trans children deserve to be loved and supported as they safely grow into trans adults, as opposed to being chopped apart until they perform an acceptable version of prescribed cisness.

This is how uglification works on a very interpersonal level. And it's hard, because of course most loving parents do not believe that they are uglifying their child. Parents are moving from a place of care, of wanting their child to be safe and protected in a world that punishes and shames people who step out of the rewarded norm. Although the critiques and modifications may look and feel like the behavior of love in the moment, that's exactly what uglification primes us to do. The belief that safety is qualifiable pending on assimilation is dangerous and affirms oppression and unbelongingness. This is the strategy my own father has relentlessly used on me for decades. It has not only caused deep spiritual and emotional distress on all of us, as I have been unwilling to release my wholeness, it has led to me choosing a loving relationship with myself over maintaining a painful relationship with him.

This same dynamic can show up with parents who have disabled, neurodivergent, or sick children. Again, from a place of love and wanting the best for their child, caretakers may encourage their child to hide their disability, train them to walk/talk/respond like people who aren't disabled, reject the different coping mechanisms that child may learn to implement for their emotional wellness, and even interfere with their ability to get the therapeutic support or learning aides they may need to navigate the world as a disabled person. Even if parents think they are teaching their child to navigate the world as it is, they aren't teaching their child how to navigate the world as the child is. They are actually teaching the child that the opinions and norms of others are more valuable than the needs and nuances of the child. Instead, look up social media influencers and educators who have similar disabilities, neurodivergences, or illnesses as your child. Learn from their joy. Read about their lifehacks. Connect with people who can inspire you and your child to live fulfilling lives.

This also applies to fat children of all sizes. It makes sense that parents want their children to be well and healthy, but this focus can begin to feel like harassment to their children. Fat children are often relentlessly made fun of at school and out in the world—at least I was. When they go home, and the focus is again on their weight or size, they may feel as if they have no safe place to be, no protection from intrusive and uglifying commentary. The voices of their parental figures get swallowed into the conglomerate of cruelty and fatphobia they deal with every day. Because of fatphobia and how "childhood obesity" has been turned into a politicized action word, parents of fat children are also uglified and criminalized as child abusers. Sometimes that uglification those parents receive is a part of why they so aggressively bully their child into losing weight.

For many young people, being constantly critiqued and assessed by their families leads to hopelessness, stress, and deeply embodied shame. If you are afraid that your child is using too many processed foods as a coping mechanism, don't shame their love for food. Food is a source of joy, pleasure, and connection for so many of us. Consider all the cooking shows and dessert competitions on television. Food is art. It's sacred. Instead of making food the enemy and uglifying it, which leads to eating disorders and other agonizing complexes, teach your child how to safely indulge in the pleasure of food.

Cook decadent meals together. Learn to savor the sensuality of food together. Indulge in the beautiful plethora of colors, the science of mixing and baking foods, the history of food diasporas, and the wacky mix and match of creating new foods. Bonding over creating and enjoying food can be an act of intimacy and joy that brings you and your child closer together. That time you share with them in this manner may save their life, especially if they are being bullied and tortured outside their home.

Fighting uglification, on all levels but especially in the family and through child rearing, is about imagination. As a parent, do you want to immediately go to a place of shame, or do you want to learn about who your child is and what they need to be their happiest and most creatively potent self? It might feel natural to us, and even just, to use shame or punishment as a tool because that is how we were disciplined and taught morals by our parents. We may have grown up in families who believed that sparing the rod, as the Bible says in Proverbs, leads to spoiling or hating your child. But we have more effective ways to discipline and educate than by using shame and spanking.

Can you imagine discipline strategies that will feed your children's life force, that will energize them to think critically about what right and wrong mean to them, that will encourage them to begin developing their own praxis of justice, liberation, and even collaboratively chosen goals? Consider children who struggle in school or with behavior, who are often made to feel like they are wrong, bad, or less intelligent than they should be. But these places of conflict could be magical portals to your child's superpowers. What if we are curious about why they make the choices they make? What if we support them to be curious about their choices and talk to them about their needs and the impacts of their actions? What if we open collaborative dialogue with our children about the people they are and the adults they are becoming?

By taking these approaches we could be saving our children from the school-to-prison pipeline, from years of self-doubt and feelings of academic failure, and from schools and educational styles that don't actually serve their creative and intellectual greatness. I was a B-C-D student in high school. In middle and elementary school, I was perpetually getting in trouble for not sitting still in my seat, for drifting off in my imaginary realm, for getting lost during field trips. It wasn't until graduate school that I realized I had ADHD, was on the autism spectrum, and had other unique ways in which my brain functioned that weren't compatible with the type of education I was getting. I was not a bad student. I was not unintelligent or lazy. It really was an issue of compatibility.

As parents, you can fight the uglification of your children's intellectual processing and personality by exploring where and when your children thrive instead of focusing on their failure. Uglification is obsessed with blaming people for not being able to survive systems that fail them. And it is systems, not people, that fail. Supporting your child to not fall prey and victim to uglification means slowing down to learn who they are, what they need, and what they desire as opposed to forcing on them the ideas that were forced on you. We need expansiveness, curiosity, and imagination. We need the time to become, to unfurl.

Very few people will want to eat only one fruit or one vegetable all the time. Our diversity, including our intellectual and creative diversity, is magic. It is this magic that can transform the world for the better. Your child, when allowed to be themselves and when uncorrupted by external standards of normal, beautiful, or brilliant, might find that they have the specific type of intelligence needed to change the world. They may grow to become something we desperately need and have never seen.

Refusing to be a one- or two-strategy parent means leaning into the courage and vulnerability necessary to allow newness to blossom in your home. It means allowing your child to become who they are, listening to them, studying them, and not just recycling the messages that you received from your parents and other parts of the world. And yes, this is taking a risk. But it is a risk you and your child are worthy and deserving of. Because when we don't take this risk, the parental behaviors we may think of as love are deeply harmful and spirit-killing.

If your child has a body, a gender, a personality, or an intellectual disposition that you know the world will be violent toward, they don't need you to encourage or pressure them to change for their safety and survival. They need a love warrior, an ally, a sacred voice who will remind them of just how beloved and valuable they are and all the possibilities they can pursue. They need iron that will keep them strong when the winds of oppression and fear, facilitated by classmates, strangers, doctors, and other relatives, try to knock them down.

Teach them to love themselves as they are. Teach them the power and fierceness of compassionate self-acceptance. Turn your home into a safe retreat, a place where they can get the fuel they need to keep going. Teach them how to survive oppression with vision and imagination, not acquiesce to it. Teach them how to choose people who will nurture their potential and joy, and how to say no to groups and individuals who will hurt them. Teach them that they don't need to be loved or accepted by everyone, that they can center the voices and embraces of people who will see just how precious and amazing they already are, and love them for that.

My mother was not perfect at this, but she tried so beautifully, and I solidly believe her attempts saved my life from the uglification I received from my father and the schoolyard bullies. A Christian, she told me this every single day: "God made you perfect, just as you are." When I came out as queer, she reminded me that I was perfect. When I told her all the reasons other kids said I was weird, she told me that her god made me perfect, and also, fuck them. When I became suicidal and homicidal in my early teens, my mother went into the most loving state of triage imaginable. She didn't attempt to shame, pray, punish, or incarcerate me into wellness or a desire to live; she collaborated with me to turn my current life into one that I felt was worth living, and she sacrificed to do it. She figured out how to sign me up for a psychiatrist, a therapist, and group counseling back when therapy and mental health were not talked about as much in the media, much less our community. When my therapist outed me to her and suggested that my queerness was the source of my struggles, she told him off in front of me, standing up for me, and reminding him and me that I was not the problem, homophobia was. And most incredibly, most beautifully, my mom realized that I needed joy, acceptance, and a safe space. She found a theatre program full of other queer and trans kids of color and drove an hour and a half, each way, three days a week, to take me to that theatre program for over a year. When I was done with that program and wanted to go to social justice training instead, she made the same commute for another three years.

My mom's love helped me realize that it was the world that needed to change, not me. Instead of focusing on the fear of a bigoted society, she built a fire of determination inside me. That fire is what supported me to create Reclaim UGLY when the acid and venom of uglification became apparent. When Pat Riarchy posted the picture and commentary of me online, I knew that there wasn't anything wrong with me. I knew that people who look like me should be able to go wherever they wanted to go. I knew that his mentality was a played-out beauty supremacy that had absolutely nothing to do with me or anyone else, and I would no longer allow that supremacy to win. I had the strength and power to speak up and do something about it because my mom made sure to let me know that I was nothing to be ashamed of. My body, my face, my hair, my smile, my teeth, and my disabilities are all little bits of the dynamic recipe of me, and I am proud. I am a magic that can save lives.

If you are a parent or caretaker, especially one who is trying or has tried to love and provide for your children the best you know how, I want you to know that you are hallowed. You are so important. You are worthy of love, praise, and empathy, first and foremost. To my mother, I love you so much and I am immensely grateful to you for every bit of life, love, and possibility that you provided for me and my siblings. I do not want to uglify you. I will try to tell my stories with dignity, with compassionate spaciousness for what I don't fully know or understand, and using my personal truths.

And if you are a person who has been severely harmed by your parents or caretakers, your anger or pain is valid, just as mine toward my father is valid. It is *not* your responsibility to have compassion for what may have led to their violence. But with the appropriate support, when you are ready and able, pursuing understanding of them will facilitate your own liberation and enable you to heal and settle intergenerational trauma. Focused and intentional knowledge paired with openhearted curiosity can create a potent and rippling foundation for transformation.

Parents, if the examples I listed earlier feel familiar, or if they remind you of other things you've said or done that may have uglified your children, give yourself a dose of love and compassion. It's not just you. While it's true that you have taught your child to love or think independently, you've also taught them some form of judgment, cruelty, shame, or supremacy—this is not your fault. Nor is it the fault of your parents who did the same to you, or their parents who did it to them. We have *all* been uglified. We have all experienced and survived horrific injustices, and we all, including you, deserve love, care, compassion, and self-forgiveness.

The teachings and practices of uglification that you have handed down to your children are influenced by the systems that rear us, alongside and within our families. They are born of circumstance and cemented in survival, a manifestation of what we have experienced, not who we actually are. You do not deserve to be shamed for this, or ashamed of it. It is just a concrete fact of the world we exist in, and we cannot shift it if shame or guilt is paralyzing our ability to self-reflect and reimagine child-adult or society-parent relations.

Transforming how we parent, and how we support and care for parents and caretakers, is critical to eradicating uglification, healing intergenerational trauma, and interrupting the violence we have come to accept as "just a part of life." Most likely, the way you engage with your children, and the way your parents have engaged with you, even when it hurts, comes from a deep place of love and a desire to protect. I absolutely know that this is true for my parents. The wounds I still bear and the ones I've managed to heal are not about what my parents have felt for me, nor is it about them being bad or abusive parents, it's about their fear of what a bad and abusive world would do to their baby girl.

## Capitalism Uglifies Parents and Their Children

Much of the harm we experience and perpetrate reflects the society that reared us, not who we are at our cores or the people who have tried to love us. This is why discussing uglification, just like discussing racism and rape culture, cannot be limited to interpersonal relationships, self-perception, and individual actions. It is a structural issue and, consequently, needs to be a structural conversation.

Parents don't use shame and punishment as a strategy because they don't care, but because contemporary adulting provides only the wealthy and privileged with enough time and resources to spend the necessary time with themselves imagining and then, with their children, doing. Due to so many different intersections of oppression and uglification, most parents do not receive the time or emotional spaciousness they need to recognize and interrupt the uglification they have learned. Who among us can spend time wondering what our child needs to stop them from bullying other kids or failing their classes when we work fifty hours a week and still can't pay our bills?

If we can decenter capitalism and lean into a culture that structurally and spiritually prioritizes mutual aid, more people will get the opportunity to be the best (and most productive) parents they can be instead of being relegated to acts of urgency and desperation. I know this is hard to imagine because most parents do not have the power or influence to create structural changes, but some of us do. Some parents employ other parents, are principals and administrators at local schools, and are on the school board and can create transformative and life-saving policy. Some parents are police officers and can reimagine safety and protection for families affected by violence and poverty. Some parents are churchgoers and have a say in which messages they expose their and other families to. Some parents are graphic and visual artists and can make designs that affirm children who are fat, disabled, sick, darker-skinned, BIPOC, or not hegemonically beautiful. Some parents work in finance and banking and can make choices that protect families' access to the financial resources they need to live.

We can choose to divest from the idea that we are only responsible for our own families—and that families are only blood relatives. What if our block, our neighborhood, and our city are family? What if we believe in making sure that everyone eats instead of hoarding wealth? I know that some people might say these questions are idealistic, that it isn't possible for local or federal governments to take care of everyone in this way. But I disagree. And even if I am wrong, what if, instead of focusing on what is not possible, we use our infinite imaginations and extraordinary brilliance to focus on what is possible and then go create it?

It's possible for our systems to support us without going under. We know what it means to see cultural structures for aid being supported. The *Washington Post* estimates that banks, credit unions, and other significant financial institutions (Wall Street) received just over $500 billion from the United States Treasury to bail out and stabilize the economy between 2008 and 2010. This is because of the Emergency Economic Stabilization Act of 2008, also called the 2008 Bank Bailout.[1] Architects and proponents of the bailout argued that this focus would protect employers' abilities to retain and fairly pay their employees (even though job loss and unemployment increased by millions) and land/property owners' ability to keep their belongings. The Treasury's willingness to offer loans and breaks to keep these institutions from going under illustrates just how revered they are to the prioritized fabric of this country. When families, on the other hand—especially families of color—fall into debt, homelessness, and destitution, their children and their parental rights are stolen from them until they can jump through the systemic hoops and navigate the agencies that didn't support them in the first place.

What if we lived in a world where the billions dedicated to bank bailouts were a part of family survival plans? What if legislative stipulations demanded that institutions benefitting from the bailouts pay all their workers a wage that allowed them to live comfortable and relaxed lives? What if people cared enough about other people to reject billionairism and pay their employees well enough to live good lives and have the spaciousness to uplift, glorify, and love themselves without legislative incentive? Can you imagine the experience of children and their parents or caretakers if systems and attitudes were established to support their wellness? Can you imagine how your own upbringing would've been different? Or how your current relationship with your own children might shift?

This is what transformative justice asks of us—to imagine and create a world in which we can all thrive and to change what isn't working, instead of trying to beat and cut ourselves down to fit in and incarcerating or uglifying people who cannot. It's why Reclaim UGLY's tagline doesn't just stop with uplift, glorify, and love yourself (or your family). We need to go beyond this and create a world in which everyone else can as well. Specifically that means using your power and resources, if you have them, to make policies and laws that not only get out of people's way when they try, but that invite them in so they can use their lived experiences and expertise to facilitate the laws and social changes that will help them access the lives they want, need, and deserve.

Oppression leads to wisdom and extreme intelligence. When we struggle, we generate answers. Because we're oppressed, however, we don't have the time, space, power, and support to implement our wisdoms with finesse. As a result, our solutions are uglified and not trusted by stakeholders. This is why the chant for Black Lives Matter has been mispositioned as an attack on and hatred for non-Black lives, instead of being embraced for what it actually is: a plea to survive and a request for institutional and policy changes that will ensure and protect that survival.

Systems-impacted people know that when intervening in and prosecuting violence is the norm, violence remains the norm. But when peace-centered prevention practices and care are the norm, when feeding and housing all families is mandatory, and when liberatory imagination and leadership are actively invested in, then peace, care, and safety become our day-to-day, and violence, stealing, rioting, and rage eventually becomes outliers. We can spend our time building instead of fighting because those who benefit from oppression will slowly, and then quickly, have fewer admirers and stewards who are willing to do their bidding and trying to enforce our participation. How we raise our children today can facilitate all of that, effectively changing the world for generations to come. But all of that is mere idealism if we don't actually create a world where it is possible.

Caring about families and humanity means ensuring that oppressed and disenfranchised people lead the political, economic, and structural discussion for change and show up to support implementing such changes. Because we haven't seen this kind of change yet, I believe that all parents, especially BIPOC or poor parents who may have caused unforgivable harm to their children, deserve grace.

How systems treat parents and families is what informs how we learn to be and survive. Establishing cultural structures that cherish the well-being and holistic education of children and that socioeconomically support the wellness and success of those who do child-rearing will create a more buoyant, cohesive, and joyfully productive society. But as of now, most parents and children are not structurally protected by the economic and justice practices of this land. We are led to believe that we are through offerings like public K–12 schools, Medicare, and breakfast and lunch programs, but these barely scratch the surface and don't remotely address the level of oppression that children and their parents encounter while they are trying to make it. We can't just ask people to uplift, glorify, and love themselves, much less create a world where others can, when they are being beaten into complacency, incarcerated, and neglected by the systems that have the potential to help, and belittled by their loved ones.

As children, we watched how our parents and loved ones struggled, how they uglified themselves and each other, and how they figured out survival. We also witnessed and sometimes bore the scars of how they responded to suffering. We were there when they drank, when they yelled at each other, when they used their fists or slammed doors, when they schemed and overworked, and when they sank into hopelessness. All of that was an education. It molded us and taught our tiny child bones instinct and survival. We were learning and processing, to an extent, exactly what our caretakers were learning and processing. Hence, reclaiming the parts of us that have been uglified by systems of oppression doesn't mean pointing our finger at our parents for being solely, or even primarily, responsible for who we are.

It means recognizing that we are all doing our absolute best with what we have and what we know. It means leaning into compassion for our parents, as they are both survivors and victims of oppression, and recognizing that the violence and uglification they may have relayed upon us is symptomatic of the world they were navigating, the lack of care they received, the uglification they suffered from, and the violence they endured.

If we are committed to the work of fighting uglification and reclaiming ugly, ultimately we have a responsibility to try to understand the circumstances and systems that uglified our parents because those are the systems that hurt and uglified us, and they are people as well. If you are a survivor of child abuse, incest, or molestation, I am not requesting that you empathize with the people who may have violated or endangered you. I'm certainly not demanding that you forgive them. But attempting to understand what they experienced and why they made the choices they made can help you create a blueprint for what better, healing, and reclamation means to you. It can be the education that will finally end the cycle of uglification and intergenerational trauma.

---

## BREAKING PATTERNS AND HEALING FORWARD

One of my best friends renamed herself Annah Anti-Palindrome shortly after her mother passed away from an addiction that caused so much hardship in Annah's, her siblings', and their mother's life. But even in her pain and rumination, I have never heard Annah shame her mother or her mother's addiction. She discusses it with care and compassion. She recognizes that her mom's using was a strategy that she—lower working class, Jewish, living in a predominantly white, Christian, rural town—used to cope with antisemitism, lack of resources and support, and surviving sexual assault and intimate partner violence.

When Annah found herself falling into the same practices of survival that stole her mother from her, Annah decided that the palindromic cycle of familial struggle and addiction ended with her. Choosing to uglify and demonize her mother for the way she handled her own pain, even though it hurt Annah as a child and as an adult, would not have ended Annah's legacy of pain or have created space for the magic of her future. It was compassion, curiosity, forgiveness, and love that ended that legacy and allowed Annah to create something else.

Annah wrote a collection of poetry about her personal reclamation of self and family called *DNA Hymn*. *DNA Hymn* was healing for so many rural feminists and queers who faced similar experiences with personal and family addiction and trauma, including and especially herself. I like to imagine that it was healing for her mother's spirit as well. Annah's story reminds me that centering our individual healing can create avenues of healing for so many other people. Liberation is truly the gift that keeps giving, and art that is rooted in love saves lives every day.

## Self-Love, Romantic Love, Platonic Love: We Are Worthy of It All

Earlier I told the story of how, in my early twenties, I fell passionately in love with a woman who, shortly after our first anniversary, began to assault me physically, emotionally, and sexually into submission. We eventually broke up, and after a gruesome and extended period of mourning and several years and thousands of dollars of therapy, I hit the dating scene—heart wide open—ready to fall into the queer partnership of my fantasies. Only this time, violence free. It took me forever to realize this, but that was where I made a naïve yet critical error—one that I know I'm not alone in making.

I internalized this idea that because I had done the tedious labor of, and spent a ridiculous amount of money on, healing from my trauma and abuse, I was finally ready for the healthy, 'til-death-do-we-part, communication style–aligned relationship that self-help/self-betterment/romance-driven/popular-media literature told me I'd achieve. I swallowed the subliminal pill that a loving, easy partnership would be my guaranteed reward for doing the hard work of getting better and getting ready. But I neglected to consider how that healing process and paradigm wasn't even created for people like me, or the sort of relationships I wanted, in the first place.

In my reaching this supposed place of being "healed and partner-ready," I didn't know to anticipate the different traumas my partners would bring, and the traumas I didn't even realize I had, and how all those traumas would collude. I neglected to consider how most of my therapists were white, middle-class or wealthy, monosexual cis women with graduate school degrees from institutions covertly practicing principles steeped in white-supremacist, capitalist, patriarchal, heteronormative, cisnormative, and other status quo–centered models of thought.

Meanwhile, my partners were Black—like myself—sometimes mixed-race and intercultural, predominantly poor or working-class, nonmonogamous, MaGe, and politically-radical-as-fuck artists and intellects. And like me, they were trying to figure out how to love themselves and others when models of nontraditional, queer, Black love are still so limited. I was using a system that inherently informs our collective marginalization to facilitate healing, wellness, and a readiness to romantically partner—and didn't even realize it. Nor did I realize that played a significant role in perpetuating the hurt and confusion I felt when things didn't work out the way I was taught to believe they would. And believe me, things were not working out.

In fact, after a few stumbles and hurt feelings too many, I decided to sit my lovelorn ass down and examine some of what I perceived to be the bruises I gathered along the way. At the time, I had what I thought of as the spirit-rash left over from the woman who told me she didn't actually find me attractive or desirable—after living in my house, letting me take care of her, and boning the heck out of me for a little over a year.

I also still had the lingering blood gush from the radical feminist of my dreams who, in her attempt to practice anti-oppression, unintentionally used her wicked-smart tongue to highlight every rhetorical mistake I ever made, who compared me to the most deliciously gluten-y bread in existence (she was gluten intolerant), and who sliced me into a few fresh shreds of heartache. And of course I had the many missing chunks of gut left over from that beautiful bawse, the one I loved with like no other before, who rode through my life like some warrior god/dess of hurricanes and, probably with the intention of fixing my faults, painfully picked at all the trauma scabs I thought I addressed and healed ages ago.

But after an exhausting period of finding and naming wounds, pointing fingers, reliving over and over again every single way I had ever felt harmed by a lover, and forgetting all the sweet times we shared in the face of my heartbreak and disappointment, my hands got cramped and gnarled with a resentment so unfamiliar, so bitter, that I stopped recognizing my own reflection. Y'all know that Erykah Badu song "Bag Lady" about the person who folks run from because of all the bags from yesterday she is still carrying? Yep, that was me.

Rather than recognizing that sometimes people are just incompatible and things don't work out, I perceived myself to be someone who was being repeatedly harmed by people who hadn't done their healing work . . . like I supposedly had. And as a result, I was angry. I was full of blame. And I was a drag—even to myself, perhaps especially to myself—and I wanted my life back. I knew something needed to change, immediately, so I started asking questions:

- What was going on internally that led me to continue to not only choose but go out of my way to wine, dine, and romance people who, in hindsight, seemed so clearly incompatible with me?

- What led me to passionately desire partners who, at best, didn't deeply appreciate who I was and, at worst, were actively antagonistic, hostile, and violent toward me?

And although those were great questions to look inward and question myself, I didn't yet trust myself, so I accepted outside answers—answers that I didn't actually solicit.

Acquaintances who barely knew me, a few occasional friends, and (sometimes) even relatives had the solutions to my spiritual pain and disconnection. I encountered all the answers—beautiful, wise, brilliant advice, *so* generically one-size-fits-all—a million times, repeatedly, on every single Facebook post, Tumblr meme, and in every country western song ever created about why hearts break, what makes relationships go astray, and why some of us take a long time to heal once they're over.

Supposedly those deeply painful partnerships were reflections of what I thought about myself. I had to learn to love and cherish myself before anyone could love and cherish me in return. I obviously needed to learn to become the woman I wanted to attract. Intimate partner violence and toxic relationships take two to tango, so, according to this pop-psych advice, it was time to stop acting like a victim and acknowledge that I was a co-creator in my own history of abuse. And according to a few, I needed to make Jesus Christ my personal Lord and Savior and trust him to take the wheel (inside my vagina) and steer me to greener pastures.

The answer was clear. I, through the power of Christ (or Iyanla, depending on who I was talking to), needed to go inward and fix whatever was broken inside me so that I could be a happier person, attract a happy person, and have the kind of partnership that happy people have. Although I completely agree that, outside of the abusive dynamic, I shouldn't have spent so much time pointing my fingers at what my exes did wrong, the problem is with the ultimate theme underlying the advice: that I needed to spend more time looking at myself and what I did wrong, and that peace would come once I made the choice to create peace.

Of course it had nothing to do with the fact that we live in a fake-meritocratic, hierarchal, victim-blaming culture dependent on capitalist myths of individualism that my partners and I had internalized and harmfully projected onto each other and our relationships, even while identifying as conscious queers who were attempting to untangle ourselves from those violent messages.

It had nothing to do with the fact that so few of us learn vulnerable, compassionate, and accountable truth-telling strategies to help us process through moments of confusion, hurt, and disconnection. And you know that all those toxic, compulsive trajectories of monogamy and what partnerships are supposed to look like had absolutely no role in influencing how I treated my partners, how I allowed them to treat me, and what I believed that I deserved.

So these conversations and suggestions led all my internal brain fingers to, once again, point back at me and what I needed to change. And even though I could recognize the subtle and overt victim-blaming a mile away, I still swallowed those messages whole, making myself even more emotionally despondent. I didn't know what other healing options I had, where else to find a sense of power and agency, and how to create a dynamic that would not only eradicate the pain but also make sure it never returned. So I took the self-deficit way out that society and pop-psychology spoon-feeds us all: I looked to myself for shame, blame, and punishment.

I told myself that all those people and their writings were correct, that I was manifesting pain in my life. I convinced myself that every romantic failure—including the ones ripe with violence and abuse—was because of my not loving myself appropriately, of my not being the best version of myself possible. And suddenly, under the guise of healing, growth, and so-called accountability, I started to pick at myself with even more vicious venom than any of the people who had hurt me before had. In fact, I began to center their opinions of me and used their critiques as a basis for what I needed to change, fix, and shift about myself.

I did this until I started paying attention to the people around me and realized that I wasn't the only person feeling this way. I wasn't the only one struggling with incessant melancholy, abandonment, and hopelessness. All around me, people were in hidden and muted agony because of feeling disconnected, deprioritized, and consistently violated by both systemic oppression and the loved ones they wanted to trust the most. All around me, people were attempting to find some way to be more slender, more "attractive," more economically successful, more fun, more articulate, and more accomplished to experience a sense of social validation, desire, and inclusion.

The answer to finding compatible partnership, or joy, or healing, is not solely that we *all* need to love ourselves better. I've reached a place where this saying does not make me want to spit tacks, but I want the world to know that it's misleading and completely untrue. This idea that self-love is the one, true answer once again puts the onus for change on the individual. Change is a collective and community effort. Self-love is a part of that effort, but self-love cannot truly blossom without support, care, and nurture from multiple facets. I crave a culture where we hold ourselves accountable to loving ourselves and other people better. Part of loving people better is choosing to divest from ideas and practices that teach people they are unworthy of love and goodness in the moment as they are.

I don't currently have the self-love that I dream of or even that I have had in the past. I am haunted by traumas that I'm working hard to heal, and I don't always feel like I'm winning in the healing process. Still, I am currently partnered with two people who love me deeply, compassionately, and in a way that sometimes jars me most beautifully. They give me random feedback and affirmation that celebrates me for who I am and how I am, including the parts of me that others have critiqued and shamed due to their internalized uglification, ableism, fatphobia, and respectability politics. They encourage me and remind me that it's okay to be myself, that I am worthy of love when I fuck up or struggle, and that I don't have to earn kindness or inclusion through perfection or beauty. They just love me because of who I am and how I love them, regardless of how I'm loving myself in that moment. And I love them for exactly who they are and how they love me.

I don't think the answer is self-love. I think the answer is self-compassion merged with deep care for the people around you. I think it's learning to love yourself in a way that does not come at the expense of the people you love, and choosing people who will love themselves in a way that doesn't come at your expense. I think the answer is allowing yourself to be vulnerable and choosing people who you can safely be vulnerable with; who will love you into greatness and not weaponize your vulnerability against you. Similarly, it's you choosing to not be the kind of person who will weaponize other people's vulnerability and struggles against them.

For me, the answer lies in acceptance. I'm not a perfect person nor communicator and I never will be. That doesn't exclude me from the possibility of healing and empowering communication. Instead, it allows me to have grace for myself and others while committing to trying my best. All we can do, at any given time, is try our best—and our best is an effort that deserves to be celebrated.

When people say "we just need to love ourselves better," they usually mean that better self-love will make us more eligible for a romantic relationship. Though I am a romantic person and enjoy dating and being in romantic partnerships, romantic love is not the only kind of love in the world—nor is it the only kind of love that most of us want and need.

Those of us who are romantic (there are plenty of people who are aromantic, which means they don't want or need romantic love) tend to prioritize romantic love for a few reasons:

- It's the type of love we most see reflected in art, literature, and media.

- Most adults primarily share their emotional energy, financial resources, time, and vulnerability with their romantic partners or spouses.

- Religious dominion and social mores tell us that we should only fulfill our sexual desires within committed, monogamous, heterosexual relationships with people we have married under the supervision of the government and church.

- It's the arena where we'll most likely receive the most nurture, support, and access to intimacy.

- We equate marriage, including sharing a home and bank account, with being grown up and settled down.

These ideals create a romantic or couples supremacy culture and limit our access to the family, love, and care we need and deserve—including the diverse kinds of life-saving love that is available to us. My friend Caleb Luna, a fat liberation scholar and activist, performance artist, and Reclaim UGLY board member, spoke to this in their essay "Romantic Love Is Killing Us: Who Takes Care of Us When We Are Single?" "Romantic love, especially marriage, is politicized and informs how resources, caretaking, and protection is dispensed. It does not have to be this way," Luna says. "We can commit to keeping each other alive despite our sexual capital. We *need* to care for each other to keep each other alive."[2]

## Life-Saving Love Will Fight for Your Humanity

While I currently have partners who love me with more care, intentionality, and pleasure than I ever expected with a romantic partner, it does not negate the fact that some of my most fulfilling, joyful, safe, and longlasting loverships have come in the form of nonromantic, nonsexual partners. For example, my mother, Kandee Rochelle Lewis, pursued every avenue she knew of to illustrate to my younger siblings and me just how much she loved us in ways that we could feel and believe it.

Each time I was sick and hospitalized as a child and adult, my mother was right there beside me, holding my hand, advocating for me, and attending to my every need to the best she could. Her love was so thick that one nurse awkwardly thought she was my romantic partner. That gave us both something to chuckle over—and speaks to the fact that we rarely see, or imagine, adult parent-child intimacy.

My mother loved us free and whole. She never expected us to assimilate to her love language or style of expression. Instead, she learned who we were by paying attention to how we moved and expressed ourselves. Her goal was to support and guide us to be the best, most amazing, and happiest versions of ourselves, not the performative hologrammed mini-me's of respectability and obedience that so many parents expect of their children.

My little sister Malinda Rochelle's love language is quality time, words of affirmation, receiving gifts. My mother sees her multiple times a week, includes her in her plans and schemes as frequently as possible, takes her on trips, and remembers to always set aside things she thinks my sister will appreciate. They don't have to be expensive. They can even be hand-me-downs. What makes them special is that they remind my sister of the fact that she is never alone and not discardable; she's always in my mother's thoughts and prayers.

My little brother Carl's love language is also quality time, words of affirmation, and acts of service. My mother celebrates his every accomplishment, lifts his brilliance and uniqueness, and shows him unlimited empathy and compassion. She strives to love him the way he teaches her he wants to be loved, listens to his hopes and dreams, and believes in his goodness unconditionally.

My love language is words of affirmation and physical touch. Even though I am bigger and taller than her, my mom will hold me in her lap when I come to visit. She will invite me to sleep in her bed with her and big-spoon me all night. She will caress my face, look at me adoringly, and tell me how beautiful I am. When we go out into the world, she and my father hold my hand the same way they did when I was tiny, because I like it. My mom reminds me every time we talk that regardless of how old I get, I'll always be her baby.

Because all three of her children are hams for public praise and adoration, she writes long essays filled with love, celebrations, and pictures for every single birthday. I can ask my mom for anything, and if she has the means, she will give it to me. If she doesn't, she will find a way. I can call her to cry. I can call her to rage. I can call her for advice. I can call her to swoon over a romantic or erotic encounter (though she has added a few boundaries to those conversations). I can call her to process through a conflict or fantasize about a new project. I know that I won't ever have to be lonely if my mother is alive.

Nor do I have to earn her love or jump through hoops to sustain it. I don't hide or repress parts of myself—including my sexual orientation, kinky lifestyle and desires, radical politics, or queer, witchy spirituality. My truth is not an insult to her god or religion, nor is it a rejection of who she is, our shared heritage, or the morals and values her parents taught her. Everything I do, say, and believe is just a beautiful part of the daughter she loves and adores.

As I have aged, the texture of my mother's love has become my romantic and nonromantic standard for intimacy. I rarely feel uglified, insecure, or as if I don't belong in her presence. Though it took a while to get to this place and truly honor how blessed I am to have her, learning to appreciate her love and recognizing just how unique and special it is has taught me how I want to live my life. My mom's love taught me what to ask for, not just what to reject. And I have never, never, never had to reach a mandate of self-love to be the recipient of her love. I just had to be open to receiving it at its fullest, and for a long time, I wasn't. I was focused solely on partnership. I gave my all to romantic partner after romantic partner, and while most of those relationships faded away, my mother's affection toward me never wavered. She has always been my safest place, and I am so grateful to finally be in a place to honor and enjoy it.

I wish a love like hers for everybody, especially those of us who know the deep-spirited angst, loneliness, and neglect that comes from uglification.

## HOW DO YOU WANT TO BE LOVED?

There are so many ways to experience love, intimacy, and care that have absolutely nothing to do with romance. Here are some questions to consider that might open your heart, time, and life up to people who will love you the way you deserve.

- What relationship behaviors feel good to you?

- In whose company do you feel the freest to be your whole and authentic self?

- Whose words and presence empower you to take creative risks or lean into personal exploration?

- When do you feel love from another person so deep in your bones that you don't even question it when they are upset with you, or you are upset with them?

- When have you experienced a love so profound in its behaviors that each conflict leads to increased healing and intimacy as opposed to pain and further uglification?

- Who are the people not related to you or in romantic relationship with you who love you to your very core?

- Who are the people you have the potential to love to their core?

- Who are the people you can imagine sharing your life with, building home and family with, and turning to when you are in need?

---

## Love Is Not a Challenge

When people say "we just need to love ourselves better," they put the onus of change on a vulnerable individual instead of questioning why a person would struggle to love themselves in the first place. When we make people the sole culprit for their suffering, we steward the ideologies that facilitate their suffering. We uglify them while protecting the systems and practices that harm them. Uglification always puts the blame on people, whereas love invites us to ask the questions that will help us create transformation and healing.

Insecurity and lack of self-love is a scapegoat for the violence, neglect, critiques, harassment, rejection, and exclusion that get in the way of people being able to love themselves good and see themselves as someone others will want to love. Low self-esteem is not a personal failure. It is not a status, location, or personality trait. It is a result of our lived experiences. It is a trauma that deserves community care.

The way to address a friend's low self-esteem, insecurity, or lack of self-love is to love them. Spend time with them, go on friend dates, explore what kinds of pleasure and intimacy feel good to you both, purchase or make them gifts, check in on them to see how they are doing, hold them when they're sad, go with them to the doctor or to visit family, treat them with the loving compassion they deserve. Provide an experience within your relationship that doesn't repeat the status quo of who is and isn't worthy of our attention, devotion, and affection. If you are both people who enjoy casual (or not casual) sex, enjoy erotic or kinky experiences with each other. Give each other massages. Wash each other's hair. Uplift, Glorify, Love them with actions and words. But a lecture on whether they need to love themselves more is not what is going to ease the pain or help them understand what self-love can feel like.

We need to experience love and feel secure in that love to truly know how to love ourselves and others the way that we desire; and some of us, because of our past experiences, can't even imagine it. Some of us have been exploited, abused, raped, trafficked, or enslaved in the name of love. We have watched our parents and loved ones die from the hands of abusive partners in the name of love. We cannot assume that everyone knows how to love themselves; we can only try our best to love other people.

Self-love is not a destination or accomplishment to be achieved. It is practice that takes intentionality, time, and the loving and supportive attention of people around us. It is not one-size-fits-all. It is not a universal expression, experience, or way of being. No person can determine how much another person does or does not love themselves, or even whether they love themselves enough. Self-love is not a performance for other people to assess, critique, or judge us by. The behaviors and practices of self-love are not uniform or always easily recognizable. **We learn to love ourselves based on the world around us, the time we give ourselves to self-reflect, and the healing resources and voices we have access to.** The way we love changes as we age, as our bodies and hearts have different needs, as we move in and out of new relationships, jobs, physical locations, access to wealth and resources, and parenthood.

Romantic, platonic, or familial love is not a trophy, and it should not be treated as an award for a set of behaviors or activities, including loving yourself in a way that fits into some arbitrary set standard determined by someone that is not you. Love is not something we earn or compete for. It is not something we receive after pursuing someone long enough or seducing them skillfully enough. It is not something we will get once we lose weight, get plastic surgery, grow our hair back, become financially successful, get a makeover or wardrobe change, or buy a fancy car. It is inherent. People give love, receive love, and are lovable to others for a delicious plethora of reasons, including simply existing.

Whether you realize it or not, you are worthy of love. You are currently loved. You will be loved in the future. People will love you even when you don't like or love yourself, and it is that love that will help you heal.

---

## WE ARE LOVEABLE.

That is a full sentence. But to be specific:

We are loveable for being alive.

We are loveable when we are depressed.

We are loveable when we are sick.

We are loveable when we don't have the resources to care for ourselves.

We are loveable when we are incarcerated.

We are loveable when we are homeless.

We are loveable when we fail or make mistakes.

We are even loveable when we are causing harm.

We are loveable to people who don't understand us or our lifestyles.

We are loveable to some people who have politics that don't support our freedom and safety.

We are even loved by people who don't always like us or what we do.

We are loved by people who don't know how to love us the way we want or the way they want to love us.

We are loved by people who are stuck in their own cycles of violence and trauma.

We are loved by people who don't have the capacity or courage to tell us how much they love us.

We are loved by people who have decided they can't be around us because of our choices and behaviors.

We are loved by people who can't safely tell us how they feel.

We are romantically loved by people who don't want to sleep with us.

We are loved by people who have lustful desires that we'll never know or understand.

We are even loved by people we don't want, folks whose love we've rejected.

---

## Are You Enforcing the Status Quo through Your Relationships?

Not everyone who struggles with self-love or low self-esteem is told that they need to better love themselves to get the love they want. Depression, sadness, and self-harm are sometimes even glorified as their own aesthetic or erotic when the person struggling fits into certain standards of beauty. Those of us who are read and treated as ugly notice this. We see the way some folks are desired and pursued, regardless of how much they do or don't love themselves. We witness the ways men and masculine-of-center people are pursued and adored, regardless of how they treat themselves or the people around them. We are aware of how much grace hegemonically beautiful people are offered when they make mistakes, cause harm, and struggle with trauma and emotion. And we are very aware of the fact that we are not offered the same kindness, support, or opportunity for redemption. When we struggle, are lonely, or have complicated needs, we are told to love ourselves better.

We know that regardless of how many times someone tells us that we need to love ourselves more, self-love has little to do with how other people will treat us and what kind of care they will offer us. When our loved ones repeat this mantra, they reinforce uglification and lookist social hierarchies. They remind us that there is something wrong with us, that we need to be the ones to change, that the world just doesn't care as much about us, that the person speaking to us, to an extent, may be in alignment with that world.

Next time you feel inclined to tell someone that they should love themselves more, consider asking yourself why. Why might this person be struggling to love themselves sufficiently? If you're ready to be vulnerable and really create change, look inward and ask yourself how your own beliefs and actions may contribute to a world where the people around you may struggle with self-love. The following questions may help:

- What sort of people, bodies, and faces do you glorify around your loved ones?

- Who do you direct your romantic and celebratory attention toward?

- What type of people do you always call fine or sexy in public?

- What messages are you giving the people around you, and yourself, when you constantly pant, fawn, and lust over the same types of people?

- Who do you call ugly, as a joke or not? What parts of people's bodies do you belittle, make fun of, or draw negative attention to?

- Who do you say would never have a chance with you based on how they look, their height, their body size or shape, their skin color, their transness or nonbinariness, or their job?

- Who do you describe as "they're nice, but . . ."?

- Are you, inadvertently, illustrating to your friends and loved ones that they are unlovable or undesirable based on the beauty you affirm and the people you dismiss in their presence?

- Do you justify who you prioritize and who you dismiss by saying you have a preference while ignoring that your preference looks just like everyone else's preference?

- Are you crushing on the same people we see plastered on magazines and in music videos?

- Do you date, crush on, or pursue people who look like the friends you believe need to love themselves more?

- Are there strangers you immediately say yes to and some you immediately say no to, solely based on appearances?

- Who are you missing out on, excluding, and dismissing because they don't look like what the world teaches us to want?

- Are you dating or fucking people in secret because you are worried about how people will judge you for your attractions? And what is the impact of that choice?

- What standards of uglification and beauty are you reinforcing for your children, friends, and loved ones?

- What are you teaching yourself about your own face and body?

- Are you resisting uglification and harmful beauty standards?

## Reclaiming Our Sexualities and Desires from Uglification

So many parts of our wild, expansive, and extraordinarily beautiful humanities are uglified, shut down, and policed by other people's morality, fear, and shame. The moon, the stars, the sky, the ocean, the rivers, and all our silenced and repressed MaGe ancestors before us asked me to deliver this message directly to you: fuck shame.

Other people's fear and moral values are theirs, designed to serve their needs, beliefs, and feelings of safety. Propriety and piety are just external standards of suppression coordinated by systems of oppression to keep you small and well-behaved. You get to be as big, as dynamic, as horny, as sensual, and as unapologetically hungry for pleasure and exploration as you want to be. Your relationship to your erotic is yours. No one gets to yuck your yums or your hungers. Your sexuality is yours and worthy of freedom, safety, and abundance at your pace.

You get and deserve to explore the rolling expanse of your flesh as you desire. You get to tease your mind and body into states of arousal that leave you emotionally high, fulfilled, and satiated. You get to chase orgasms if that feels good to you. You get to love, kiss, make out, cop a feel, flirt, tantalize, and romance in all the ways that you and your partners consent to and desire. You get to decide that sex is not what brings you pleasure, and you get to change your mind as frequently as you wish. Do not allow anyone to uglify your asexuality or your process of understanding what sex means for you. You get to be nonromantic and fill your world up with the sweetest of platonic intimacies. You get to cuddle with friends, pets, and stuffed animals all you want. You get to be nonmonogamous and polyamorous. If you have a heart big enough and desire dynamic enough to share them with multiple consenting partners, it's your world and you deserve to live it as you desire. You get to be monogamous and explore the depths and peaks of one love, one romance, one partnered intimacy for as long as you both desire. Do *you*.

If your sexuality is kinky and experimental, grab the ropes, the chains, the latex, the collars, the paddles, the claws, the feathers, and share your safe word as far and as wide as your blissed-out self desires. Exploring what feels good for you and the people you share sex, kink, or sensuality with is a beautiful and liberating thing. If you liked to be called names, regardless of how profane others perceived them to be, please dig deep into the trenches of your feel-good and find the people who will talk to you exactly the way you desire. If you are a dominant who loves to be doted on by luscious submissives who call you Mistress, Master, God-dexx, Sir, Ma'am, and more, be free and keep exploring all your erotic power and leadership. If your greatest desire is to be owned, collared, trained, and in service to a person or a couple you trust, then please don't let any social uglification or misunderstanding keep you from indulging in the beautiful empowerment of honoring yourself and your needs.

If you want to be in a poly triad (a throuple) with two other people who mean the world to you, keep negotiating and creating a beautiful love affair that serves you all and any children you may raise. If you are a tender hedonistic art hippie like me who fantasizes about traveling the world in a luxurious bus or trailer and exploring love, sex, and friendship with whoever moves you, stay honest and respectful, allow your shared bliss to be reciprocal and dynamic, and keep hitting up those sexual health clinics. If you are monogamous and your partner is polyamorous, and you both have figured out how to make it work, don't let other people's insecurities or opinions interfere with your joy parade. Keep exploring what love and freedom means for you and your sweet love. If you want to wine, dine, court, and romance a sweet and tender faerie princess named Vanessa and her gorgeous cuddle daddy mercreature spouse named Eri, find us online, send us food and art, take us on vacations near the water, and play games and karaoke with us, and be respectful.

You have every right to be a slut, to explore every flavor and sensation of sex and attraction that your precious brain can generate. Just be honest and safe with your partners. Don't hurt yourself or other people in the name of pleasure, release, or healing. If you have sexual desires that make you uncomfortable or that might lead to the harm or death of another person, you get to find the professional and emotional support to live your best, most joyful life without hurting other people. There are people who won't judge you but who might have some really good resources and suggestions for ways that you, too, can have a safe, violence-free, erotic life.

Perhaps you are someone who wants to skip romance and be the best possible worker, visionary, artist, parent, or anything ever else you desire. I hope you go all out for your dreams and imaginings. This is also an erotic. If you know you don't ever really want to have sex, but you do it every now and then because you love your partner and they want sex, keep making choices rooted in your joy, happiness, and self-advocacy. If you don't desire sex and you've met another person who also doesn't desire sex, y'all's all-night cuddling sessions are no one's business but yours—unless you choose to share. It's more than okay to explore your erotic alone, with robots, dolls, toys, pornography, or anything else that makes you happy and keeps you and others safe.

Being ashamed of who we are and what we crave does not serve our safety and protection. It does not keep us from getting raped or becoming rapists. It is not a statement about our moral character, an assessment about how we deserve to be treated, or a reflection of our self-worth or self-respect. We, and our sexualities, are diverse and deserving of exploration, actualization, and liberation.

Honoring your erotic is honoring the full and whole exploration of you. It is an invitation to visit your brightest bubble of possibility and those dark parts that you might want to love or understand a bit more. Sex, with yourself and others, is a portal, a prayer, and a grounding. It is a place and activity that generates ideas, creativity, self-understanding, and radiantly magical energy. And it, alongside your body and desires, does not belong to anyone but you—not your partner, not your parents, not your church, and not the whispered judgments of your community.

You are yours. Your freedom is yours. Your joy is yours. Your pleasure is yours. Your decisions are yours. Each yes, no, maybe, each uncertainty, curiosity, or kinky craving that flits through the supple matter of your brain and/or genitals is yours. Do not internalize other people's uglification of what's yours to explore and embrace as you choose. Unless you or another person is in danger (and anything nonconsensual is putting someone in danger), invite and encourage them to mind their own business.

Beloveds, do you.

Be you.

Love you.

Enjoy you.

Pursue you.

And try your best to not project your values on to other people. Your desires are not "the" normal. Your preferences are not more objective, universal, moral, or sane than anyone else's. And what turns you on is not problematic (unless you are harming and exploiting others or pursuing sex with children as an adult—if you're having these urges, there are people you can talk to). What's problematic is judging others, attempting to control people who don't want to be controlled, being dishonest with the people who share their body and trust with you, putting others at risk or in danger without their consent, uglifying people's freedom and self-exploration, and shaming their attempts at pursuing and defining their own romantic and sexual liberation.

## For People under Eighteen

Sexuality, desire, and even horniness (giggle) are not limited to adulthood. Your sexuality, body, and desires are beautiful, and they matter. If you are a young person under the care of an adult, I am not advocating for you to break the agreements or rules your parents, school, or caretakers have set up for your safety and well-being. If the adults in your life are asking you to wait, there is a reason for that. As urgent and alive as your desires are, your brain and ability to make decisions that serve your long-term joy, freedom, and safety are still developing. You are vulnerable right now.

But that does not mean you don't get to have an active sex life with yourself. Bless yourself with the space and opportunity to explore yourself and your body autonomously for a while. Figure out what feels good to you, what turns you on, what you don't like in relationship with yourself. Visit educational websites and read sensual and erotic books that honor where you are in your life and enable yourself to reach adulthood as safely as you can.

If you are a young person in a relationship that feels good and safe, and you are ready to take that next step into sexual exploration and desire with a partner, *talk to each other*. Read those same erotic books and visit those same educational websites with each other. Have embarrassing, nerve-wracking, heart-sharing conversations with your sweetheart until you feel like you can talk about anything and everything to each other. You might be surprised, but that deep level of dialogue and emotional vulnerability is an intimacy and lovemaking of its own. So much can happen and unravel in the wonderful world of words, breath, and eye contact.

There is a sensuality to so many parts of our bodies other than our genitals. There is the whisper of breath along our neck. The shiver of a gentle caress to the ear. The marvel of fingers slowly tracing hands, palms, other fingers. There is the magic of storytelling, of taking each other on erotic adventures that don't yet involve touch. There is the trace of a flower petal along the flat or rippled terrain of a belly or the soft part behind our knees. There is the decadence of a foot rub and the erotic feel of a million butterfly kisses along your shoulders.

Young folks, allowing yourselves to move slow, to take your time, to uncover your desires with yourself and then with a lover, to ensure that you are making choices that are truly in service to your precious safety and sexual liberation (which includes abstinence and asexuality as well as sexual expression), is not uglifying or repressing yourself. Quite the opposite, it's allowing yourself to wade into a wonderful world of your own erotic feelings and desires slowly, safely, and confidently. This world is yours. Explore it at a pace that honors your precious magic.

And if you have adults in your life that you trust to truly be present with you and not take advantage of you or uglify you in any way, talk to them. Ask them questions. Tell them about your feelings. Ask for the resources to stay safe—whether those resources include literature, vibrators and other sex toys, condoms, gloves, or dental dams. Reclaiming your ugly does not mean submitting to the binaries of no sex or yes sex, it means blessing yourself with the time, space, and resources to figure out what feels right to you.

## For Parents, Guardians, and Caretakers of People under Eighteen

Start out early with supporting young people to love the parts of their body, development, and desires that others may uglify. This means, first and foremost, do not uglify yourself, your desires, your sexuality, and other people's sexuality and sexual expression in front of them.

Don't kink, sex, slut, or body shame the characters on television or the people in your shared lives. Instead, talk honestly and lovingly with the young people you are supporting and protecting. You may think they are too young for these conversations, but chances are, they are far more exposed to sexuality than you were at their age. They are watching the television and films you watch, and some things you don't watch. They listen to the music you listen to and the music their friends listen to. They are reading books and poems and websites. Our world is filled with so many messages and lessons about sex, not all of them liberating, joyful, or rooted in consent.

Regardless of the gender of your child, when you have loving and honest conversations with them about sex and desire, you can help create a world for them and the people they eventually choose to date, have sex with, and love that is free of rape culture, trafficking, exploitation, lying, abuse, insecurity, body hating, and other forms of sexual violence. Not discussing sex inadvertently uglifies and shames it, as well as the development of our desires and the changes of our bodies. We live in a sexual world and many of us have sexual bodies and desires. Even if we don't, other people will sexualize us. Loving, responsible, and respectful conversations and practices will keep your precious dumpling far safer than silence and performances of innocence.

Let them know that other people, including you, may critique, uglify, fear, and not understand their sexuality or desires. Explore the many ways to navigate that when it happens. Maybe that looks like them choosing not to share information about themselves, maybe it looks like them asking questions of the people uglifying them, and maybe it looks like speaking up for themselves and educating others. Give them as many different tools as possible and the opportunity to practice determining when they want to use which tool given the circumstance.

Talk to them about your values, where they come from, and how they protect your happiness. This doesn't mean conditioning them to embrace your values, but it does mean giving them the tools to engage with your values as well as the tools they need to think critically and expansively enough to decide their own values and to change them as they age and mature. Help them embrace and understand what it means to be curious, to do research, and to ask questions.

As they mature, expose them to sexual ideas, practices, bodies, and genders that are not a part of your household. If you are heterosexual and cis, bring your queer, trans, and asexual friends into your home, and engage in literature and media created by those communities. If you are thin and not disabled, bring fat, disabled, and sick friends over to talk to your children about how they navigate sexuality, especially if you have a fat, sick, or disabled child. Help guide and expose them to bodies, genders, sexual orientations, and lifestyles that reflect their desires and that don't. Help them learn not to become uglifiers of themselves or people different from them. Remind them that all bodies deserve sexual pleasure, not just those that are glorified as beautiful, desirable, and healthy within our cultural imagination.

If you care for a disabled child, or an adult, please remember that you are not in control of their sexuality. Disabled people, including mentally disabled and nonverbally communicative people, also have bodies with sexualities and desires that deserve safe and autonomous (as possible) exploration and actualization. Figure out ways to support the people you care for to articulate and access the pleasure or romance they crave. This might look like hiring an attendant who has experience supporting disabled people to masturbate and express their desires to people with whom they share mutual attraction. It also may look like hiring a sex worker who knows how to create a safe, blissful experience for people who have bodies and disabilities like the adult child you care for. It may look like examining your own prejudices, fears, and anxieties, understanding what they mean and where they come from, and releasing or learning from them to create more space for your child to have a whole and liberated life.

Create opportunities for your child to practice saying no, hearing no, and responding to no in other parts of their lives, alongside opportunities to practice saying yes, asking for what they want in detail, and asking other people for what they want. Explore what it means to create consent culture in your household. Even if these practices are not attached to sexuality, your child will learn and embody consent enough to bring it into their sexual negotiations. If you are raising children who identify as cis boys, this is especially critical. So often the responsibility for sexual safety and avoiding rape is placed on MaGes. Teaching boys the beauty, safety, and pleasure of consensuality will increase their own access to safe and joyful sex, and they will become stewards of that within their friendships with other boys and in romantic relationships with whomever they pursue.

If you are raising children of color, help them understand the way their bodies may be hypersexualized, sexually villainized, sexually targeted, exploited, policed, stereotyped, and fetishized by people of their own ethnicity and others. Introduce them to their ancestral histories of sexual expression and liberation as well as the legacies of oppression and violence within the different cultures and societies they navigate. Help them determine practices that will protect them from white supremacy, misogyny, rape culture, and rape accusations while still pursuing their pleasure, sexual agency, and actualization. Teach them what it means to not allow white supremacy, colonization, and fear to dictate and inform how they relate to their body or consensual connections they have with other people. Help them understand that they have less safety and protection in this country, so it's important that they choose partners they feel safe with, not just partners with bodies and identities our society lifts up as being the most important. Talk to them about intersectionality without enforcing compulsive heterosexuality and cisnormativity on them.

Remember that while you have wisdoms your child is still learning, you also come from a different generation. They may experience a freedom, safety, and awareness that you weren't offered during your sexual development, that perhaps you still feel like you can't access. Learn from your children and from people who experience the world differently from you. You might find yourself feeling a bit freer and more expansive in the process.

Lastly, I understand that having these conversations may be nerve-wracking for you, especially if it is different from the ways your parents and caretakers spoke to you. It's okay to be nervous and unsure. Take your time. Practice being vulnerable with yourself, your partner, your therapist, and even your own parents while or before having these discussions with your children. Explore your own sexual desires, the ones that have scared you, the ones you were taught were not acceptable, the ones that visit you in your dreams or when you feel your most relaxed. If you have the income, purchase sex toys, manuals, literature, and films that take you to places of wild abandon and possibility. If you want to prevent or heal the uglification of your child's relationship to their sexuality and body, you must start with yourself. You are just as deserving.

Feel good, be safe, don't hurt anyone, practice consent, and fuck shame. We are all worthy.

---

## EROTIC EMBODIMENT AND SELF-WORSHIP EXERCISE

Practice reclaiming your body, erotic feelings, and desires from uglification *and* familiarizing your body with the treatment it deserves. This is a private-time writing and embodiment activity. It was designed specifically for people who haven't had much opportunity to access the erotic beauty of their bodies and worship of them in a safe way. Practice this exercise with a friend, partner, or by yourself. Indulge in the glory of your precious and decadent self. Modify this exercise to make it yours. You are worthy.

1. Find a place where you can sit comfortably while writing, and then easily adjust yourself to sit comfortably while deep breathing and meditating.

2. Write down things that you, personally, find beautiful, sensual, erotic, tantalizing, and stimulating about who you are. Silently reread what you wrote.

3. Write down what it feels like to embody your erotic, sensual, and tantalizing self. What does your body and spirit feel like when you are in the throes of pleasure and stimulation, unconcerned about how others perceive you? Silently reread what you wrote.

4. Breathe and relax into a comfortable seated position for your body. Allow your root and groin to guide how you align the rest of your flesh, including your spine. Gently rock. Keep breathing nice and slow.

5. While rocking, take your time and sign your list, read it aloud, or listen as your communication device reads it aloud. If you are reading, enunciate and fully breathe into each word you say. Feel where they are the most alive and activated in your body, where they build the most tantalizing and concentrated energy. Share that energy with your root, your groin, your fingers, and your tongue.

6. Once you are done reading, soften your eyes, go inward, and stay with the succulent energy of your words. Keep breathing nice and slow. Allow your muscles and body to soften and become as open and relaxed as possible.

7. Invite your divine, erotic energy to become a part of your breath, your skin, and your crown.

8. Keeping your eyes closed and continuing to rock, try to open your groin and root more and more with each back-and-forth rock. Allow your groin and root to breathe, in and out, alongside your breath.

9. Starting with your feet, if possible, or the lowest part of your body that you can reach, begin to gently caress and massage yourself and slowly work your way up. Spend time with each part of your body that you touch. Affirm its beauty, its sacredness, how much pleasure and joy it brings you, its importance

to you. Whisper the sweet nothings you deserve to be told every day.

10. As you caress and embrace yourself, breathe and feel the erotic energies that you wrote about earlier moving underneath your skin. Remember that this energy is a power, a force, a resistance against the uglification of your body, and a pleasure. You are a treasure worthy of worship, exaltation, and adoration.

11. Remember that you, as you are, are a masterpiece. Any hands that touch you, including your own, need to know and move like they are touching God.

12. While breathing and rocking, say out loud or sign five times: *This body of mine deserves to feel good and cherished.*

13. Say out loud or sign five times: *This body of mine is beautiful and feels so good to touch and explore.*

14. Say out loud or sign five times: *I love myself so much.*

15. Say out loud or sign five times: *This body of mine is perfect exactly as it is and I love it.*

16. Say out loud or sign five times: *I love myself so much.*

17. Say out loud or sign five times: *I am worthy of all the glory and all the praises.*

18. Say out loud or sign five times: *I am not too much. I cannot get enough of myself.*

19. Say out loud or sign five times: *I am sexy and beautiful. I love myself so much.*

20. When you are ready, start breathing normally again. While you may keep your hands on your body in a way that feels comforting, stop rocking, open your eyes fully again; if you are seeing, take your time to look around. Notice the texture, colors,

beauty, and erotic in your environment, even the things you'd normally consider to be mundane. Remember that the erotic is divine, not just sex, and that divinity is power. Seeing the erotic around you is embracing that power.

21. If you can, stand up at your own pace or settle into your mobility device. Feel your power. Keep your root and your groin open and breathing.

22. Move around your space. Allow your divine energy and curiosity to guide you. Touch the objects you encounter. Caress them. Smell them. Breathe them in. Taste what feels safe to you. Notice the beauty you recognize and the experience.

23. Remember that you determine how to recognize beauty with your senses and perception. Remember that your body is a universe of its own, not a scribe to be dictated beauty and sexuality. Remember that this earth is your playground, and your body is a portal to bliss. Remember that you can carry this energy, passion, erotic feelings, and freedom you may be experiencing anywhere and everywhere with you. Remember that you are free, that you love yourself, and that you are worthy of feeling good and sensual in your flesh.

# Imagination Is the Ultimate Weapon against Uglification

One of the juiciest and most joy-inducing terms I've ever encountered in the liberation movement spaces is *radical imagination*.

This concept is decadent to me, so filled with unapologetic hope and breathtaking possibility. It feels like a step away from the trigger and pain of reactionary politics (when we organize solely in response to the structural violence and disenfranchisement that is currently and has historically been harming, oppressing, and killing us), and several steps closer to the empowered erotic of establishing a collective vision of the world we actually want to experience and collaborating across difference as well as within affinity coalitions to achieve and taste that vision in our lifetime. Radical imagination is a healing-informed praxis that helps us recover from the impacts of oppression, violence, and other traumas in the moment. It's the exploration of self-ordained wellness and pleasure, which is revolutionary and redeeming for those of us stuck in the spirit-draining muck of constantly encountering and analyzing the pillars of our own disenfranchisement and emotional exigency.

Reactionary politics and persistent oppression analysis are as contagious and virulent as a shame spiral, and similarly ineffective when it comes to personal healing and collective visioning. It is a trauma leash that squeezes tighter and tighter with each reflection. We want to understand what we experienced, and so we dig into it, paint it around our present and future selves like creative researchers at their most vigorous, dissecting each lash, analyzing each wound, until it completely consumes our lives and colors every person and incident we encounter. It teaches us how to be and transforms the beauty, the whimsy, and the magic that could have been into burning rage.

This is the slow, seeping uglification of our future, of community members and associates who might very well be our allies and potential friends, of the outrage and demands of people who experience even more uglification than us, and sometimes even of the beautiful expression of other people's chosen freedom. This uglification is a coping and defense mechanism that shape-shifts simple misunderstandings into community-ripping conflicts, spreading rumors and social media call-outs like wildfires in a California summer. It makes gentle people think violence is their only option. It makes butterflies want to cut their wings. It makes us devastated and terrified enemies of our own liberation. I believe that radical imagination, and its reclaim ugly cousin, transformative inclusion, is the antidote.

*Transformative inclusion* is what happens when creatives, writers, organizers, artists, educators, administrators, culture and structure builders, media creators, policymakers, medical professionals, child-rearers, bankers, and anyone else in a supervisory or service position decide to step away from the status quo and jump off the reform train; they instead use their brilliance, leadership, and platform or position of power to dissolve any exclusive aspect of their project, practice, or organization and transform it to be not just inclusive but liberating for all. Transformative inclusion is a massive and courage-demanding aspiration. It requires participants to recognize and publicly acknowledge that they benefit from someone else's oppression, exclusion, or uglification and to denounce it with actions. Our culture is accustomed to performances of political care.

We have Memorial Day and so many gorgeous monuments to our fallen soldiers, and yet we've made no significant effort to end war or to create a military culture that strives for healing over vengeance and slaughter.

When it comes to the personal work of reclaiming ugly and eradicating uglification, radical imagination encourages us to envision what consistent joy, safety, resource security, and societal inclusion might feel like and to turn that into our liberatory blueprint, which is such a phenomenal, uplifting, and non-draining (because regardless of how pure and beautiful the goal, fighting *is* exhausting) weapon to combat uglification.

For example, consider class mobility. *Class mobility* is utilizing acquired skills and resources, alongside making lucrative connections, to increase your income, raise your tax bracket, and have access to what folks born into more privilege than you have. It's a capitalism and meritocracy mirage show, fireworks and all. Class mobility functions to elevate and tokenize a few marginalized outliers, making the machine of capitalism seem like it's functioning for the greater well-being of everyone and effectively gaslighting those who suffer from poverty and various glass ceilings into believing their inability to climb up the money ladder is their fault. Radical imagination is dreaming up a different system of food production and resource sharing so compelling in its abundance and so feel-good in its functionality that people inherently gravitate toward it instead of the capitalistic idea of class mobility, leaving the whip where it belongs, in a defeated and desecrated past.

As a Black girl, born to semi-radical parents in the '80s, who went to small Christian schools actively invested in Black liberation, I find that the imaginative scope I was exposed to was solely in response to where we as Black people have been and the strategies we used to survive—not all the miraculous places we had the potential to be. Our praxis continually justified that we deserved to have what we perceived white and affluent people to have just as much as they did: safe and pristine communities, competitive educations, and economic ease.

This ideology is a threat to the contemporary and evolving radical Black imagination because the privilege of whiteness and affluence was birthed on the backs of our ancestors' suffering, and nest eggs of trauma are still crusted in our own spinal subconsciouses. Oppression colonizes our brains, mines them of their genius and brilliance, and teaches us to celebrate our ability to thrive in complacency to or surpass projects that exploit and degrade most of us to privilege a small few.

I wasn't taught to imagine models of existence free from the violence of white supremacy. I was taught to survive white supremacy, to figure out how to understand it, and to use that system for my benefit. For example, I learned early on how to avoid the police and how to respond if they came for me, not to imagine a life without police violence or abuse, much less how to strategize to get there. I learned the importance of going to tutoring and dedicating as many hours of my day and night to my grades as possible, not to talk to my teachers about creating academic environments that made learning accessible to and enjoyable for me. I was reminded of how to talk and dress in mixed company so that I didn't give men the wrong impression, not that rape and sexual assault are grave crimes against humanity that can and should be addressed through cultural change and community-building strategies. These beliefs and social training about how to not succumb to the reaching arms of oppression are known to most as *respectability politics*. They put the levy of survival in the hands of the people most targeted and only give them the spike-studded tools of the systems already weaponized against us.

Respectability politics polish our brains smooth of dissent, and reactionary politics render us submissive bedfellows to our most victimized and unchanneled anger. Both are a subconscious masochism, a slow and suicidal massacre of the radical Black imagination. Embracing capitalism as a respectable strategy for freedom teaches us to think small, to focus solely on ourselves and our families, to embrace the timid thralls of succeeding amid mediocracies. Reactionary politics protects the patriarchy— the culture of male dominance, leadership, and supremacy. It protects white supremacy by allowing white ideology to determine what we fight toward and what we fight against. It relies on the cultural and religious values our ancestors were forced to embrace to stay living. Embracing reactionary politics pillages our emotional well-being, tramples us with competition, exhausts us with constant and unwavering stress, and turns our comrades and allies into enemies. Tearing things down, even things that desperately need to be destroyed, is a short-term and unsustainable quest.

I am not an anarchist. We need systems, structures, and processes to support our survival and wellness. We just don't need the systems that exist in our current governmental and social stronghold. Those systems, like prisons, the death penalty, policing practices, credit lenders, and banking institutions, are relics of slaughter, devastation, and exploitative economies that keep on killing. Striving to not succumb to them or pandering to the hopelessness of people afraid to imagine something different does not heal their impacts or mollify other transgressions that hurt and uglify us. We need to cultivate our ability to dream. We need models built from our most hopeful and liberatory imaginings. Some of these exist but are smothered by the sensationalist stories spoon-fed to us through our daily social and news media dosages. Extraordinary stories of mutual aid, resource sharing, and revolutionary healing strategies are overcast by the terrified white imagination of militarized Black looters and pregnant, gun-wielding illegal immigrants.

While these fears are not limited to people with white bodies, they prevail because of how so many of us have internalized some nuanced tendril, big or small, of white supremacy. They are familiar. Then some radically imaginative models only exist in conversation, in bedroom journals and Facebook statuses. These ideas are untapped by the masses because their owners exist in bodies sometimes devalued by their own communities.

In California's Black community, so many of the faces of spiritual, educational, political, and even radical leadership share a similar skin color, hair texture, cisgendered expression, and body shape. Theirs are the bodies and voices we trust because we were socialized to see them, in their adjacency to white validation, as leaders, as safe, and as desirable. Their skin and presentation are less linked to the uglified stereotypes of darker skin, Afro-Indigenous features, fatter bodies, and disability, so they haven't had to imagine liberation in the same ways as people who experience more intersecting forms of oppression. This doesn't mean they don't understand racism or oppression; it means they haven't had to navigate the same struggles from within their marginalized communities, and hence, they haven't been forced to learn to love themselves or understand others with the same critical voracity.

Liberating our radical imaginations, regardless of which groups we mobilize with, invites us to see, hear, and dream beyond the colonial norms of beauty and propriety established early on by systems of dominance and hierarchy. When it comes to the Black radical imagination, it means unpacking colorism, lookism, fatphobia, and ableism to explore the thoughts and ideas made invisible and suffocated by internalized oppression and respectability. As a larger, fat, darker-skinned, queer Black woman, I have had to imagine myself beautiful and worthy of respect even though I have been told, throughout my entire life, that I am less worthy of care, protection, love, and of being heard—both within and outside of my marginalized racial group. Because of the systems we live in, queer people like me are less likely to escape their cis-heteronormative households and find love, acceptance, desirability, and a chosen family in the queer liberation landscape. Because of these systems, I am highly unlikely to be a chosen and adored representative of body positivity.

Because of these truths, I, like so many others in my shoes, have stepped into leadership to create spaces and environments where people like us can feel welcomed, cared for, and included. The more intersectionality marginalized we are, the greater mind work, creativity, and community building we must undertake to sustain ourselves. The spaces I have created that center the inclusivity, leadership, and comfort of the most intersectionality marginalized community members have been transformatively healing and uplifting for all the people who participated, regardless of race, age, gender, or sexual orientation. The radical imagination of those with the most uglified bodies is an untapped superpower that might leave oppression and stewards of oppression with something unfathomable to reckon with, much less fight.

Many of us have figured out methods of joyful existence independent of the validation of a social system we already know embraces certain bodies and experiences at our expense. We have realized that we live better lives when we bond together for our collective well-being rather than competing for scraps. We have created our own feast halls and constructed our own standards of courtship and desire, love and family making, health and wellness. We have engineered a community, economy, and entertainment like one I've never experienced before. It's a magical realm that has opened my heart and brain to all I have to offer, all that I can create, all the ways that I can be and become, and it feels so good that I want to share it with the rest of the world with a fierce and passionate determination.

This is not an endeavor rooted in capitalist profit or power gain. I don't have a product or service to sell. *But* I know that if more people learned to love themselves and others the way that I have learned to love myself and others, we would have a much more caring, compassionate, and nonviolent world. I know that a world that can accommodate bodies like mine, bodies like my friends' who use mobility devices, thought processes like those of my autistic friends, families like those that belong to my trans and nonbinary parent homies, and a vigor for communication access like that of my Deaf and hard-of-hearing beloveds is a world where we can all prosper. I know that a world in which all Black and Indigenous families can eat well and have a sacred connection with the earth is a world where *all* families, even those of the most viscerally violent of white supremacists, will be eating well—and maybe less stress and fear might lead to fewer reasons for hate. I know that within my survival, in the survival of undocumented migrants, in the survival of sex workers, in the survival of unhoused folks, in the survival of super- and infinifat people, in the survival of all our disabled siblings, and in the survival of the entire LGBTQIA+ spectrum lies a brilliant answer to so many of the world's stressors, and as such, our imagination transports us the liberation we all deserve.

To my fellow survivors of isolation and ostracization, we have a powerful magic that needs to be revered, explored, and utilized. Now is the time to dream and create, among each other and willing beloveds, a world where we can joyfully thrive in the moment. Our hopeful, rested, and pleasure-centered imagination is one of the most extraordinary weapons against uglification we have. Our ability to see our beauty and worth in a world that keeps telling us how unwanted we are holds the spiritual resilience and creative potency of religion. It can mastermind culture. Your imagination *needs* and *deserves* to be fierce, bold, and unapologetic. We already know that what has been does not work, and we cannot allow the ghost of fear to terrorize us out of our power. Unleashing your imagination and engaging with people who will listen to, respect, and collaborate with your offerings is a fight for our collective freedom; and it is a fight that leaves no broken bodies or rivulets of blood streaming down our streets. It is root and regeneration over machine gun and manipulation. Trust yourselves and surrender to your brilliance. You, me, *we* are the antidote to uglification.

We can tap into, explore, and release our radical imaginations in so many ways:

- Examine the sorcery you're already undertaking.

- Determine where you see the greatest exchange of love and care in your community.

- Pay attention to when your joy and sense of comfort are most activated.

- Search for and honor time to rest and nurture your emotional, spiritual, and embodied wellness.

- Feed your brain and body the company of other people pursuing collective liberation, especially those who also have uglified bodies.

- Allow your body to move at the pace of its own joy and access.

- Explore being untethered by fear.

- Center indulging in the creative and performance art of inter-sectionality-marginalized people.

- Explore the beauty and erotic of other people whose bodies have been uglified by oppression.

- Choose relationships on the basis of who makes you feel like the safest, most magical versions of yourself.

- Journal and archive your own ideas and thoughts.

- Meditate to connect with your intuition and desires.

- Create your own performance, visual, or literary arts.

- Step into leadership as frequently as you can, and create structures and systems that you and all your friends can navigate with joyful ease.

- Employ curiosity instead of defensiveness.

- Move at the pace of your pleasure and the pleasure of everyone you collaborate with.

- Instead of asking how people will respond to your choices, ask how people will be affected.

I know that we can co-create experiences of joy and inclusivity that transcend way beyond ourselves, our family units, and our local or chosen communities. I know we can create peace and access with the same rigor and comprehensiveness that we've created commerce and government. And I know, without question, that my belief in a humanity that creates systems and structures of care is just as pragmatic as it is optimistic. We are brilliant and capable of far more than our current circumstances have taught and allowed us to imagine.

Can you imagine what we could create, dream, and do if we trusted ourselves and supported each other, if we did not believe in the ideology or concept of ugly? I want us all to reclaim the ability to enjoy our lives, our time on and with this earth, and our relationships with each other. This means we need a dynamic and unparalleled transformation.

It means we need to learn to have everything we want and need without monetizing other humans. This means reclaiming our brilliance from the coercion of oppression. Can we imagine developing systems of love and inclusion with the same attention to detail and fervor as the scientists who developed nuclear bombs? What if all of us who had these visions invested in collectives of liberatory scientists and engineers as much as we invest in politicians?

Concretely, this means that everyone has access to safe housing, whole foods, and joy regimens, regardless of their income, education level, or employment status. It means that all parents can raise their children without worrying about how to fund their child's life and growth. It means that people can choose careers or other forms of societal/ global contributions that are accessible to how their unique brain and body works, their differing needs for rest, their family obligations, and of course their creativity and pleasure. It means that we can commute to wherever we need to go and know that our city's infrastructure was designed to accommodate all our bodies, regardless of size or disability. It means that people contribute to an economy that supports everyone's ease and survival, as opposed to strategizing how to profit off each other and have more than the next person. This is a world where people don't have to worry about rejection because of how their body looks or what they are wearing, because of who and how they choose to love or make love, or even because of the amount or type of labor they are able to produce. It means that all people get access to healthcare providers and educators who genuinely care about their holistic wellness and who are trained, supported, and offered the spaciousness to build authentic relationships with the people they serve.

Can you imagine going to the doctor, to school, or to work and knowing that you will be seen and cared for as an individual, rather than as a number, an illness, a means toward an end, or a representative of someone's prejudices and assumptions? Can you imagine having the spaciousness and encouragement to learn who you are and what you believe and to be able to shift and change as you gain more knowledge and life experience—as opposed to being taught what to believe, how to exist, and how to participate in systems that don't serve your joy, wellness, relationships, and the earth? Can you imagine having a relationship with your elders or local leaders/stewards where you can ask questions, negotiate your needs and desires, and know they have the means and desire to spend this time with you? Can you imagine not being pressured, shamed, or threatened into behaviors and beliefs that harm, violate, stagnate, or repress you and all your magic? I believe this is possible.

I imagine a world where there are more gardens filled with well-cared-for fruit, herbs, vegetables, and living animals than concrete and metal shopping malls. In this world, we aren't afraid of losing the sort of jobs that make only a small few wealthy, because we have decided that we care more about each other and the planet than the systemic capitalism we've been taught to think of as the "real world." We have stepped into our collective power and pleasure and have imagined and explored economies that allow us to live the lives we self-determine to be good, moral, and accessible. In this world, people get to tend to the gardens and animals if that's what they love and to know that their community will ensure they have all they need. Here people get to imagine earth-friendly sewage, cleaning, and recycling systems that honor our oceans, rivers, lakes, wetlands, and rainforests without pushback from billionaires who care more about money than the lives of the people who make their money. Others get to maintain those systems in a way that truly honors their physical and emotional well-being and not carry the stigmas that classism or corporatism teaches us to apply to certain types of employment. In this world, artists, healers, nurturers, educators, and joy-makers are recognized as the exquisite treasures they are—because joy sustains us and keeps us going.

I believe that if we move away from compulsory ideas of success and achievement, of what good work is, and of equating certain work with certain worth, we will find that people can create dynamic and sustainable economies that save lives. We will live longer and get to genuinely enjoy our bodies. We will realize that we don't need policing (as we have experienced it thus far) because we have learned that a culture that feeds, shelters, and supports the self-actualization of all its members *is* the antidote to violence, crime, poverty, cruelty, exploitation, and struggle. This is a world where people know they are valued and cared about, both by the way other people treat them and by the systems they navigate. A world where people see other humans as friends, family, neighbors, collaborators, and equals, not as a means to an end, as competition, or as a threat they need to overpower and control.

I imagine a world where people are encouraged to be curious as opposed to being judgmental or standardizing their thinking and opinions. When we can slow down to research or ask questions, to self-reflect, and to think critically as opposed to assimilating into and complying with narrow standards and expectations of what is normal or respectable, legal or illegal, appropriate or moral, we tend to make more loving, compassionate, and generative decisions. We think toward solutions and possibility rather than punishment and limitation.

Feelings get to be seeds of possibility to nurture, museums and library archives of ourselves and our surrounding world to explore, and ingredients that lead to creative and social masterpieces. Our feelings are the stirring spoons of imagination and truth. Don't they deserve the space to blossom, to take up space, to mature, and to reveal themselves? Don't we deserve the space to understand our feelings, to listen to and learn from them, to know how to take care of them so that they don't lead us to hurting ourselves and others? Feelings are a brilliant intelligence that should be harvested, not set to the side for the sake of productivity or systemic norms.

Similarly, imagine a world where the systems we create also get the space to grow and evolve as we grow and evolve, and that these systems water the soils of human survival—as opposed to causing people to bend over backward, struggle, and run at a pace that their hearts-brains-bodies cannot accommodate. Imagine a world where the systems are failures rather than people being failures. Imagine a world where no one is ever told or led to feel as if they were a failure ever again.

I imagine a world where no one believes that they are ugly; where no one feels unwelcome or unsafe; where no one has the urge or inclination to uglify another person; where everyone knows they are loved, held, and capable of healing and forgiving. I believe in us, and I believe in what we can create.

## Forgiveness as a Path to Healing

The last few years of activism culture has seen many arguments about the merits and dangers of what some people call cancel culture, call-out culture, or accountability processes. I believe that everyone needs to be heard to heal, but not everyone needs to have a platform. People who use their platform to uglify others, cause harm, or gaslight the people they have hurt are sustaining the power of patriarchy, and that power must be eliminated. But unless those people are murdering, trafficking, abusing, or otherwise abetting in the structural exploitation and subjugation of others, we cannot uglify them out of their humanity or their capacity to reclaim ugly. Some people, power-backed or not, are absolutely dangerous to humanity, and those folks need to be handled. Some people, however, are stripped of their own survivorship, nuance, and humanity in the process of a mob-based accountability. This is also a form of uglification. Reclaiming ugly means meeting ourselves and others in the messy nuance oppression and all its symptoms.

Canceling individuals and other offsets of uglification don't address the problem of systemic or interpersonal violence, they exacerbate the problem. It's the systems and practices that facilitate the dangerous beliefs harmful people spew and enact that need to be banned. And those systems and practices are sustained by all sorts of people—including those of us disenfranchised by them. Systems, structures, and institutions are nothing without people, so addressing structural issues without creating the space, tools, resources, time, and incentive for people to heal, change, and then decide what will be best for their wellness will achieve nothing but chaos and a re-creation of the power dynamics we already know.

To my Black, Indigenous, and people of color siblings and loved ones reading this book, I pray daily for our healing. I want the systems that have hurt us and our ancestors so badly to burn, and I also know that even if we completely destroy every semblance of the capitalist white supremacy built into every infrastructure of the US, the islands claimed by it, and any other place colonized by European countries, what was done to us will continue to live on in our bodies, on our tongues when we talk to each other, in our semen and wombs when we create and birth each other, through our relationships when we attempt to collaborate with and love each other, and in our own eyes when we look in the mirror. Nothing will change until we take our healing into our own hands.

We need to heal from what was done to us and what we've done to each other. We will only taste liberation by determining that liberation for ourselves, dreaming it, imagining it, painting it, poeming it, turning it into plays and films, songs and novels, and acting it out with every single choice, action, thought, and word we make. We must feed it to our children and friends with our words and caresses, we must rub it into our own flesh to push out the anchored memories of subordinating hierarchies.

White people must also center their healing from centuries of colonial racism, especially those who want to liberate themselves from uglification and the inclination to uglify. White supremacy devastates us all in so many ways. While it is a perpetrator and beneficiary of the uglification of people of color and all the death, grief, trauma, and loss we have experienced because of it, it is also an ancestral and intergenerational trauma response to the economic and monarchal hierarchies of its European motherland.

Because most of us were primarily or solely exposed to history through the archive and gaze of European and eventually white American colonizing experiences in American primary and secondary schools, we know that many Europeans did not just immigrate here for opportunity; they were escaping the class- and religion-based uglifications that sentenced people to poverty and murdered those who stepped out of line. And after suffering the heavy hand of uglification in their homeland, they immigrated to Turtle Island and reenacted the same oppressive dynamics. Colonizers immediately went to war with the people indigenous to this land, as well as their European counterparts, for political and religious dominance, control of trade, and land and water ownership.

Whiteness as an American culture and creation never healed from the trauma of all the oppression and war that poor and oppressed white people from Europe experienced. Instead, white immigrants settled into it. Contemporary white supremacy, from the wealthy white supremacists in government and media to the more apparent ones wearing MAGA hats and KKK robes, is still activated in a war-like crisis for power.

We all need to heal if we want to fight it and survive the fight. Nothing will change until we prioritize and fund healing for everyone, not just the people who can afford the process. Reclaiming ugly, in its grand totality, is about having the audacity, courage, and determination to choose to heal our minds and spirits from the impacts and inclinations of historical uglification in a permanent and strategic way over the false safety of complying with the status quo and all its familiarity and privileges.

White European Americans died for the right to own this land from "sea to shining sea," enslaved six million Black people to cultivate it, killed almost everyone they perceived to be a threat—and they did it all with the force and fear of uglification. Like I mentioned before, most of them were fighting with the urgency of a people desperate to finally taste freedom.

I dream that we—Black and Indigenous people of color who want to finally feel safe and free, white allies who know they can do better than white supremacy, fat and disabled people who are ready to be treated with inclusion and respect, LGBTQIA+ people hungry for the opportunity to be our whole and full selves in every aspect of our lives, MaGes who deserve and demand the chance to finally be perceived as autonomous and treated with equity, and poor and undocumented people fighting for safety and access—that we all *commit* to working together to create the space in which we can heal from what was done to us and what we have done to others.

Unlike systems of white-supremacist and patriarchal oppression, I dream that we use our brilliance to think of ways to create this space without committing genocides, exploding mountains, dropping bombs, and poisoning the earth with radiation in the process. I believe that fighting uglification can only happen if it is an act of togetherness, and that means figuring out how to reallocate the power and money to people who will help us heal from what's happening and work across the deep and damaging divides that centuries and centuries of structural uglification have created both within us and between us.

## Reclaiming Ugly as a Spiritual Practice

While political organizing, protest work, and education can sometimes feel urgent and focused on achievable goals, reclaiming ugly is a practice. Like spirituality, it can't be taught. You can't learn a specific amount of information and become an expert. It must be practiced with commitment and intentionality. The transformation reveals itself, steadies itself, heals us, and opens our hearts and imaginations to our personal magic through the practice. We can't just commit to stop uglifying others. We need community to support us to figure out how to do it in the real world we live in, a world where we get hurt, feel angry, and encounter walls. We need reminders and encouragement when we want to give up.

I have the wording *Reclaim Uplift Glorify Love Yourself* written on a wall in my bedroom. When I am ruminating in my trauma, I try my best to look at those words and remember that they are instructions and not just witty phrasing. I can reclaim my brain back from the trauma. I don't have to uglify myself or internalize the uglification I've experienced. I can uplift myself, remind myself of how worthy I am of compassion and ease, that I don't have to accept behaviors or circumstances that feel hurtful to me. I can glorify myself, see myself as precious and important enough to protect from harm and harmful people. I can love myself, softly, sweetly, and gently through it. I can choose to stop what I'm doing and do loving things for myself in the moment. And when I feel inclined to justify harmful behavior of my own doing, even if I feel wronged by the person I want to hurt, I can ask myself, "Am I in alignment with my spiritual and political values?" I'll admit, there have been times when the answer was "absolutely not," and it tortured me to not do what I wanted to do. I'm human. The answer is not to perform perfection or be a martyr, the answer is try to lessen your own violent footprint in the world.

We have been participating in uglifying beliefs and practices for as many years and decades as we've been alive. Those beliefs and practices are embodied, especially when you have lived thirty, fifty, seventy years. They inform every choice we make and the choices we allow others to make for us. We build community and ritual around them, and use them to determine how we vote, build family, raise children, eat, treat others. It's where we go for guidance. Imagining outside of what we know and what we've been exposed to requires more than a choice, it requires a commitment to those choices, rituals, and community to help with capacity, and a pull toward investment that's bigger than the merits of how capitalism, patriarchy, white supremacy, and ableism privilege you. Consequently, the first step to reclaiming ugly is not studying systems of oppression or other people's ideas of liberation, though this knowledge is important. The first step is choosing to be present, still, and curious with ourselves.

Treating reclaiming ugly as a spiritual practice and commitment has helped me connect with my own source enough to know myself, trust myself, and honor my intuition with choices and actions. I've asked myself the following questions and invite you to do the same:

- If you studied your feelings, desires, and actions with the same commitment that people study religious texts, what would you learn from your morals, values, dreams, standards, and life purpose?

- If you were committed to praying gratitude and love to yourself every morning when you wake up and each evening before you go to sleep, how would that love and gratitude start to take root in your body?

- If your body is a temple, what does it mean to respect yourself as your worshipper? What would you say during a service for yourself?

- What songs of praise and worship would exist in your hymn book, and how often would you sing them? What would they remind you, and how would you use those reminders?

- How would you thank yourself for the blessings and miracles that you make happen in that life?

- What would you perceive to be sin?

- What would be your rituals around birth, redemption, grief, transformation, gratitude, romance, family, and death?

- How would you assess your commitment, actions, and hearts in the process?

- How would you walk your paths in the face of temptation? How would you hold yourself accountable to this walk?

- How would you practice your divine when the world around you makes divinity so hard to access?

- What do you need in order to trust and honor your divine daily?

The discussion of ugly and ugliness is so tender, so deeply connected to self-worth (which I believe is a fragile and delicate thing for many people), and brings up so much emotional nuance that it cannot be divorced from the spiritual or the body. It cannot just be intellect, politics, or demonstration. It requires a vulnerability that must dig past our bones and into our ancestors, our dreams, and our magic. Allowing myself to go toward that spiritual, vulnerable place gave me the courage to share my vision with my community without the pressure to be perfect. It helped me understand what was ego and what was heart, what was fear and insecurity versus an actual reason to pause. It's what kept me from allowing pauses to become full stops. It's what moved me to start healing. It is what holds me steady and accountable enough to return to healing when I lose my way.

## Healing Takes Time; You Are Not in a Rush

It is exceedingly difficult to heal trauma when your oppressors, bullies, and uglifiers are still assaulting you at the knees, the gut, the heart, and through your memories. It is impossible to heal when they surround you, when they call themselves families, friends, lovers, community, and comrades but use the same strategies and practices of uglification that colonized the lives and enabled the deaths of our ancestors. Though we are told that Manifest Destiny has ended, that the Civil Rights Movement is over, that women and MaGes have finally found equity, that we are in a better and more progressive state, that all is untrue. The structures of oppression are still in place, and they have gripped many of us by our necks and our values. We live in a world that actively stands in the way of our ability to release, breathe, and grow.

I say this so you know that if you're struggling with healing, if rage is constantly coursing through your bones and blood, if the hurt and pain of yesterday's hardships and betrayals won't seem to go away—your feelings and struggles are valid. Your rage, in fact, is self-love. It's dignity. It's a conscious respect for yourself and others. It's the rational rage of knowing that you are being slapped and murdered for someone else's pleasure and greed. It's what self-worth looks like when the systems and structures of the world consistently intervene with your ability to actualize your worth and exist, safely, in the wholeness of your humanity.

I don't yet have the answers for how to hold this. I don't know what the solution is to end this continuous and viciously careless violation of humanity and earth, of safety and legacy.

But I do know that none of us deserves it.

I also know that:

> If we recognize the embodied dignity in our anger,
>
> If we gather, frequently, compassionately, and ritualistically in our anger,
>
> If we hold each other in our anger,
>
> If we love each other through our anger,
>
> If we acknowledge and tend to our anger,

If we remember that, despite our anger, *we are not each other's enemies*,

If we sing, dance, pray, play, poem, art, and write our anger,

If we dream and strategize in our anger,

If we meditate with our anger,

If we collectively ask questions of our anger,

If we study and explore our anger,

If we stop uglifying our anger,

Eventually our anger will birth liberation, freedom, and release from the circumstances that facilitate and motivate it.

Our anger will transform into vision and motivation that will surprise and strengthen us. It will help us examine what has been done to address our oppression, what has been successful, what can be successful again, and what we can do to modify it so that it protects our lives, our well-being, and our ability to collaborate toward the creation of something better.

It will rearrange itself and foster the focus and direction we need to nurture our joy and connection. It will become a resource that can introduce us to new, more sustainable tools for protection and toward the triumph of liberation and healing. It will help us have increased grace for each other and a desire to care for and honor both our autonomous and collective selves.

Rage is here to protect our access to joy, to well-being, to self-love, to community, to creativity, to dignity, and to being full and whole. But for rage to do its purpose and fight outward instead of inward, we have to honor the divinity of the joy, well-being, and community we're attempting to protect.

We must create continuous, sustainable, and imaginative spaces for it to exist, heal, and thrive. We must surrender to forward movement, to the frenzy of change, to expansion and self-reflection—even in the midst of everything else happening in the world. We have to be able to command our time and move slowly enough to witness the beauty that continues to exist and persist in spite of uglification, to uplift that beauty as a part of ourselves and our neighbors, to glorify that beauty as a part of the universe, and to love that beauty so much that we protect it with every word we speak, every kiss we honor, every item or service we purchase, every vote we cast, and every choice we make.

When your hackles rise, when your heart starts racing, when you feel rage start to build, when you are unsure about someone's intentions, trust yourself and your intuition. That does not mean you are automatically correct, just as it does not mean you are automatically wrong. But it does mean something is telling you to slow down, to create the emotional and psychic space to assess and reflect, to figure out which questions need to be asked and asked of whom, and to understand what inside you may need more examining and unpacking.

Most likely, you are right—something is happening that you need to better understand, something that's not clear. For me, sometimes simply acknowledging the validity of that sensation is enough, especially when uglification and oppression work so hard to gaslight us out of our truth.

Sometimes I might need to dress my candles with sandalwood and cinnamon and meditate, pray, dance, or beg my ancestors for some answers via my faerie tarot. Sometimes I just need to briefly push the urgency of my worries out of my brain, take a shower or a nap, smoke a joint, microdose some mushrooms, and be shocked when the answer or appropriate question is revealed the next day while I'm walking to the bus stop or making my lunch. Sometimes the answer comes in the middle of a song or a conversation with my bestie, a kiss with my beloved, a stroll around the park.

I often feel the need to figure out a solution and answer for every concern, every bump, every hiccup, every confusion, and every conflict right away. It is the capitalism and consumerism of our culture that makes me feel that way. It's the hierarchies and competitions we learn in school. It's the colonization of our earth—the unwillingness to move with seasons in the face of privileging commerce and wealth. It's the uglification of not knowing, of not controlling, of not dominating, of allowing life to be.

I have learned that if I rush myself into a solution or attempt to conquer my problems, I limit my access to my own creativity, to my natural and inherent perceptiveness, to my ability to read and perceive that which is invisible to many, and to my compassion and empathy for myself and others. I have learned that when I rush, I stumble, I miss out, and I settle for behaviors and ideas that are not aligned with my joy, values, or liberation. I am too much glory and magic to settle. My vision is too precious and critical for me to settle. So is yours.

If you are angry and you can't seem to let go of it, it's okay. Be with yourself and your rage. Don't discount, reduce, or villainize your rage. Love yourself enough to heal it, and bring power in you to the surface.

Beloved, give yourself the opportunity to really know where you are and what you really feel. Honor it. Heal at your own pace. Time is an extraordinary gift, and regardless of what all the inner voices and social systems say, time belongs to us. You are not in a rush. You get to heal, shine, grow, learn, unlearn, and fall in love with yourself at your own pace.

One day, your rage and your beauty will set us all free.

## (U)plift, (G)lorify, (L)ove (Y)ourself: And Create a World Where Others Can as Well

### U—Uplift Yourself

Legacies and lifetimes of uglification have convinced most of us to believe that we need to fix ourselves from fault or imperfection, prove we are worthy of life, earn the right to comfort, and fit in to access safety. We are done with that. Now is the time to reject the traditions privileging oppressive ideals, regardless of how traditional and familiar they are, at the expense of our ability to be safe and live good lives. Reclaiming ugly is uplifting the fact that we are all inherently worthy of protection, safety, access, resources, and love simply for being alive. No one is more or less worthy.

But everyone—especially people in positions of wealth, influence, and leadership; people who employ other people; admit people into colleges and institutions; teach medical and law students; hire teachers and professors; educate children; work in law, social services, banking, government, and peace fields; make movies and television shows; create music; write books and comics; develop video games; and work in any sort of human resources—must uplift the voices, leadership, safety, and inclusion of the people who experience the most intersections of oppression and uglification.

It is time for us, the uglified, to lead the way for change. People who are privileged by systems of oppression can never be in the forefront of change. Privilege makes the stones that kill invisible. The people who have borne the wounds of uglification and learned the strategies to heal them and imagine different must guide the way. And we must be protected, heard, nurtured, fed, and financed by the people who have privileged from our oppression. Trust that in our leadership, you will be safe—and not because we've protected your privilege. You will be safe because we will dismantle the systems and practices that perpetuate any and all oppression or uglification. You will be safe because we know that power doesn't have to come at the expense of someone else's freedom. We are smarter than that.

## HOW TO UPLIFT YOURSELF FROM THE CLUTCHES OF UGLIFICATION

- Prioritize your needs and joy over the opinion of anyone who doesn't want to see you determine your own happiness. When you are inclined to suppress yourself into painful cubes for the status quo or the comfort of someone who is afraid of your freedom, fight for yourself the way you would fight for a bullied friend.

- Fight for yourself the way you would fight oppression. That fight doesn't have to be violent, it shouldn't resemble the tools of oppression, but it does need to be compassionate and courageous enough to help you achieve the peace and feel-good that is your birthright. Lift up your peace. Release anything that tries to push your peace down or knock you out of safety and joy.

- Lift your feelings, safety, and intelligence up above any naysayer or gaslighter who attempts to silence you. Lift your joy, your pleasure, your rest, your creativity, your art, your imagination, your rage, your concerns, your grief, and your needs when patriarchy tells you to be silent or judge yourself.

- Stop silencing, suppressing, or downplaying your feelings. It doesn't serve your freedom or healing. It will not keep you safe from those who don't care. It only makes you attractive to people who aren't invested in your full humanity. You deserve to explore your whole self, to grow, to be big, to unfurl, to find yourself again and again. You deserve to be your own.

- Trust and believe with your entire body that you deserve better and can experience better. Build vulnerable and trusting friendship with the people who are invested in a similar better, and who want to support and experience better with you.

- Affirm that you deserve to be invested in and advocated for, and that your needs, dreams, comfort, value, joy, desires, growth, and humanity should be honored.

- If you are a leader, allow yourself to be a leader. Center your time to heal, learn, and prepare. Uplift yourself as someone worthy of being heard and protected. People who are in alignment with you, who are searching for ideals like yours, want to see you shine. They want to learn, support, and build community and possibility with you. They will be ready for you when you are ready. Take your time, but don't hide from your destiny.

- Say no anytime you want to say no. No one is entitled to your time, attention, body, or freedom. You can say no to harmful relationships and practices. You get to change your mind without being questioned. Your needs and feelings are just as important as other people's and can be met without suppressing someone else's safety or wellness. You are not second-class, second-rate, or second-tier. There are no tiers. Rewrite the story.

- Embrace your right to protect yourself from and reject any internalized message that limits your freedom or confidence. Cushion every thought you have about yourself with compassion, generosity, amnesty, and care. Celebrate your uniqueness. Honor that the parts of you that someone else uglified are majestic—regardless of what they did.

## G–Glorify Yourself

Uglification conditions us to perceive ourselves as worshipper, worker, and selectee while glorifying someone or something else as God, leader, boss, chooser. In our subordinate condition, we are coerced and manipulated into underestimating our brilliance, denying our divinity, and shutting off our ability to lead and create.

When we stop acquiescing to following the programs that sustain our suppression and steal our access to joy, safety, resource, and wholeness, we are uglified as dangerous, as bad, as nasty, as terrorist, as a threat to our family and nation. When we speak up for ourselves, live our lives the way we want to live, or glow too bright for people who are afraid of difference or freedom, we are uglified as an abomination against God, as attention seekers, as threatening tradition and morality, as having gotten too big for our britches, as bitches and man haters, as radical.

Reclaiming ugly means recognizing that uglification is used to keep oppressed people (MaGes, people of color, LGBTQIA+ people, people made poor by capitalism and white supremacy, Indigenous people, disabled people, fat people, migrant and systems-impacted people, youth, elders, and freedom fighters) small, obedient, ashamed of their situations, and constantly looking for permission from folks in authority and leadership. We will no longer uglify ourselves for what other people have done for us. We will no longer wait for the world to decide that we deserve better. We will consort with each other to create the better that we need.

We glorify LGBTQIA+ POC creativity, innovation, and imagination as the pathways to freedom—where we can rest and center our right and need to heal.

We glorify disability justice, fat liberation, and prison and military abolition frameworks as the blueprint for systems, structures, processes, governments, buildings, schools, and healthcare. They're the frameworks to eradicate poverty and violence, reduce stress and stress-related illnesses, and rescue humanity from the traumatized imagination that continues to tolerate and justify gender-based violence, medical injustice, criminalization and war, body shaming, exploitation, and self-hatred.

We glorify the collective wisdoms of Indigenous, Black, Brown, Asian, and refugee womanist and feminist MaGe scholars (especially those who have raised children who were stolen from them due to criminalization born of uglification), regardless of whether they graduated from school or not, what language they speak, what their sexual proclivities are, if they are parents or not, what their gender expression is, how easy they are or aren't to get along with, how quickly they get along with, or how close they are to death. These scholars are the experts on the morality and consciousness that will sustain our freedom and center our healing as we metaphorically march into the future we deserve.

We glorify our ability and desire to be kind together through actions, behaviors, thoughts, strategies, and the redistribution of power and resources. We know that white, cis, able-bodied, neurotypical people can choose to say no to the systems that privilege them (and their opinions, their wisdom, their political and spiritual leadership) at the expense of our lives and safety. We support their ability to step back, imagine anew, protect, and honor our leadership styles and brilliance. We demand their investment in our healing, so that we can be resourced and grounded enough to create the world that serves us all, building at the rate of pleasure, trust, and ability instead of urgency.

We glorify our bodies. We glorify our names. We glorify our voices. We glorify our hearts. We glorify our joy. We glorify lives.

## HOW TO GLORIFY YOURSELF BEYOND THE CLUTCHES OF UGLIFICATION

- Be so relentless about uplifting yourself that centering your joy, pleasure, peace, and dreams becomes your creed, your religion, your daily practice. You get to learn and practice them with the same dogma that we have been taught to study religion. Uglifying any part of you or your desires is sin and sacrilege.

- Embrace being your own standard of greatness, preciousness, and beauty. You are entitled to celebrating and lauding yourself without justification or concession. You can adorn yourself with lathers of praise, toot your horn so much that you make a song. Write your ideas and publish them. Archive your experiences and thoughts. Gift yourself to the world.

- Sing praise and hymns to your existence, history, body, brilliance, personality, and passions. Get the spirit for how magnificent you are. Scream and shout testimonies to the parts of yourself you love and the parts of yourself you were taught not to love. Paint your body on the largest canvas. Turn billboards into altars of your magnificence. Write down your desires and give them to yourself. Allow other people to swoon and be mesmerized in the face of your glory. Let people appreciate you with the same reverence that has been reserved for those previously chosen as leader and deity.

- Allow yourself to recognize and flamboyantly honor the divine that keeps your heart beating, your blood flowing, and your dreams glittering with life. There is no such thing as another person or entity being greater than you, better than you, or out of your league. There is no space for supremacy in liberation. You are vast and infinite in the moment.

- Tune in to the incomparable decadence that is you. Enjoy your smell, the way your body moves, the words and sensations that marvel and shimmer across your brain, the feeling of earth and decadence underneath your feet. Do the things that are fun for you. Tantalize your taste buds and the pleasure receptors on your skin. Dance with the flames of bonfires. Let the sun make naked love on your skin in a garden of living luxury.

- Create an energetic or physical altar to the magnificence of who you are in the moment and the glory of all that you can become, at your pace and by your choosing. Exalt every bit of you—especially the parts of you that have been criminalized, monsterized, uglified, ridiculed, violated, abused, and targeted by other people. Glorify yourself piece by piece, pound by pound, inch by inch, as frequently as possible, with adoration and reverence, poetry and art, film and photography, affirmation, and decision. Choose people who will bring gifts to your altar, who will protect it, who will maintain it when, for whatever reason, you cannot.

- Pray to yourself with glory and gratitude for every beautiful decision you make and every gift you've been blessed with and allowed yourself to cultivate. Talk to your spirit. Remind yourself that you are great more frequently and passionately than anyone who tells you otherwise. Convince yourself that you are deserving of the best, and make that your standard for yourself and others. Lift yourself up and honor your divine so fiercely that no one will ever be able to steal it or desecrate it.

---

## L–Love Yourself

Uglification manipulates us to think that we must do something to be worthy of love, that we have to be chosen by someone as loveable, that we are difficult to love, that we are indebted to the people who love us, and that love is compensation for some achievement. When we reclaim ourselves from the clutches of uglification, we reclaim our ability to love the parts of us that someone else attempted to convince us were unlovable. We reclaim our right to love ourselves hard, loud, and without apology in the face of external hate and uglification.

We commit to loving the parts of our bodies, identities, desires, and legacies that were stolen from us and our ancestors, that were weaponized against us, that were dehumanized and painted as inferior, that were abused by the stewards of the patriarchy.

Reclaiming ugly is loving our bodies and spirits with actions and choices. We choose to divest from any practice or system that interferes with our ability to love ourselves the way we want, including loving ourselves by resting, loving ourselves with clean drinking water and fresh air, and loving ourselves by saying no to those who don't love us.

We recognize civil rights movements as expressions of self-love. Boundaries are expressions of self-love. Saying no is an expression of self-love. Demanding accessible work and educational spaces, as well as teaching styles, is an expression of self-love. Divesting from capitalism is self-love. Telling our stories—of both pleasure and deep harm—is an expression of self-love.

Feeding and unleashing our sensuality is self-love. Carving out the space to care for our bodies as they are is self-love. Demanding that our medical professionals listen to and respect us is self-love. Speaking up about rape culture is self-love. Following our most grand dreams is self-love. Choosing our joy over our fear is self-love.

We demand the space, the time, and the right to love ourselves well. We demand a shift from work structures that detract from the time we can spend loving ourselves. We demand an end to the harassment, microaggressions, and violent political practices that turn self-love into a battle.

We want the world to understand that self-love cannot exist in a vacuum. Those of us who have been violated, traumatized, neglected, and unprotected by uglification want more protected and privileged people to know that we are not solely responsible for creating the environment where we can love ourselves. Screen and comedy writers, radio show hosts, and other content creators must stop promoting uglification. Uglification is not funny. People's looks, bodies, identities, and experiences are not the butt of the joke. We will no longer be silent. We love ourselves too much for complacency.

We want to be loved with actions, with intentionality, and with compassion and investment in our belonging and sense of safety. We understand that our loved ones have every right to their own politics, beliefs, expectations, values, and friendships. We don't want to control other people. We simply will no longer tolerate love that does not consider our feelings, respect our boundaries, or care for our personhood.

We reserve the right to ask for more and better than people are accustomed to giving us. We know that it only seems like too much because uglification has conditioned us to believe that we are too discardable and not precious enough to ask for what we want.

Now that we know better, we won't settle for anything less.

## HOW TO LOVE YOURSELF THROUGH
## THE CLUTCHES OF UGLIFICATION

- Take time to learn how you like to be loved, what sweetness you need to thrive, what softness you need to heal, what encouragement you need to grow. Give it to yourself without limits.

- Tend to the small, hurt, and tender parts of yourself. Wash them gently. Hold yourself close. Pray sweet soothing words to them, for them. Imagine them happy, whole, protected, and fully actualized.

- Award yourself for your self-selected accomplishments. Decide your living rubric and allow it to shift and change as you shift and change. Protect your image of yourself with actions and choices that you choose and respect. Shelter your sweet soft parts from any force that wishes to disturb, hurt, or interfere with your ability to care for and protect yourself. Have empathy for yourself, your process, your grief, your hurt, and your mistakes.

- Be your own minister and choir. Invite others who genuinely love you the way you need and want to be loved to join the choir. Get to know yourself in wondrous new ways: your true desires, your true feelings, your true pleasures, your true values—divorced from capitalism, oppression, and other controlling forces of hierarchy, supremacy, and hegemony.

- Choose you and direct all your loving energy toward you until you are full enough to spill over and love others with the same care and integrity. Ritualize your love. Burn it into your forever. There is no shame in choosing yourself.

- Do not be a martyr for anything. We need you to live a happy and fulfilling life of your choosing. Your joy heals far more people than does your exhaustion, resentment, pain, suffering, and frustration. You living in the thick, juicy, fullness of your body keeps other people's bodies alive in the face of shame and judgment. Your love for yourself is the fortitude and pillars of your ability to love others, whether they are your children, your friends, your parents, your siblings, your partners, or strangers across the globe.

- Know that healing cannot happen without you. Liberation cannot happen without you. Transformation cannot happen without you. We can't and don't want to leave you behind.

- Remember: You are worthy of your dreams. You can absolutely be the star of your life. While we encourage growth and healing, you do not need to change your brain or body to be worthy of love, acceptance, safety, inclusion, or hope.

- Don't let anyone convince you that you are not enough. *You are enough.* Reclaim yourself from any voice that tells you that you are theirs. You are your own.

## Create a World Where Others Can as Well

No one's liberation can come at the expense of someone else's liberation. We are not in competition. We must create a plethora of freedoms that do not depend on someone else's slavery, servitude, repression, or injustice.

We can laugh without laughing at other people, especially people in pain, turmoil, and hardship. We can celebrate our beauty without castigating anyone else's face or body. We can be smart without belittling another person's consciousness or brilliance. We can pursue our dreams and ambitions without standing on the feet of someone who doesn't consent. We can exist without competition. There is enough for us all. We can nurture joy, life, work, and dreams that uplift other people alongside ourselves and that create space for them to lift themselves up. We can surrender to a glory that holds space for all of us who are trying.

We can love people for who they are, even if they are different than us, even if they don't make sense to us.

This loving practice of reclaiming ugly means collective, collaborative, and intersectional liberation. It means we figure out *how* to work together. It means we slow down enough to honor each other and the nuances that come from diverse and cross-issue solidarity.

It means we create workspaces, classrooms, entertainment arenas, buildings, and homes where all bodies fit. It means centering the practices that are invested in the freedom of *everyone*, especially those of us who are excluded and targeted the most.

It means reimagining what normal is, what beautiful is, what intelligence is, what time is, what power is, what family is, what community is, and what love is. It means being honest enough to recognize that we exist in a system and social structure that don't serve *any* of us except for a small few, and on many levels, it's a disservice to them as well. It means we *must* figure out how to create changes that support everyone to be kind, to create systems of inclusivity, and to honor human life far more than we can ever love money or possessions. It means radical transformation and change.

Reclaim ugly believes that these shifts can happen, will happen, and are destined to happen. And you, fellow humans, have the power to make these changes happen locally: in your homes, your relationships, your workplaces and classrooms, and your neighborhoods.

## Closing Practice: UGLY Affirmations

Just like the Black, Brown, MaGe, disabled, trans, queer, nonbinary, bruja, witch, priestess, artist, weirdo, tender, and survivor ancestors who sparkled, glittered, and shined before me, I *am ready* for this world and for the people of this world who are salivating for a magic, vision, and voice like mine. My openhearted creativity is medicine for myself and others.

I am a masterpiece of joy, connection, and prosperity when I am in intimate collaboration and vulnerable solidarity with other people I care about and who I allow the opportunity, space, and time to genuinely care about and love me as well.

I experience the most peace, joy, and creativity when I slow down, pay curious and compassionate attention to myself, learn when I am the happiest with myself and the people around me, and make choices that prioritize our shared pleasures, desires, and boundaries. I can and will fill my own cup. When I have enough, I graciously spill over into the cups of people who cherish and reciprocate my energy. And if I need to, I trust my loved ones to help me fill my cup when I need a bit more than life will allow me to generate.

Whether it's a new relationship, project, family addition, personal practice, or vision, I can define what success means to me and actualize it. I am supported by my family, chosen and given, and committed to the nuanced work of self-reflection and collaboration.

Like a god, I define beauty for myself. It is made of my flesh, image, and imagination: lush-bodied and perfect; mermaid thighs and growing; a universe of belly built to be loved and lavished.

I am stronger, smarter, and more creative than oppression, uglification, and the insecurities and trauma those systems bestowed upon me. With the support of my beloved community, I will fight, scream, battle, rage, and roar for my liberation and yours.

I choose to eat without fear or apology. My body is precious and deserves to be fed with earth-born decadence that lifts my soul, nourishes my flesh, and flavors heaven and orgasm on my tongue. I have no shame in my pleasure or my body, and I will not tolerate other people's attempts to project their own internalized shame on me.

I am a body divine with freedom, curiosity, and fire. My pleasure is the soundtrack of liberation, and I will moan, whimper, thunder, scream, and shout my desires and joy without fear or inhibition.

My body is pliant, able to expand and shift in miraculous ways that *only* I can. I honor my body by living in it fully, moving it to my own rhythm, and defining health, beauty, and joy for myself.

I bless myself with the spaciousness to know where I am and what I feel. Time is an extraordinary gift, and regardless of what the inner voices of shame and capitalist hierarchies dependent on my labor and complacency say, my time belongs to me. I will not push myself faster than the pace of pleasure, trust, or accessibility.

I have a dream, a plan, and a vision that I know I can pursue and achieve. I will not let fear anchor me to untruths, insecurities, or stagnancy. My agency, self-efficacy, and commitment to my vision are liberation against a system that depends on me not believing in myself enough to pursue those dreams. Honoring my plan for myself is a buttery magic spell for me, my future, and so many doors that I am darn determined to knock down and replace with wide open portals of possibility.

I get to reject opportunities, no matter how amazing they may seem, when they don't align with my vision for my life or my understanding of happiness and freedom. I deserve more than the status quo, complacency with other people's visions and expectations of me, and the elite limitations on how success has been previously defined. I will find what I need. It's out there. Settling might be an accessible, rewarded, and lucrative option, but that doesn't make it the only or best one. My possibilities are as abundant as my imagination.

I surround myself with other tender-hearted warriors who carry mirrors way stronger than any antagonism or uglification clinging to my shoulders. I choose friends, lovers, comrades, and other relationships that remind me of how brilliant and loved and dynamic I am, no matter how much my traumatized retentions or negative self-talk may fight my ability to believe in my worth. I build with people who I trust to lay hands and words of magic and love on me and with people who help me exorcise the demons of internalized oppression and yesterday's agony out of today's flesh.

I sparkle. I sing majestically. I glow against the heavy of my yesterday. I belly big laughter, smile wide-mouthed, face fat and lush with the victory of my survival. I create space with my body, make portals with my imagination, build countries from sandcastles, swim past the moat of outer space, find faerie kindred in every galaxy, and art nightmares into healing.

I am fire with roses blooming out my mouth. I will keep talking pollen because the sweetest bees are trying to collect my flavor, bring it back to their queen, feed it to their young, and turn that shit into honey.

I am the kind of magic that keeps the earth lubricated, that turns dirt into soil, passion into love, and fear into freedom. I am a damn good thing and will not stand in the way of my own blessings.

# Acknowledgments

To my mother, Kandee Rochelle Lewis, executive director of the Positive Results Center, I love you SO much. Thank you for always being the most extraordinary love warrior and advocate I could ever imagine. Thank you for validating me and holding me alive when I couldn't imagine myself living. Thank you for the work you do to love, care for, and protect so many uglified, abused, and under-loved people. Thank you for always welcoming my queer and trans friends and partners into our home. Mom, you are glorious, and I worship you. I would not know the best of me if it weren't for you.

To Annah Anti-Palindrome and Eri Kiyoko Oura, thank you for being the best friends and life partners I have ever imagined. Thank you for loving me unconditionally, for caring for me when I was sick and at my worst, for seeing past the uglification of the world and recognizing my beauty, for fighting for me when I didn't believe anyone else would. Annah, thank you for always being my home, my safe respite, my queen of sweetness and imagination. You restore me simply by breathing, love, because your breath carries the same sweetness of mine. You remind me free. Thank you for helping keep me alive. Eri, thank you for feeding me while I worked hard to write this book. Thank you for all the labor you have put into this partnership so that I can share my art and heart with the world. Thank you for holding me at night and being my cuddle daddy. Thank you for making sure I get to the doctor and stay on top of my medication. Thank you for being a critical part of my healing. Thank you for growing and expanding with me. Thank you for loving my kinky, ho'ish ways. Our relationship transitioned during the creation of this book, but know that my love for you, my devotion to you, and my gratitude for you has done nothing but blossom. I love you so much.

To Amira, Prerna, and Bri, you three are so new to my life and yet so very instrumental to me completing this book!!!!! Thank you for all the ways you encourage, love, and protect me with all of your mer-alien-goddess-femme-royalty fierceness. Thank you for being with me during tragedy and through moments of heavenly sweetness. Thanks for listening to my stories, my heartache, and reminding me that I need to tell my stories, that I deserve to be honest about who I really am, that I am worthy of love. Y'all are all family, all neurodivergence superheroes, and creative geniuses in every way. I love y'all so much.

To the members of my Bay Area queer and trans community, my former College of Alameda learning community, the Oakland community, and my social media community, thank you for your love and support during the most buoyant and difficult of times. I have become a woman with you. I have moved into my power and strength because of you. There are so many of you and I love you. To Mia McKenzie, thank you for seeing something extraordinary in me and inviting me to be an editor for Black Girl Dangerous. That might have been one of the most empowering experiences of my life. I love and appreciate you always. To Edith and Debbie from College of Alameda, thank you for seeing something special in me and for hiring me to be a twenty-five-year-old community college teacher. Thank you for training, mentoring, supporting, and loving me, and even buying me food and clothes when the going got tough. Y'all are the best. To Karen and Anna-Pia, thank you for being sacred beloveds and heart flames. I love you soooo much.

To my Reclaim UGLY and Creating Freedom Movements (CFM) team, each and every one of you. Y'all are my future. Y'all are my strength. Y'all are my passionate loves. Thank you for dreaming so beautifully with me, for executing those dreams with such finesse, for helping me be kind to and patient with myself while creating this book. I love growing with you all. I love being a gentle revolution with you all. I love healing with you all. Lauren, thank you for helping me put this project on the map. Lilac, for being a voice as fierce and nurturing as the ocean. Anna, for being the best faerie cheerleader friend a femme could imagine. Gina and Taylor, for your magical editing support and deep care. Amira, for being my work wife and hopefully our new ED and the most wonderful and creative friend/colleague. System Hatfield and Joah, for the revolutionary gift of you funding our movement. For everyone on the board who stood with us and helped us make this happen. I love y'all.

Shayna, Janelle, Matt, Adaobi, and everyone at North Atlantic Books, thank you deeply for your patience and advocacy in this process. Ya'll are such an amazing editorial and publishing team, and each of you helped make this book beautiful and coherent. I trusted you all to hold me through the process, and you gave more and better than I could ever ask for. I appreciate all the compassion and all the skill you brought to this practice. I hope this book blesses your life the way each of you have blessed this book. I am forever and ever on your team.

To all the people striving to reclaim their ugly, I want you to know that you deserve better than the best you've ever had.

You deserve love, peace, freedom, adoration, company, safety, and to live a damn-good life.

You deserve joy and oodles of pleasure.

You deserve to create the world in which you want to live.

We are in this together, family.

# Notes

## Chapter 2: An Introduction to Uglification

1 "The Typical Black Woman Is Unattractive. Period," Afro Futurism, January 13, 2017, https://jointron33.wordpress.com/2017/01/13/the-typical -black-woman-is-unattractive-period/.

2 "Hampton University Business School Dean Bans Cornrows and Dreadlocks," Black Youth Project, August 24, 2012, http://blackyouthproject .com/hampton-university-business-schol-dean-bans-cornrows-and -dreadlocks/; Elizabeth Korver-Glenn, "Compounding Inequalities: How Racial Stereotypes and Discrimination Accumulate across the Stages of Housing Exchange," *American Sociological Review* 83, no. 4 (Aug. 2018): 627–56, https://doi.org/10.1177/0003122418781774; Khristopher J. Brooks, "Redlining's Legacy: Maps Are Gone, but the Problem Hasn't Disappeared," CBS News, June 12, 2020, https://www.cbsnews.com/news /redlining-what-is-history-mike-bloomberg-comments/.

3 Sarah L. Webb, "Colorism in Casting Call for 'Straight Outta Compton' NWA Film," July 19, 2014, https://colorismhealing.com/colorism-casting -call-straight-outta-compton/.

## Chapter 3: Uglification and Other Forms of Oppression

1 Mia Mingus, "Access Intimacy: The Missing Link," May 5, 2011, https:// leavingevidence.wordpress.com/2011/05/05/access-intimacy-the -missing-link/.

2 Natasha Lennard, "'Why Are Black Women Less Attractive?' Asks Psychology Today," Salon, May 17, 2011, https://www.salon.com/2011/05/17 /psychology_today_racist_black_women_attractive/.

3  Associated Press, "Police Guide That Calls BLM a Terrorist Group Draws Outrage," *Tampa Bay Times*, December 2, 2020, https://www.tampabay.com/news/nation-world/2020/12/02/police-guide-that-calls-blm-a-terrorist-group-draws-outrage/; Cheryl Corley, "Black Lives Matter Fights Disinformation to Keep the Movement Strong," NPR, May 25, 2021, https://www.npr.org/2021/05/25/999841030/black-lives-matter-fights-disinformation-to-keep-the-movement-strong.

4  "The World Is Watching: Mass Violations by U.S. Police of Black Lives Matter Protesters' Rights," Amnesty International, August 4, 2020, https://www.amnesty.org/en/documents/amr51/2807/2020/en/.

5  Alan Feuer and Juliana Kim, "'Occupy City Hall' Encampment Taken Down in Pre-Dawn Raid by N.Y.P.D.," *New York Times*, July 22, 2020, https://www.nytimes.com/2020/07/22/nyregion/occupy-city-hall-protest-nypd.html.

6  Jonathan Levinson, Conrad Wilson, James Doubek, and Suzanne Nuyen, "Federal Officers Use Unmarked Vehicles to Grab People in Portland, DHS Confirms," NPR, July 17, 2020, https://www.npr.org/2020/07/17/892277592/federal-officers-use-unmarked-vehicles-to-grab-protesters-in-portland.

7  Melissa Chan, "These Black Lives Matter Protesters Had No Idea How One Arrest Could Alter Their Lives," *Time*, August 19, 2020, https://time.com/5880229/arrests-black-lives-matter-protests-impact/.

8  Helen Regan and Jessie Yeung, "Myanmar's Military Is Killing Peaceful Protesters," CNN, March 25, 2021, www.cnn.com/2021/03/16/asia/myanmar-protesting-coup-explainer-intl-hnk/index.html.

9  "Charlottesville: One Killed in Violence over US Far-Right Rally," BBC, August 13, 2017, https://www.bbc.com/news/world-us-canada-40912509.

10  James Doubek, "Oklahoma City Police Fatally Shoot Deaf Man Despite Yells of 'He Can't Hear,'" NPR, September 21, 2017, https://www.npr.org/sections/thetwo-way/2017/09/21/552527929/oklahoma-city-police-fatally-shoot-deaf-man-despite-yells-of-he-cant-hear-you; Shaun King, "North Carolina Police Kill Unarmed Deaf Man Who Was Using Sign Language," *New York Daily News*, August 22, 2016, https://www.nydailynews.com/news/national/king-n-police-kill-unarmed-deaf-mute-man-sign-language-article-1.2760714.

11  Adrienne Phelps Coco, "Diseased, Maimed, Mutilated: Categorizations of Disability and an Ugly Law in Late Nineteenth-Century Chicago," *Journal of Social History* 44, no. 1 (Fall 2010): 23–37, https://www.jstor.org/stable/40802107.

12  Katie Dowd, "San Francisco Once Pioneered America's Cruelest Legislation: Ugly Laws," SF Gate, March 2, 2020, https://www.sfgate.com/sfhistory/article/San-Francisco-once-pioneered-ugly-laws-15098902.php.

13  Margo Schlanger, "Prisoners with Disabilities," in *Reforming Criminal Justice: Punishment, Incarceration, and Release*, ed. E. Luna, 295–323 (Phoenix, AZ: Academy for Justice, 2017), https://repository.law.umich.edu/cgi/viewcontent.cgi?article=1114&context=book_chapters.

14  Luz Pena, "There Are an Estimated 46,000 Vacant Homes in the Bay Area, but Why?," KGO, January 6, 2020, https://abc7news.com/realestate/there-are-an-estimated-46000-vacant-homes-in-the-bay-area-but-why/5820129/; "Homeless Population: Point-in-Time Homeless Counts, 2005-2022," City and County of San Francisco, https://sfgov.org/scorecards/safety-net/homeless-population; "City of Oakland Homeless Count and Survey, Comprehensive Report," ASR, 2019, https://everyonehome.org/wp-content/uploads/2019/12/2019HIRDReport_Oakland_2019-Final.pdf (Oakland number is from 2019).

15  "Food Waste FAQs," US Department of Agriculture, https://www.usda.gov/foodwaste/faqs; "Food Security Status of U.S. Households in 2021," Economic Research Service, US Department of Agriculture, https://www.ers.usda.gov/topics/food-nutrition-assistance/food-security-in-the-us/key-statistics-graphics.aspx.

## Chapter 4: Dangerous Uglification

1  Jenn Walton, "Black Women's Biggest Health Issue Is the System," *Hopkins Bloomberg Public Health*, Fall 2020, https://magazine.jhsph.edu/2020/black-womens-biggest-health-issue-system.

2  "Black Women and Domestic Violence," Blackburn Center, February 26, 2020, https://www.blackburncenter.org/post/2020/02/26/black-women-domestic-violence.

3  *Global Study on Homicide*, United Nations Office on Drugs and Crime, 2013, https://www.unodc.org/documents/gsh/pdfs/2014_GLOBAL_HOMICIDE_BOOK_web.pdf.

4  "Women in Prison: An Overview," ACLU, https://www.aclu.org/other/words-prison-did-you-know.

5  "Women's Safety: Facts and Statistics," Brookview, https://brookviewhouse.org/womens-safety-network/facts-statistics-2.

6  "More than 1,200 Americans Die in Murder-Suicides Each Year, VPC Study Finds," Violence Policy Center, October 29, 2015, https://vpc.org

/press/more-than-1200-americans-die-in-murder-suicides-each-year-vpc
-study-finds/.

7  "Domestic Violence Statistics," Hope: Domestic Violence Homicide
   Help, https://domesticviolencehomicidehelp.com/statistics/.

8  "Eighteen Months after Leaving Domestic Violence Is Still the Most
   Dangerous Time," Battered Women's Support Services, June 11, 2020,
   https://www.bwss.org/eighteen-months-after-leaving-domestic-violence
   -is-still-the-most-dangerous-time/.

9  "Racial and Ethnic Disparities Continue in Pregnancy-Related Deaths,"
   September 6, 2019, Centers for Disease Control and Prevention, https://
   www.cdc.gov/media/releases/2019/p0905-racial-ethnic-disparities
   -pregnancy-deaths.html.

10  Lauren Camera, "Black Girls Are Twice as Likely to Be Suspended, in
    Every State," *US News & World Report*, May 9, 2017, https://www.usnews
    .com/news/education-news/articles/2017-05-09/black-girls-are-twice-as
    -likely-to-be-suspended-in-every-state.

11  Jack Harrison-Quintana and Sharon Lettman-Hicks with Jaime Grant,
    "Injustice at Every Turn," National Center for Transgender Equality,
    https://transequality.org/sites/default/files/docs/resources/ntds_black
    _respondents_2.pdf.

12  Marissa Rewak et al., "Race-Related Health Disparities and Biological
    Aging: Does Rate of Telomere Shortening Differ across Blacks and
    Whites?," *Biological Psychology* 99 (May 2014): 92–99, https://doi.org
    /10.1016%2Fj.biopsycho.2014.03.007.

13  "Qandeel Baloch's Brother Arrested, Says He Killed Her for 'Honour,'"
    Pakistan Today, July 17, 2016, https://archive.pakistantoday.com.pk/2016
    /07/17/qandeel-balochs-brother-arrested-says-he-killed-her-for-honour/.

14  Clark Mindock, "Trump Sexual Assault Allegations: How Many Women
    Have Accused the President?," *Independent*, November 6, 2020, https://
    www.independent.co.uk/news/world/americas/us-politics/trump-sexual
    -assault-allegations-all-list-misconduct-karen-johnson-how-many
    -a9149216.html; Monica Lewinsky, "Emerging from 'the House of Gas-
    light' in the Age of #MeToo," *Vanity Fair*, March 2018, https://www
    .vanityfair.com/news/2018/02/monica-lewinsky-in-the-age-of-metoo;
    Sheryl Gay Stolberg and Carl Hulse, "Joe Biden Expresses Regret to
    Anita Hill, but She Says 'I'm Sorry' Is Not Enough," *New York Times*,
    April 25, 2019, https://www.nytimes.com/2019/04/25/us/politics/joe-biden
    -anita-hill.html; Clare Foran and Stephen Collinson, "Brett Kavanaugh

Sworn in as Supreme Court Justice," CNN, October 6, 2018, https://www
.cnn.com/2018/10/06/politics/kavanaugh-final-confirmation-vote/index
.html.

15 Nicole Reinert, "Why the Celeste Guap Scandal Isn't Only about Her,"
KQED, September 29, 2016, https://www.kqed.org/news/11106467/why-the
-celeste-guap-scandal-isnt-only-about-her-case; Fiona Keating, "Woman
Sues Police Department for 'Failing to Stop Officers from Sexually Trafficking Her,'" *Independent*, August 24, 2017, https://www.independent.co.uk
/news/world/americas/woman-jasmine-abuslin-celeste-guap-bay-area
-richmond-chris-magnus-chris-magnus-sex-trafficking-underage-sex
-slavery-a7902921.html.

16 Breanne Fahs, "Daddy's Little Girls: On the Perils of Chastity Clubs, Purity
Balls, and Ritualized Abstinence," *Frontiers: A Journal of Women Studies* 31,
no. 3 (2010), https://doi.org/10.5250/fronjwomestud.31.3.0116, https://www
.breannefahs.com/uploads/1/0/6/7/10679051/2010_frontiers_fahs.pdf.

17 Lee Suckling, "Why Being Called a 'Ho' Is No Longer an Insult,"
*New Zealand Herald*, October 2, 2018, https://www.nzherald.co.nz
/lifestyle/lee-suckling-why-being-called-a-ho-is-no-longer-an-insult
/HCM4ZULT7NVYJM4D7HX2257BJA.

18 Sam, "There Are 64,000 Missing Black Women in the USA," Medium,
November 23, 2019, https://medium.com/the-blight/there-are-64-000
-missing-black-women-in-the-usa-222001806a6e.

19 Gregory D. Smithers, *Slave Breeding: Sex, Violence, and Memory in African
American History* (Gainesville: University Press of Florida, 2012), www
.jstor.org/stable/j.ctvx070kn.

20 Christopher F. Petrella, "Wealth, Slavery, and the History of American
Taxation," Black Perspectives, April 20, 2017, https://www.aaihs.org
/wealth-slavery-and-the-history-of-american-taxation/.

21 Robin L. Einhorn, "Tax Aversion and the Legacy of Slavery," University of
Chicago Press, 2006, https://press.uchicago.edu/Misc/Chicago/194876.html.

22 Jennifer McMahon-Howard, Jody Clay-Warner, and Linda Renzulli,
"Criminalizing Spousal Rape: The Diffusion of Legal Reforms," *Sociological Perspectives* 52, no. 4 (Winter 2009), https://www.jstor.org/stable/10
.1525/sop.2009.52.4.505.

23 Kim Russell, "This loophole could let a husband get away with sexually assaulting his wife in Michigan," WXYZ Detroit, October 24, 2019,
https://www.wxyz.com/news/this-loophole-could-let-a-husband-get
-away-with-sexually-assaulting-his-wife-in-michigan.

24 *Free CeCe!*, dir. Jacqueline (Jac) Gares, 2018, https://www.freecece
documentary.com/; Sabrina Rubin Erdely, "The Transgender Crucible,"
*Rolling Stone*, July 30, 2014, https://www.rollingstone.com/culture
/culture-news/the-transgender-crucible-114095/.

25 Marcus Brock, "Coalitions and Community Members Support CeCe
McDonald," GLAAD, June 13, 2012, https://www.glaad.org/blog/coalitions
-and-community-members-support-cece-mcdonald.

26 "CeCe McDonald," Barnard Center for Research on Women, http://
bcrw.barnard.edu/fellows/cece-mcdonald/.

27 Ana Coughlin, "The Brutal Murder of Gwen Araujo," Medium, December 27, 2020, https://medium.com/the-crime-center/the-brutal-murder-of
-gwen-araujo-fce7d95b6560.

28 "FBI Seeking Assistance Connecting Victims to Samuel Little's Confes-
sions," Federal Bureau of Investigation, October 6, 2019, https://www.fbi
.gov/news/stories/samuel-little-most-prolific-serial-killer-in-us-history
-100619.

29 Ibid.

30 D. Ojanuga, "The Medical Ethics of the 'Father of Gynaecology,' Dr. J.
Marion Sims," *Journal of Medical Ethics* 19, no. 1 (1993): 28–31, https://jme
.bmj.com/content/medethics/19/1/28.full.pdf.

31 Shankar Vedantam, Maggie Penman, Jennifer Schmidt, Tara Boyle,
Rhaina Cohen, and Chloe Connelly, "Remembering Anarcha, Lucy, and
Betsey: The Mothers of Modern Gynecology," NPR, February 7, 2017,
https://www.npr.org/2017/02/07/513764158/remembering-anarcha-lucy
-and-betsey-the-mothers-of-modern-gynecology.

32 Kelly M. Hoffman, Sophie Trawalter, Jordan R. Axt, and M. Norman
Oliverb, "Racial Bias in Pain Assessment and Treatment Recommenda-
tions, and False Beliefs about Biological Differences between Blacks and
Whites," *Proceedings of the National Academy of Sciences of the United States of
America* 113, no. 16 (2016): 4296-301, https://doi.org/10.1073%2Fpnas.1516047113.

33 Steven Briggs, "How the 'Father of Gynecology' Experimented on
Enslaved Women," *Scrubs*, February 2021, https://scrubsmag.com/how
-the-father-of-gynecology-experimented-on-enslaved-women/.

34 "Ending Violence against Native Women," Indian Law Resource Center,
https://indianlaw.org/issue/ending-violence-against-native-women.

35 Grace Segers, "Congress Tackles Crisis of Missing and Murdered Native
American Women," CBS News, June 12, 2019, https://www.cbsnews.com
/news/congress-crisis-missing-and-murdered-native-american-women/.

36 "Policy Insights Brief: Statistics on Violence against Native Women," NCAI Policy Research Center, February 2013, https://www.ncai.org /attachments/PolicyPaper_tWAjznFslemhAffZgNGzHUqIWMRPkCD jpFtxeKEUVKjubxfpGYK_Policy%20Insights%20Brief_VAWA_020613 .pdf; Abaki Beck, "For Indigenous Women, More Pipelines Mean More Threats of Sexual Violence," The Revelator, October 10, 2019, https:// therevelator.org/fossil-fuel-indigenous-women/.

37 "Fact Sheet: Missing and Murdered Aboriginal Women and Girls," Native Women's Association of Canada, https://nwac.ca/assets-knowledge-centre /Fact_Sheet_Missing_and_Murdered_Aboriginal_Women_and_Girls.pdf.

38 Jessica Rizzo, "Native American Women Are Rape Targets Because of a Legislative Loophole," Vice, December 16, 2015, https://www.vice.com/en /article/bnpb73/native-american-women-are-rape-targets-because-of-a -legislative-loophole-511.

39 Timothy Williams, "Higher Crime, Fewer Charges on Indian Land," *New York Times*, February 20, 2012, https://www.nytimes.com/2012/02/21/us /on-indian-reservations-higher-crime-and-fewer-prosecutions.html.

40 "Introduction to the Violence Against Women Act," Tribal Court Clear- inghouse, https://www.tribal-institute.org/lists/title_ix.htm.

41 "On Violence Against Women Act Anniversary, Udall Calls for Senate Vote on VAWA with Tribal Provisions, Public Safety Bills" (press release), US Senate Committee on Indian Affairs, September 13, 2019, https:// www.indian.senate.gov/news/press-release/violence-against-women-act -anniversary-udall-calls-senate-vote-vawa-tribal; "Fact Sheet: Reauthori- zation of the Violence Against Women Act (VAWA)," The White House, March 16, 2022, https://www.whitehouse.gov/briefing-room/statements -releases/2022/03/16/fact-sheet-reauthorization-of-the-violence-against -women-act-vawa/.

42 Joaquin Sapien, "Guards May Be Responsible for Half of Prison Sexual Assaults, ProPublica, January 23, 2014, https://www.propublica.org /article/guards-may-be-responsible-for-half-of-prison-sexual-assaults.

## Chapter 5: Future Histories of Reclaiming Ugly

1 Yamiche Alcindor, "Trayvon Martin: Typical teen or troublemaker?," *USA Today*, December 11, 2012, https://www.usatoday.com/story/news /nation/2012/12/11/trayvon-martin-profile/1761373/.

2 Jim Salter, "2 Views of Floyd Onlookers: Desperate to Help, or Angry Mob?," Associated Press, April 19, 2021, https://apnews.com/article

/george-floyd-derek-chauvin-closing-statements-bystanders-141c718d48
5194c5ab9737c4b96b8e18.

3  "The Challenge of the Black Brunch Movement," *Seattle* magazine,
   April 9, 2015, https://www.seattlemag.com/article/challenge-black
   -brunch-movement.

4  Jaclyn Diaz, "Florida's Governor Signs Controversial Law Opponents
   Dubbed 'Don't Say Gay,'" NPR, March 28, 2022, https://www.npr.org
   /2022/03/28/1089221657/dont-say-gay-florida-desantis.

5  Anne M. Coughlin and Naomi Cahn, "Texas Is Trampling Parents'
   Rights in Its Investigations of Trans Kids," *Washington Post*, April 8, 2022,
   https://www.washingtonpost.com/outlook/2022/04/08/texas-transgender
   -family-law/.

6  Jack Holmes, "An Expert on Concentration Camps Says That's Exactly
   What the U.S. Is Running at the Border," *Esquire*, June 13, 2019, https://
   www.esquire.com/news-politics/a27813648/concentration-camps-southern
   -border-migrant-detention-facilities-trump/.

7  "Black Indiana Doctor Died of Coronavirus Weeks after Accusing Hospital of Racist Treatment," WTVD, December 28, 2020, https://abc11
   .com/dr-susan-moore-md-covid-coronavirus-covid-19/9094278/.

8  "Obese, Unattractive Students Are Less Likely to Land Med School Resi-
   dencies," Duke Health, June 4, 2019, https://corporate.dukehealth.org
   /news/obese-unattractive-students-are-less-likely-land-med-school
   -residencies.

9  C. E. Parsons, K. S. Young, N. Kumari, A. Stein, and M. L. Kringelbach,
   "The Motivational Salience of Infant Faces Is Similar for Men and
   Women," *PLoS ONE* 6, no. 5 (2011): e20632, https://doi.org/10.1371/journal
   .pone.0020632.

## Chapter 6: Surviving Uglification

1  Eldra P. Solomon and Kathleen M. Heide, "The Biology of Trauma:
   Implications for Treatment," *Journal of Interpersonal Violence* 20, no. 1
   (January 2005): 51–60, https://doi.org/10.1177/0886260504268119.

2  Michelle Dean, "The Story of Amanda Todd," *New Yorker*, October 18,
   2012, https://www.newyorker.com/culture/culture-desk/the-story-of
   -amanda-todd.

3  Jonece Starr Dunigan, "McKenzie Adams' Suicide Caused by School's Failure to Stop Racist, Sexist Bullying, Lawsuit Claims," AL.com, January 21,
   2020, https://www.al.com/news/2020/01/mckenzie-adams-suicide-caused
   -by-schools-failure-to-stop-racist-sexist-bullying-lawsuit-claims.html;

Elizabeth Chuck, "Bullying Drove 13-Year-Old Rosalie Avila to Kill Her-self, Parents Say," NBC News, December 5, 2017, https://www.nbcnews .com/news/us-news/bullying-drove-13-year-old-rosalie-avila-kill-herself -parents-n826281; Sunnivie Brydum, "San Diego Mourns Third Trans Teen to Die by Suicide," *Advocate*, November, 17 2015, https://www .advocate.com/politics/transgender/2015/05/25/san-diego-mourns-third -trans-teen-die-suicide; Fallon Fox, "Leelah Alcorn's Suicide: Conversion Therapy Is Child Abuse," *Time*, January 8, 2015, https://time.com/3655718 /leelah-alcorn-suicide-transgender-therapy/; Mitch Kellaway, "Trans Teen Activist, Former Homecoming King, Dies in Charlotte, N.C.," *Advo-cate*, March 24, 2015, https://www.advocate.com/obituaries/2015/03/24 /trans-teen-activist-homecoming-king-dies.

4   "Prescott v. Rady Children's Hospital-San Diego," Transgender Law Center, https://transgenderlawcenter.org/legal/youth/prescott.

## Chapter 7: Love and Family as Tools against Uglification

1   Matt Taibbi, "Secrets and Lies of the Bailout," *Rolling Stone*, January 4, 2013, https://www.rollingstone.com/politics/politics-news/secrets-and -lies-of-the-bailout-113270/.

2   Caleb Luna, "Romantic Love Is Killing Us: Who Takes Care of Us When We Are Single?," The Body Is Not an Apology, September 18, 2018, https:// thebodyisnotanapology.com/magazine/romantic-love-is-killing-us/.

# Index

# About the Author

Born and raised in South Central, Los Angeles, Vanessa Rochelle Lewis (MFA) is a queer, fat, Black, femme performer, facilitator, educator, writer, activist, healer, joyful weirdo, and Faerie Princess Mermaid Gangsta for The Revolution.

Vanessa has danced across many professional and creative stages. She has been a writer and co-managing editor for acclaimed feminist magazines Everyday Feminism and Black Girl Dangerous; a community college instructor at multiple Bay Area schools and radical transformative justice programs; a fundraiser and events coordinator for the Queer Women of Color Media Arts Project; the artist-in-residence for the Young Women Freedom Center, where she facilitated art healing workshops and a master class for formerly incarcerated women, trans, and nonbinary people; and so much more.

She is currently a core team member for Creating Freedom Movements (a yearlong social education project that supports grassroots visionary leaders to incubate healing and joy projects while learning more about the art, theory, and practice of social justice movements) and a creative and programming consultant and facilitator for the Positive Results Center (a family-run organization founded by her mother, Kandee Rochelle Lewis, that addresses the impacts and sources of bullying, sexual abuse, dating, domestic or interpersonal violence, and sex trafficking). Vanessa has spoken at UC Berkeley, Hampshire College, Mills College, the 5 Colleges Queer Conference, California College of the Arts, California Institute of Integral Studies, and more.

After experiencing her appearance being weaponized against her on too many occasions, Vanessa began to write articles about ugliness and uglification. Many people responded with their own stories of being bullied and harmed due to their appearance. This exchange inspired Vanessa to create the organization Reclaim UGLY: Uplift Glorify Love Yourself—And Create a World Where Others Can as Well! Her vision is to co-create a world where everyone knows that they are a safe, welcomed, and valued member of their communities; has the support to dream authentically and exist in their truths; and accepts that there is no face, no body, and no person who is ugly or unworthy of love and acceptance. The organization hosts conferences, heal-ins/teach-ins, and other uplifting events. Please visit www.reclaimugly.org to learn more.

When she's not trying to save the world, Vanessa loves listening to audiobooks; flirting with her friends, her partner, and strangers; and swimming in every body of water she can find.

# About North Atlantic Books

North Atlantic Books (NAB) is an independent, nonprofit publisher committed to a bold exploration of the relationships between mind, body, spirit, and nature. Founded in 1974, NAB aims to nurture a holistic view of the arts, sciences, humanities, and healing. To make a donation or to learn more about our books, authors, events, and newsletter, please visit www.northatlanticbooks.com.